Maximizing the Power of Microlearning

ROBYN A. DEFELICE

I0109662

atd
PRESS

ALEXANDRIA, VA

© 2026 ASTD DBA the Association for Talent Development (ATD)
All rights reserved. Printed in the United States of America.

29 28 27 26   1 2 3 4 5

No part of this publication may be reproduced, distributed, or transmitted in any form or by any means, including photocopying, recording, information storage and retrieval systems, or other electronic or mechanical methods, without the prior written permission of the publisher, except in the case of brief quotations embodied in critical reviews and certain other noncommercial uses permitted by copyright law. For permission requests, please go to copyright.com, or contact Copyright Clearance Center (CCC), 222 Rosewood Drive, Danvers, MA 01923 (telephone: 978.750.8400; fax: 978.646.8600).

ATD Press is an internationally renowned source of insightful and practical information on talent development, training, and professional development.

ATD Press
1640 King Street
Alexandria, VA 22314 USA

Ordering information: Books published by ATD Press can be purchased by visiting ATD's website at td.org/books or by calling 800.628.2783 or 703.683.8100.

Library of Congress Control Number: 2025948817

ISBN-10: 1-960231-56-1
ISBN-13: 978-1-960231-56-7
e-ISBN: 978-1-960231-57-4

ATD Press Editorial Staff
Director: Sarah Halgas
Manager: Melissa Jones
Content Manager: Alexandria Clapp
Developmental Editor: Shelley Sperry
Production Editor: Katy Wiley Stewts
Text Designer: Shirley E.M. Raybuck
Cover Designer: Rose Richey

Text Layout: PerfecType, Nashville, TN

Printed by BR Printers, San Jose, CA

Contents

Foreword

Writing *Microlearning: Short and Sweet* was a fun project. After many long discussions and debates, Robyn and I built a consensus about what microlearning was and could be. We then put those thoughts to paper and eventually wrote the book. Our goal was to cut through the buzz and hype to get to the meaningful elements of microlearning. It was a grueling process but, in the end, we thought we'd nailed it. We thought it was a book that could define the field.

But the concept of microlearning had its own ideas.

It turns out, microlearning is not a static concept, idea, or implementation; instead, it continues to evolve. It's both exciting and a bit overwhelming to see where the field has taken microlearning and how it continues to change. And that's why this book matters. It captures another moment of time in the evolution of microlearning. It's the next natural step.

We've seen some dramatic changes in work, technology, organizations, and learners, and it's time for a fresh and more mature look at microlearning. Who better to write about microlearning than Robyn? She's been knee-deep in L&D practice, research, and consulting. She's been working with and listening to frustrated practitioners, watching organizations stumble and succeed, and cataloging every lesson learned. She's seen firsthand that while microlearning sounds like it should be quick and easy ("just make it shorter!"), the reality is anything but. Microlearning isn't a shortcut—it's a design choice. And like all good design, it requires strategy, science, and, yes, a lot of discipline.

This book highlights Robyn's abilities to simultaneously be analytical and practical. She dug deep into research, frameworks, and data to uncover the principles that make microlearning work, while also providing insights into real-world applications that L&D practitioners have actually implemented. She also takes the time to separate fact from fiction, to challenge the industry's most persistent myths, and to say out loud what many practitioners have quietly suspected. It's this unique combination that makes her voice both trustworthy and refreshing.

The nuances of microlearning can be a bit hard to understand; fortunately, Robyn has an antidote for that—cooking and food analogies. For example, she mentions that she learned to eyeball seasonings in chicken salad by assessing the depth of the bowl, the circumference, and the desired flavor profile. She then uses that analogy to describe the creation of microlearning. This not only makes the concepts accessible, it makes them sticky. You'll walk away not only understanding the principles but also remembering them the next time you step into a design challenge. (And yes, you may even find yourself a little hungry.) But don't mistake the lightness of her cooking and food analogies for a lack of rigor. Behind each one is a deep well of experience and insight.

Robyn doesn't just theorize about microlearning. She's lived it. She's worked alongside leaders making strategic decisions, instructional designers under pressure to "make it micro," and developers eager to build experiences that stick. She's seen where the confusion lies, she's spotted where the opportunities are hidden, and she's translated those observations into actionable insights. No matter where you fit into the world of talent development, this book will help you create effective microlearning.

If you're a learning leader trying to make microlearning strategic, this book will help you connect microlearning initiatives to organizational goals, build readiness within your teams, and push past the myth that short equals effective. You'll gain language to use with stakeholders, frameworks to assess readiness, and strategies for scaling microlearning as part of your long-term performance plan.

If you're an instructional designer, you already know the pressure to shorten a long course into a small course and how that can lead to ineffective instruction. Robyn shows you how to resist that trap. You'll learn design principles grounded in cognitive science, strategies for managing cognitive load, and approaches to ensure microlearning products truly drive behavior change.

If you're a developer, you'll find practical tools for turning concepts into digital reality. Robyn offers ways to use current tools effectively without overcomplicating production, advice on piloting microlearning in real-world environments, and methods for assessing results that go beyond vanity metrics. You'll come away not just with recipes but with the "seasoning sense" to adjust to your unique context.

And if you're a consultant, this book gives you research-backed arguments and frameworks to take directly to your clients. You'll be able to cut through stakeholder myths, set realistic expectations, and guide organizations toward microlearning content that improves performance rather than just adding another shiny object to the mix.

The strength of this book is in its versatility, examples, and common-sense approach. In short, Robyn has given L&D professionals a gift. My advice is simple: Read this book, put its principles into practice, and then, like any good cook, make the recipe your own.

Karl M. Kapp, EdD, Professor of Instructional Design and Technology, Commonwealth University, Bloomsburg, PA

Preface

When I was young, my mom gave me my first cooking lesson. I had no idea how much that experience would forever shape how I approach learning. As I began measuring oil for a boxed cake mix, Mom gently tapped the back of my hand and said, "Pour it freely." I was terrified. How could I possibly know how much to add? Come to think of it, how did my mom know?

Fast-forward to me as an adult, when my little brother pushed a bowl of partially prepared chicken salad toward me the moment I walked through his door. "I was waiting for you to arrive so you could season it," he said. "You can make it taste like Mom's."

When he asked how I did it, I initially shrugged and replied, "I don't know; I just learned to eyeball it because that's how Mom taught me and how her mom taught her."

But then I stopped and paid attention to what I was actually doing. I was assessing the depth of food in the bowl, its circumference, and the flavor profile I wanted to create. I wasn't just dropping seasonings in the center; I was intentionally coating the surface, adjusting the coverage based on the intensity I wanted. I was intuitively balancing ratios of wet ingredients to ensure that none overpowered the others or made the mixture too *goopy*. (I'm choosing to say *goopy* here because *runny* chicken salad just sounds gross.)

By breaking down the process, I was able to teach my brother how to do it himself. He quickly mastered our family's classic chicken salad and went on to create his own amazing variations, including one with garlic-herb almonds.

He didn't need me to help him anymore because he had learned the principles that allowed him to create confidently on his own.

My mom's initial lessons turned me into the confident cook that I am today, and I continue to experiment with new recipes, none of which I ever write down. What most people don't realize is that behind my seemingly effortless cooking are hours of research. I usually study 20 or more recipes from a variety of sources, test batches of my own creations, and practice multiple techniques while working on a new dish. I can make a traditional red sauce that tastes like my mom's, my own shortcut version, or a new version using just four ingredients, one of which is pasta water.

Although my knowledge appears simple on the surface, the foundation goes deep.

You now might be wondering how my life as a devoted cook compares with my professional life as a learning strategist and to this book about the power of microlearning. First, I don't just "eyeball" my learning projects. I write *everything* down. My approach to microlearning is systematic, unlike my intuitive approach to cooking. I've meticulously documented my journey with microlearning, spending years observing, cataloging challenges, and recording solutions.

There is also an important similarity between my cooking and my professional life: Both require a deep understanding of principles and techniques. And just as I had to break down my intuitive process into teachable principles to explain a recipe to my brother, I've worked hard to carefully unpack the practice of microlearning for students, colleagues, and now for you, as a reader.

Why I Needed to Write This Book

Within days of publishing my first book, *Microlearning: Short and Sweet*, with Karl Kapp, questions and stories about people's struggles began flooding in. One exasperated reader told me, "My client wanted microlearning, but now our five-to-seven-minute pieces have ballooned to 45 minutes because stakeholders think each one is missing important content." I listened to so many more stories like this before I recognized that part of the challenge of microlearning was the wide variance in expectations and conflation of terms in our industry.

I gradually realized that without a shared understanding of what microlearning actually is, organizations would continue to struggle to implement it effectively.

Some L&D practitioners see microlearning purely as one of many new options—one that requires "shrinking" their usual learning solutions. Others view it as the salvation of performance growth. Some are adamant that microlearning must be a digital-only option, while others remain fixated on shortening duration, despite the fact that so many of our goals cannot fit neatly into one-time, three-to-five-minute training chunks. Many leaders believe microlearning alone will solve the problem of setting aside time for professional development—but it won't.

Perhaps most concerning to me, as I've talked with colleagues over the past few years, is the fact that in many organizations, the process of learning is often overshadowed by enthusiasm for the convenience of delivering shorter training experiences. Terms such as *bite-sized*, *digestible*, and *snackable* are common, and they do a disservice to L&D professionals' efforts to craft more effective and powerful microlearning products. And don't get me started on the fact that our human brains don't *eat* information to create memories that turn into knowledge, skills, and performance.

It's not just the problematic language around learning that spurred me to take a new look at microlearning. I often wonder if organizations are considering that their employees need time to acclimate and adapt to microlearning in their work environments. Do stakeholders simply assume that if their employees are much too busy to leave their desks, microlearning will somehow solve that problem? Do any of the leaders asking for microlearning solutions understand that to create and sustain a series of microlearning products, the L&D function needs time and resources to plan and engage others in the organization before developing those solutions? One of the most frustrating, persistent myths I encounter is that shorter content means *less* development time, when in reality, crafting concise, effective microlearning often requires much *more* planning and design time than traditional formats. I hope this book will go at least a little way toward resolving some of these issues.

Despite the challenges, I am as enthusiastic about microlearning as I was when I was writing *Microlearning: Short and Sweet*. In this book, I have a chance to share a more comprehensive perspective based on years of accumulated insights, qualitative data, and statements from fellow professionals in the field. I've assembled a variety of research and talked with dozens of friends and colleagues about learning science and universal design. I hope the information here will help you create thoughtfully designed microlearning initiatives and incremental approaches to learning that meet your organization where it is today and grow alongside your L&D and organizational capabilities (and capacity!).

Whether you're an L&D leader seeking strategic approaches, an instructional designer determining what might work for your company or client, a developer honing new skills, or a consultant exploring possibilities, these pages will help you develop your own "seasoning sense" for microlearning. I invite you to join me in exploring microlearning as a multifaceted approach that, when properly understood and implemented, can transform how your organization builds knowledge, develops skills, and improves performance.

Let's discover the art of the possible together.

Introduction

> Microlearning is an instructional unit that provides a short engagement
> in an activity intentionally designed to elicit a specific outcome from the
> participant.
> —Karl M. Kapp and Robyn A. Defelice, *Microlearning: Short and Sweet*

When Karl Kapp and I published that definition in 2019, we hoped to provide clarity amid the growing buzz around microlearning. We thought that a precise definition, like a well-crafted recipe that specifies exact measurements, would help everyone create consistent results. In the years since, I've realized that even the best recipe can be interpreted differently by different chefs—just as *microlearning* continues to mean different things to different people.

Those interpretations remind me of a meringue—seemingly simple, made with just two ingredients: egg whites and sugar. Yet anyone who has attempted to make a meringue knows that success depends on numerous factors: Is your bowl perfectly clean and free of any fat residue? Did you separate the eggs carefully, ensuring that no yolk contaminated the whites? Is the humidity too high in your kitchen today? Have you achieved stiff peaks, or are they still soft?

Microlearning also seems to be straightforward: "Just make it shorter!" But like a perfect meringue, successful microlearning requires understanding many interconnected variables and continuously reflecting on your approach. This includes recognizing that performance improvement through learning isn't just about fixing problems or addressing skills gaps. Performance improvement can also mean building foundational knowledge for better decision making, developing new capabilities for changing roles, supporting compliance and safety requirements, or enhancing job satisfaction and retention.

The questions I encounter daily about microlearning reveal a focus on just one aspect of a multifaceted process:

- Is microlearning limited to one-minute or five-minute sessions?
- Isn't it just breaking longer training content into smaller chunks?
- Can I create microlearning with my current tools?
- Should our microlearning products live in the learning management system?

The most important elements of microlearning—organizational readiness, L&D capabilities, strategic alignment, and learning science foundations—are often unaddressed in discussing the most common questions, which focus on the duration of the learning experiences. Just as baking smaller meringues doesn't make them easier to create, shorter learning experiences don't automatically improve knowledge retention, skills development, or performance.

This book aims to help you develop a more complete recipe for success. It's written for a broad audience of chefs in the learning kitchen: L&D leaders, instructional designers, educators, consultants, and anyone interested in creating more effective experiences. Whether you're planning an entire learning menu or perfecting specific techniques, you'll find ingredients and methods to enhance your approach. The book unfolds in three distinct but complementary parts:

- **Part 1, Assessing Readiness,** defines the essential ingredients of microlearning by examining its characteristics as a concept, method, and product. This foundation leads to the Microlearning Readiness (MLR) Framework—a comprehensive assessment that helps you evaluate what your organization can realistically produce right now.
- **Part 2, Design Principles,** explores the science behind effective microlearning. Cognitive load theory and Robert Gagné's framework, the Conditions of Learning, support seven design principles for creating microlearning that succeeds consistently.
- **Part 3, Launching Microlearning,** focuses on applying what you have learned, including running pilot initiatives, assessing results, and scaling successful approaches based on your organization's current capabilities. This part provides practical guidance for turning conceptual understanding into actionable results.

Throughout this book, you'll follow Be Natural (BN), a fictional health and beauty company whose challenges and solutions I've created based on the many organizations I've consulted with over the past 20 years. BN's story shows how theoretical concepts play out in realistic scenarios.

How to Use This Book

You don't need to read a cookbook from cover to cover before preparing a meal, and the same is true for this book. Depending on your professional role, different sections will be more immediately useful:

- **Learning leaders and chief learning officers** who are planning their learning strategies may want to focus on part 1 and part 3, with special attention to chapter 7, L&D Capacity and Scaling.
- **Instructional designers and developers** who are creating learning solutions may want to start with the design principles in part 2.
- **Learning architects** thinking about design and implementation may want to begin with part 3 to understand how to effectively launch, measure, and scale microlearning initiatives based on their organization's current state.

Regardless of your approach, I consider chapters 1, 8, and 16 essential reading because they provide a strong foundation for all the other chapters. Chapter 1 establishes what microlearning is, chapter 8 grounds everything in learning science, and chapter 16 ties the preceding chapters together with implementation strategies. Because this book can be read in any order, key points may be reinforced throughout, but always through the lens of the chapter's core topic.

Each of the book's three parts opens with an activity to help you prepare your own mental *mise en place* (the preparation and organization of ingredients before cooking). These activities focus your attention on your specific context, making the concepts immediately relevant to your work. You'll find reflective activities throughout the book, as well as templates in part 3 that are practical guides for applying what you're learning to your own environment.

Throughout the book, I also point out connections between chapters where appropriate, to encourage you to see how the elements work together. Seeing the relationships between microlearning principles will make you a more adaptable, successful learning designer.

My goal is not to give you rigid recipes you must follow to the letter, but to help you develop your intuition for creating your own version of micro-learning and satisfy your organization's appetite for improved performance.

Let's dig in!

PART 1

Assessing Readiness

Is Microlearning Right for Your Organization?

Before you read another word, grab a pen and paper.

1. Write your current definition of *microlearning*. Don't worry about getting it "right." Just capture your honest thoughts about what microlearning means and the way you and your organization view it right now.

2. Think about a microlearning initiative you're interested in implementing at your organization. This could be something you're currently planning, have considered in the past, or think might be valuable in the future. Briefly describe this initiative.

3. Consider these questions about your initiative:
   » What problem or opportunity would it address?
   » Who would be the primary audience?
   » What would success look like?

As you progress through part 1, you'll develop a clearer understanding of whether your organization is ready to implement this type of initiative and what you might need to do to prepare. Hold on to these thoughts as you read. I hope your perspective will expand and evolve as you learn more about maximizing microlearning's potential. By the end of part 1, you'll have a clear framework for assessing your organization's readiness for any initiative.

CHAPTER 1
Microlearning (Re)Defined

By the end of this chapter, you should be able to answer these questions:
- How do people define the term *microlearning*?
- Why can placing too many rules on microlearning create strategic constraints?
- How can understanding microlearning as a concept, method, product, or campaign help L&D professionals?
- What are the three types of microlearning and how do they serve different learning purposes?
- How can you tell if microlearning is understood by your colleagues and stakeholders as a concept, method, product, or campaign?

Imagine walking into my Pennsylvania kitchen on a late-summer day. The counters are covered with fresh tomatoes from my garden, and I'm preparing to make what my family has always called "sauce," although just across the state in Philadelphia, many Italian American families would insist it's "gravy."

My method of making sauce is different from my mother's. She keeps her recipe simple—with just tomato, basil, and garlic—while I add carrots for a touch of sweetness. Although my four brothers and I all learned sauce-making from my mom, we each use an entirely different technique. Despite the differences, we're all creating delicious tomato-based toppings for pasta.

Since publishing *Microlearning: Short and Sweet* in 2019, I've met hundreds of L&D professionals who approach microlearning in the same way my family approaches pasta sauce, with firm convictions about what it is, how it should be made, and what it should be called. Here's what some of them have told me:

- "Microlearning must be digital to be effective," said a digital learning strategist at a global manufacturing firm.
- "It needs to be broken into bite-sized pieces and provided over a period of time," explained an instructional designer developing onboarding materials for a regional healthcare system.
- "Microlearning has to fit into the flow of work," a chief learning officer at a midsize tech startup told me.
- "I was certified in microlearning, but I was taught you don't always have to assess it," said a learning manager overseeing retail training programs.
- "This will resolve our employee engagement issues about not being given time for professional development," a chief human resources officer at a financial services company explained.
- "Videos have to be between three and seven minutes long to be effective," said an e-learning developer creating safety training for warehouse workers.

These competing perspectives reveal different ways of thinking about microlearning's purpose, implementation, and format. Just as members of my family have our own sauce variations, many L&D professionals emphasize different aspects of microlearning. Some focus on its conceptual value, others on methods of delivery, and still others on specific product formats.

In this chapter, we'll explore these three aspects of microlearning—concept, method, and product—and how understanding each can help your organization start with a stable foundation. We'll also explore three distinct types of microlearning—knowledge-based, skills-based, and performance-based—each designed to serve different learning outcomes. Understanding the three aspects and three types of microlearning gives us clarity as we try to maximize its potential in your organization. When you recognize which aspect one of your stakeholders is emphasizing, you'll be better equipped to align expectations and create shared understanding.

First, let's consider why seeking rigid rules about microlearning might actually limit its potential.

Do We Need Rules for Microlearning?

Rules around learning strategies and solutions can have benefits by providing structure without constraining creativity. Rules can:

- Provide clarity and consistency for your project team, stakeholders, subject matter experts, and everyone else involved.
- Ensure fairness by defining how violations of rules and norms will be managed.
- Reduce the risks of noncompliance.

However, most of us who create and facilitate learning experiences don't like to be constrained by too many rules. We want latitude to craft solutions that resolve the actual problems, align with our organization's strategic outcomes (the business goals and measurable results that drive organizational success), and meet the needs of our employees. Too many rules can adversely affect our ability to creatively solve problems, innovate in dynamic environments, and take risks that could result in new insights and solutions.

What about the "rules" described in the quotes from L&D pros? Would creating a firm, universal definition of microlearning that is rules-based and inspired by those descriptions allow us to be more creative and solve problems in diverse learning environments? Which of the quotes defining microlearning would be "wrong" and which would be "right"? Is the digital strategist correct that digital microlearning is the *only* way to ensure good results? Is the e-learning expert's rule that every learning objective should be addressed in three to seven minutes realistic?

The answer to all those questions is *no*.

To help us navigate and direct conversations so we can produce best practices tailored to the needs of our diverse organizations and employees, let's dig into the three aspects of microlearning that I derived from my research, discussions, and conversations. In doing this, we will set the table for the many decisions that you need to make about the use and application of microlearning for your organization or clients. Going back to our sauce analogy, we know that the core ingredients might be similar, but the specific methods, seasonings, and serving approaches can be tailored to your unique situation. As a microlearning designer or an L&D manager, you may follow some general guidelines, but you can also adapt the specifics to meet your needs.

Our Common Ground: The Three Aspects of Microlearning

How can we find a balance between following helpful guidelines (not rigid rules!) and freeing ourselves from unnecessary constraints to maximize how we use microlearning? We can start by developing a shared definition of microlearning that acknowledges its three aspects: It is a concept, a method, and a product. When organizations lack this common ground, many struggle to maximize the potential of microlearning. As L&D professionals, we need this solid foundation to develop effective microlearning strategies. This is similar to understanding that sauce-making involves three aspects: the concept (what makes a good sauce), the method (how it's prepared), and the product (the finished sauce itself). Without this shared understanding, conversations about "sauce" or "gravy" can lead to confusion—just as discussions about microlearning often do when people are focused on different aspects.

Let's start by making sure you can distinguish among the three aspects of microlearning—concept, method, and product—and then we can move on to understanding the different types of microlearning your organization might implement (knowledge-based, skills-based, and performance-based). Understanding both aspects and types creates a complete foundation for effective microlearning decisions.

Microlearning as a Concept

As I was starting to outline this book, I met a vice president of learning for a large international delivery service. "Help me understand what you're talking about," they said. "Tell me about all the various benefits of microlearning."

The delivery company's L&D function was being pressured to convert as much training content as possible to microlearning, as fast as possible, while continuing to maintain the company's original long-format training courses. I started with a simple answer about microlearning as a concept, explaining that it encompasses its overarching purpose and potential as a solution to achieve *outcomes*, whether they're organization-wide, department-specific, or individual. Understanding microlearning as a concept is critical for assessing an organization's readiness to implement effective solutions.

When people discuss microlearning as a concept, they're focused on its purpose (the problems it will solve or opportunities it will create) and its potential (the outcomes it can deliver). Many organizations that have implemented microlearning and believe it has failed think this because they don't consider its purpose, ask too much of it, or aren't ready to support that level of potential.

Your organization's concept of microlearning shapes how you will use it to achieve specific strategic goals. For example, an organization might view microlearning conceptually as:

- A way to foster continuous learning while increasing employee retention and innovation
- An approach to developing more internal candidates for management roles
- A solution for knowledge acquisition, skills development, or performance improvement

Unfortunately, fewer than half of L&D functions align initiatives to organizational outcomes. Even if that's the case in your organization, you can still be successful by creating a current-state conceptual definition like one of those I just listed.

While understanding microlearning as a concept helps us grasp its purpose and potential, we also need to consider how to put these ideas into practice. This brings us to our second aspect: microlearning as a method.

Microlearning as a Method

One of the questions I'm asked most often is, "Can you explain what makes microlearning different?" Here's my short answer: The characteristic that sets microlearning apart from more traditional ways of developing employee performance is the method of delivering content. Microlearning as a method focuses on implementation and delivery, or how content will be distributed, when it will be available, and how participants will access and engage with it.

Every organization decides how participants will engage with learning experiences based on anticipated outcomes and other factors, including delivery, frequency, duration, and access—as explained in Table 1-1.

Table 1-1. Four Key Factors of Microlearning as a Method

Factor	Meaning
Delivery	How do microlearning products reach participants?
Frequency	How often are products distributed?
Duration	How long does the campaign run?
Access	How do participants engage with the content? Is it pushed out on a schedule or pulled in when they are ready?

Each organization must determine if participants will:
- Integrate microlearning into the daily flow of work (frequency and access).
- Have flexibility in choosing when to engage with a microlearning product (access).
- Be able to use a mobile device to participate or engage with microlearning products (delivery method and access).
- Have personalized learning pathways, including microlearning, that expire like annual compliance training or exist in perpetuity (duration).

These method-related decisions directly affect your organization's readiness to implement different types of microlearning. Let's look at how these factors could play out differently in practice, depending on the organization and its outcomes. For a medical ethics review, for example, instructional designers might choose to:
- Distribute content through the organization's learning portal (delivery method).
- Release one scenario-based question daily (frequency).
- Allow up to two hours to complete each scenario (duration).
- Push notifications when new scenarios are available, but let participants complete them anytime within 24 hours (access).

In contrast, a marketing team learning to use artificial intelligence (AI) tools might:
- Receive content through a mobile app (delivery method).
- Get new content weekly for six weeks (frequency).

- Find that each lesson is designed to take 15 to 20 minutes (duration).
- Discover that the campaign allows self-directed engagement, with content available on demand (access).

While many organizations rely solely on their learning management system (LMS) for delivery, microlearning opens opportunities to meet employees where they are. Consider these alternative delivery methods, which can support different approaches to access:

- Team-based portals for daily access as needed by the individual (pull)
- Email notifications with direct links to the target audience (push)
- Mobile-friendly apps combining scheduled releases with on-demand access (push-pull)
- Strategic placement of physical materials, such as posters, throughout the work environment (push)

Throughout this section, I've emphasized the terms *deliver* and *delivery* and key characteristics of delivery and implementation to describe what's distinctive about microlearning as a method. When we turn to microlearning as a product, in the next section, you'll notice different terminology, including the terms *design*, *designed*, and *developed*.

Microlearning as a Product

With a clear understanding of both the concept and method of microlearning, we can now examine what it looks like in its most tangible form: as a product. Just as my mother's finished sauce reflects her specific ingredients and methods, microlearning products reflect specific design choices and implementation approaches. Microlearning as a product is a tangible, self-contained learning experience intentionally designed to elicit a specific outcome from the participant.

At one of my conference presentations, an instructional design specialist spoke up during the Q&A to ask, "How do I get the leaders at my organization to understand what microlearning is and is not?" This is a common challenge because business leaders often think in terms of products. Certainly, defining microlearning as a product is legitimate, but it's not the whole story.

Recall the definition of microlearning from *Microlearning: Short and Sweet* that we discussed in the introduction. This still holds true when considering microlearning as a product; it's a tangible, self-contained learning experience with which the participant interacts.

Microlearning products can take many forms, including:

- Interactive modules and simulations
- Short videos
- In-person one-question quizzes or team huddles
- Mobile learning activities
- Performance support tools

All microlearning products share a few essential characteristics, which we will discuss at various points throughout this book:

- **In design,** they are created for specific outcomes.
- **In scope,** they are self-contained learning experiences.
- **In scale,** they can either stand alone or work as part of a larger campaign.

Their flexibility makes microlearning products adaptable to different needs and preferences. It's important to note that our product-focused definition is no longer attempting to capture the full scope of microlearning, because microlearning is a multifaceted concept that encompasses the strategic intent (the concept), the delivery approach (the method), and the learning product. By separating microlearning as a product from broader conceptual and methodological considerations, you can be more targeted in your conversations and decision making with stakeholders. When it's time to discuss the design of a specific microlearning asset, our original, "short and sweet" definition provides a clear guideline, but when considering microlearning at a strategic level, the more expansive and organization-specific understanding comes into play.

Microlearning Campaigns

Just as restaurants might serve individual dishes or create a tasting menu, learning designers often pair multiple microlearning products together to achieve specific outcomes. We call these collections of products "microlearning campaigns" or "drip campaigns." Think of a campaign as a carefully curated selection of small plates that work together to create a complete dining experience. A campaign can include several products, each focused on a specific topic, skill, or behavior. These campaigns can be designed to build knowledge, develop skills, or support performance, depending on your organizational goals and readiness.

We will now deepen our discussion to help you recognize more distinctions among the three aspects of microlearning and which aspect your colleagues and stakeholders are emphasizing. Being able to recognize which definition is in play at any given time will help put you, your L&D function, and your organization on the same page when it comes to microlearning.

Recognizing Distinctions

Most microlearning initiatives falter as a result of poor communication; everyone thinks they're talking about the same thing when they're usually not. Table 1-2 highlights ways people frequently discuss each aspect of microlearning and what they may really be asking.

If you tune in to conversations carefully, you'll be able to tease out a better understanding of what microlearning means to the people with whom you interact regularly. You will then be able to talk with one another rather than past one another. For example, pay attention to the words that different colleagues use to describe microlearning. Their roles often influence the aspects they prioritize.

- **Strategic decision makers (learning leaders, strategists, and suppliers):**
  - » Usually discuss microlearning as a concept or product
  - » Focus on purpose (what problems it can solve), potential (what value it has), and strategic vision (how it helps to drive business)
  - » Want alignment on overarching goals and outcomes
- **Directors and managers:**
  - » Typically approach microlearning as a method and product
  - » Concentrate on execution and implementation
  - » Align processes and procedures with strategic objectives
- **Designers and developers:**
  - » Generally work with microlearning as a product and then its method

» Create tangible learning experiences

» Transform strategic vision into tangible deliverables

Table 1-2. Recognizing Aspects of Microlearning in Conversation

Aspect of Microlearning	Statement or Question	What It Means
Concept	Explain the various benefits of microlearning.	I need to understand the purpose and potential of microlearning.
	This will resolve our employee engagement issues about not being given time for professional development.	I'm envisioning purpose and potential as related to time constraints.
	I was certified in microlearning, and I was taught you don't always have to assess it.	I'm informing you that its purpose does not have to help with achieving desired potential.
Method	Can you explain to them what makes microlearning different from what we currently do?	I'm trying to build comprehension around the differences in exposure to and engagement with training compared with our current delivery methods.
	Microlearning fits the flow of work.	I'm thinking this is where and how microlearning is implemented.
	Microlearning needs to be broken into bite-sized pieces and provided over a period of time.	I'm suggesting this is how microlearning is created (product) and delivered (method).
Product	How do I get them to understand what microlearning is and is not?	I'm struggling to make this concrete and need examples.
	Videos have to be between three and seven minutes long to be effective.	I'm recommending these parameters for designing and developing microlearning.
	Microlearning must be digital to be effective.	I'm excluding nondigital microlearning solutions.

By recognizing these patterns, you can bridge gaps between different perspectives, guide conversations toward shared understanding, and ensure alignment across all levels of implementation.

Creating a shared definition of microlearning is your first step toward developing an effective strategy. The second step is to make sure that everyone understands what types of microlearning are possible.

Listen for "Performance Improvement"

The term *performance improvement* is used frequently in this book. Much like the word *microlearning, performance improvement* can mean different things to different people.

For example:
- A chief HR officer might use performance improvement to mean increased employee engagement and retention.
- A frontline manager could want faster task completion or fewer errors.
- A compliance officer likely means meeting regulatory requirements.

So, listen carefully to how your stakeholders are using this term. Their definition will determine the type of microlearning they actually need and what success looks like to them.

Types of Microlearning

Microlearning types or categories, based on how knowledge and skills are put to work, help qualify or refine the purpose and potential of microlearning. Organizations often conflate the terms *knowledge, skills, performance,* and *competency,* but as an L&D professional, you probably see these terms as completely different. Let's make sure we are all on the same page by looking at the definitions and examples in Table 1-3.

Table 1-3. Defining Knowledge, Skill, and Performance

Type	Guiding Question	Primary Purpose	Moment of Use
Knowledge-based microlearning	What does the participant need to understand or recall?	Build awareness or foundational understanding	Before application or decision making
Skills-based microlearning	What can the participant practice safely?	Build fluency or procedural accuracy	In structured practice or rehearsal
Performance-based microlearning	What must the participant do in real time?	Support action in a real-world context	During the task or decision moment

In this book, we will focus primarily on knowledge, skills, and performance because, based on my experience and recent research, fewer than half of surveyed organizations align learning initiatives with business outcomes, and only 13 percent of those are ready to execute on that alignment (Wentworth 2021). While this book focuses on knowledge, skills, and performance as the three primary types of microlearning, it's worth noting that competency represents a broader integration of these elements.

A *competency* combines related knowledge, skills, and behaviors that enable successful job performance and aligns directly with business objectives. Think of competencies as the higher-level capabilities that emerge when knowledge is understood, skills are mastered, and performance is consistently demonstrated in varied situations. As your organization builds proficiency with the three fundamental types of microlearning, you may naturally progress toward competency-based approaches that unite all three in service of comprehensive professional development.

Forklift Safety Addressed Three Ways

Let's consider how each type of microlearning might address the topic of forklift blind-spot awareness:

- **Knowledge-based microlearning.** A three-minute animated video would explain the four main blind spots of a forklift (front load, rear corners, immediate rear, and mast area), with clear visuals showing each blind spot's dimensions and why they exist. Operators would watch this video before operating equipment to understand blind-spot fundamentals.
- **Skills-based microlearning.** A series of five-minute practice scenarios on a tablet would ask operators to identify blind spots in various warehouse configurations and practice proper scanning techniques. These scenarios would provide immediate feedback on decision quality and technique, building muscle memory before actual operation.
- **Performance-based microlearning.** Before operating the forklift, the operator conducts a verbal safety walk-through with their supervisor, explaining their planned route and how they'll navigate blind spots. The supervisor may ask situational questions to assess real-time judgment and decision making in their actual work context.

The In-the-Flow Fallacy

A common misconception is that "in-the-flow-of-work" microlearning automatically equals performance-based microlearning. For example, you might hear leaders say, "Let's give them microlearning because they don't have time for dedicated professional development. That way, it can fit into the flow of work and help them improve their performance."

This misunderstanding conflates timing (when learning happens) with purpose (what the learning does). While performance-based microlearning does happen during workflow, simply scheduling learning during work hours doesn't make it performance-based.

My opinion is that performance-based microlearning is specifically designed to provide support at the moment of need—exactly when someone is performing a task. It's not just about fitting learning into busy schedules but about delivering precisely what's needed when the work is happening (Torgerson and Iannone 2020). Some may blend the idea of *skill* and *performance*, but it's important to recognize that *performance* is the use of knowledge and skills in a work context.

Knowledge- or skills-based microlearning might also be delivered during work hours, but if it's focused on building awareness or practicing skills rather than supporting immediate task execution, it's not truly performance-based—regardless of when it's accessed.

In addition to cognitive load, there are other factors to consider surrounding an individual's work environment and the ability to hold attention versus being distracted. These are all discussed in part 2.

Assess Readiness With the Microlearning Readiness Framework

The Microlearning Readiness (MLR) Framework helps assess your organization's readiness to determine, design, develop, deliver, and evaluate microlearning. Effectiveness begins with readiness. How does your organization know that it can successfully determine, design, develop, deliver, and evaluate a microlearning initiative aimed at improving knowledge, skills, performance, or competency? L&D functions must first assess their current capabilities, along with the capabilities of the organization as a whole, to establish a baseline understanding of the learning ecosystem and what types of microlearning it can support. The learning ecosystem is simply the interdependent collection of resources and infrastructure that supports employee training and development.

I'll share more details about the MLR Framework in chapter 2. Its six components include:

- **Outcomes.** The department- or organization-level measures that the microlearning initiative will inform
- **Purpose.** The problems the microlearning initiative will solve or the opportunities it will create
- **Potential.** The possible outcomes that can be derived from the initiative
- **Evaluation.** How and what will be evaluated in alignment with the outcomes, purpose, and potential
- **Spaced learning.** The duration and frequency of the microlearning initiative using techniques that spread learning experiences across time rather than delivering them all at once
- **Implementation.** How, what, when, and where a participant will engage with microlearning

By auditing these factors, L&D functions can gain a clear understanding of their strengths and limitations in relation to microlearning. For instance, some organizations may find that they are well equipped to develop knowledge-based microlearning products but lack the resources or expertise to create more performance-based solutions. Or, an organization might have the capabilities to execute a knowledge-based microlearning campaign using its LMS, but lack the capacity because the LMS administrator can't commit the time required.

The MLR Framework is linked to the three aspects of microlearning (concept, method, and product) and three primary types of microlearning discussed in this chapter (knowledge, skill, and performance). By using the MLR Framework to establish your baseline understanding of what types of microlearning your organization can support, you can make informed decisions about the initiatives you can realistically pursue and the metrics you can use to measure success.

Maximize Microlearning's Potential

Like perfecting your sauce recipe through practice and adaptation, maximizing microlearning's potential requires understanding both fundamentals and nuances. To maximize microlearning's potential in your organization, you'll need to understand how microlearning supports performance development as well as knowledge and skills acquisition; its true power lies in its ability to drive performance. By focusing on the application of learning in addition to retention, microlearning can help bridge the gap between knowing and doing.

Consider a sales training example. A traditional e-learning course might teach reps about handling objections using a mnemonic like LAER (listen, acknowledge, explore, and respond), but just memorizing this acronym doesn't guarantee that participants can apply it effectively in real customer conversations. A microlearning approach could provide short, scenario-based practice opportunities for reps to hone their objection handling (skills) in realistic contexts. For performance support, reps could access decision trees during actual customer calls to help guide them through objection handling in real time.

Chapter Summary

In this chapter, we've explored how microlearning is much more than just short learning experiences. By examining microlearning as a concept, method, and product, we've developed a more comprehensive understanding that can inform better strategic decisions about when and how to use microlearning effectively. Understanding these three aspects helps L&D professionals:

- Align microlearning initiatives with organizational outcomes.
- Choose appropriate implementation methods.
- Design effective learning products and campaigns.
- Communicate more clearly with stakeholders.

The specific definition of microlearning as a concept and method will vary based on organizational factors, such as learning culture, performance goals, and L&D capabilities. Each organization will craft its own unique perspective on how microlearning fits into its ecosystem to drive business impact. The tangible microlearning product, while important, is just one component of a larger microlearning strategy. Campaigns that combine multiple products can address more complex learning needs and create sustained results over time.

The distinction between showing and knowing plays a crucial role in maximizing microlearning's impact and determining organizational readiness. Understanding the three types—knowledge-based microlearning to build understanding, skills-based to develop capabilities, and performance-based to support work in the moment—helps organizations choose the right approach for their current capabilities and goals.

Like a well-equipped kitchen that enables a chef to create their best work, having the right organizational foundation helps ensure that microlearning initiatives can achieve their full potential. In chapter 2, we'll explore how to assess your organization's readiness for different types of microlearning using the MLR Framework.

Food for Thought

Is chapter 1 a microlearning product?

Let's analyze chapter 1 against the three aspects of microlearning:
- **As a concept.** The chapter aligns with the purpose of creating shared understanding about microlearning definitions.
- **As a method.** The chapter is delivered as part of a book, which may be paper or digital.
- **As a product.** The chapter is a tangible learning experience with clear boundaries and objectives; it uses text and visuals.

Now let's evaluate it against the three types of microlearning:
- **Does it build knowledge?** Yes. It helps you understand what microlearning is and how it can be defined.
- **Does it develop skills?** Somewhat. The chapter includes the part 1 opening activity, which helps you examine your ability to identify how you define microlearning and what type or types of microlearning you may be using.
- **Does it support performance?** Not directly. While it builds a foundation for later application, it doesn't provide in-the-moment support during actual implementation.

While chapter 1 exhibits some characteristics of microlearning, its length and complexity exceed what would typically be considered "micro" in most implementations. It's more accurately a traditional learning chapter that teaches about microlearning rather than being a true microlearning product itself.

This analysis demonstrates how the three aspects (concept, method, and product) and three types (knowledge-based, skills-based, and performance-based) of microlearning provide useful lenses for evaluating any learning experience.

CHAPTER 2
Assess Readiness With the MLR Framework

By the end of this chapter, you should be able to answer these questions:
- What is the Microlearning Readiness (MLR) Framework and why is it essential for microlearning success?
- How do the framework's six dimensions work together to assess organizational readiness?
- How can you apply the framework at different levels—from specific initiatives to broader organizational readiness?
- How does organizational readiness influence your approach to change management?

In chapter 1, we explored the three aspects (concept, method, and product) and the three types (knowledge-based, skills-based, and performance-based) of microlearning. This foundation sets the stage for understanding why implementing microlearning requires careful assessment of your organization's readiness.

Implementing microlearning in your organization is like introducing a new cooking technique in a restaurant kitchen. Just as a chef needs to assess whether the kitchen has the right equipment, staff skills, and processes before adopting a new cooking method, you need to evaluate your organization's readiness before implementing microlearning. Without this assessment, your microlearning initiatives might not deliver the expected results.

Many organizations struggle to develop effective microlearning strategies despite recognizing their potential value. Consider these experiences shared by fellow L&D professionals:

- "I totally see how this is important, but we don't even have a strategy for learning in general," a higher ed instructional technologist told me.
- "We cannot help align measures because the organization doesn't measure for more than proof that the training program was passed," explained an e-learning supplier focused on SaaS.
- "Our learning strategy is the LMS. It gathers all the measures we need to prove success," a training director for a small manufacturer said.
- "There's no point in introducing our own strategy. Whatever priority a department gives us is what we have to attend to first anyhow," shared a vice president of talent management at a startup company.
- "Now I have three times the amount of content to maintain because we kept the original training and converted it to microlearning," a support technician at a large nonprofit organization complained.

These perspectives highlight a common challenge: the disconnect between understanding microlearning as a concept and implementing it effectively. Even organizations with a clear understanding of microlearning may struggle with implementation because of gaps in infrastructure, processes, or capabilities. This is why assessing readiness is a critical component in the foundation for microlearning success. Organizations take many different approaches to implementing microlearning. Some conduct comprehensive organizational assessments first; others start with specific initiatives, as you did in the opening activity of part 1; and still others simply implement microlearning without any formal assessment.

🐝 Be Natural: Company Profile

Throughout this book, we will follow the efforts of the L&D function at Be Natural (BN) whose experiences illustrate common microlearning challenges and solutions. BN is a health and beauty company that uses raw honey as an essential ingredient in all its products. Its story, while fictional, is based on real-world scenarios experienced in multiple organizations.

BN has a signature line, the Bee's Knees: a collection of four products designed to revitalize skin, hair, nails, and lips. Other products include healing and pain relief ointments, dry skin treatments, and deodorants.

Challenges

BN is a rapidly growing company on all fronts, from sales to customer care, manufacturing to marketing. Company leaders are concerned about the overall performance of the organization as it scales to meet current and future demand for products.

Key challenges include:
- **Manufacturing.** Accidents have increased dramatically in the past two quarters because of the rapid promotion of newer employees (in their roles for less than two years) into management and supervisory roles.
- **Sales.** The sales team has a high turnover rate, particularly among new hires. A recent analysis comparing entry-level sales job descriptions with new hires over the past nine months found that the majority of these hires lacked the minimum required soft skills BN seeks.
- **Leadership development.** Rapid promotion of inexperienced employees into management roles has created leadership gaps and knowledge loss, contributing to safety incidents, quality issues, and increased turnover.
- **Onboarding.** New hires take two months longer than expected to become competent. This is due in part to knowledge gaps from being hired without requisite skills; inconsistent BN processes have also created barriers to effective performance.

Goals

BN would like to see a stabilization of its profit margin and a reduction in safety infractions at its manufacturing plant in the next quarter. Additionally, BN has set a goal to increase retention of new salespeople beyond nine months over the next two quarters. Globally, BN would like the onboarding process to better integrate new hires into their job context to reduce the onboarding time by at least two months.

Taking Action

BN is piloting multiple microlearning initiatives throughout different parts of the organization to determine which approaches work best for its specific challenges and if these efforts will help it meet any of its goals. These pilot programs will also help inform which microlearning methods can most effectively be scaled across the entire organization. As we explore the MLR Framework and its application, BN's experiences will provide practical context for how readiness assessment leads to better microlearning outcomes.

The MLR Framework: Your Guide to Readiness

Think of implementing microlearning like opening a restaurant. Success requires more than talented chefs and good recipes—you need the right kitchen equipment, efficient processes, and coordinated staff. The MLR Framework provides a structured approach using six specific dimensions (which I introduced in chapter 1) to assess readiness across your organization's learning culture, technological systems, processes, and people capabilities (Figure 2-1). The dimensions are organized into two groups to help you determine what you want to accomplish (intent dimensions) and how you can accomplish it (execution dimensions).

Figure 2-1. Dimensions of the Microlearning Readiness Framework

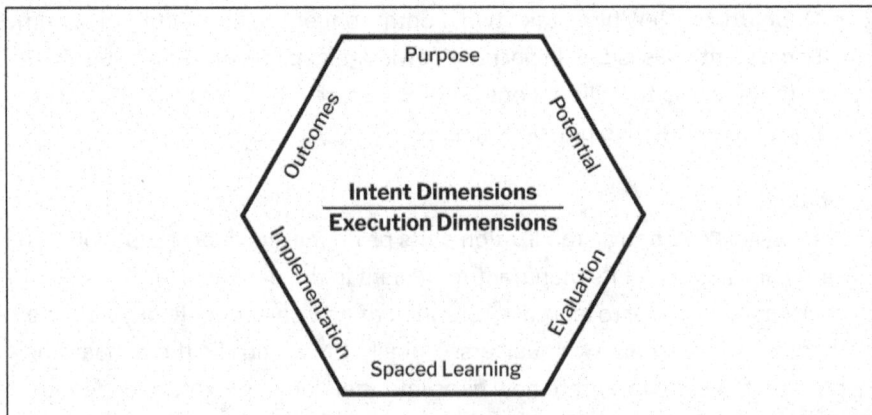

The intent dimensions are:

- **Outcomes.** The specific, measurable results you aim to achieve for your organization
- **Purpose.** Your organization's strategic reason for using microlearning
- **Potential.** The anticipated impact and benefits

The three intent dimensions work together to establish a strategic triangle, which serves as the foundation for your microlearning efforts. (We'll explore this in more detail in chapter 3.)

The execution dimensions are:

- **Evaluation.** Your methods for measuring success
- **Spaced learning.** Your strategy for distributing microlearning over a period of time
- **Implementation.** Your approach to design and delivery

Within this framework, outcomes and evaluation are constant variables, anchoring your strategy to measurable results. The other components—purpose, potential, spaced learning, and implementation—are flexible, based on your organization's specific context and capabilities. (Chapters 4 through 6 provide quick readiness inventories for each dimension and identify common barriers and enablers that can affect your ability to support different types of microlearning.)

Note: While establishing clear outcomes is important, not all microlearning initiatives require formal evaluation systems. Organizations with limited assessment capabilities can still implement effective microlearning by focusing on well-defined outcomes and purpose, even if measurement remains basic or informal.

Framework Application Levels

The MLR Framework can be applied at three distinct levels:

- **Pilot initiative level** is about assessing readiness for a specific microlearning project (the focus of chapters 3–6). This level:
  - » Represents the most manageable entry point for organizations new to microlearning

» Helps determine if a particular initiative can succeed, given current capabilities

» Asks, "Can your manufacturing division successfully implement safety microlearning?"

- **L&D function level** is about evaluating your L&D team's overall capabilities to support microlearning (explored in detail in chapter 7). This level:

  » Helps L&D assess and build its own readiness by examining what types of microlearning your team can create and sustain

  » Asks, "What microlearning types can your L&D team effectively support right now?"

- **Organizational level** is about determining broader organizational readiness (touched upon in chapter 7). This level:

  » Is the ultimate application once L&D has established its own capabilities and examines how well the entire organization can adopt and integrate microlearning

  » Asks, "Is your organization ready for microlearning as a standard approach with your current learning ecosystem?"

L&D must first develop its own microlearning capabilities before helping the broader organization implement them. This method ensures you will build from a position of strength.

The three levels inform one another. A pilot assessment reveals the L&D function's limitations, while the L&D assessment exposes organizational constraints. By starting where you have the most control, usually with a focused pilot initiative, you can gain practical experience that informs broader applications. Organizations are encouraged to progress through these levels sequentially:

1. Start with pilot initiatives that match current capabilities (chapter 16).
2. Build L&D function capabilities based on pilot program results (chapter 7).
3. Expand to organizational readiness once L&D can support various microlearning types.

The MLR Framework Establishes Your Baseline

The MLR Framework is a diagnostic tool to help you understand what types of microlearning initiatives your organization can support. The assessment process involves three steps:

1. **Evaluate your current state.** Examine your organization's or L&D's capabilities and constraints for each consideration point. At BN, this revealed strong outcome alignment in manufacturing but weaker evaluation capabilities in sales. Take these actions at each application level:
   » For pilot initiatives, focus on specific project requirements.
   » For the L&D function, assess overall skills and resources.
   » For the organization as a whole, evaluate cross-functional readiness.

2. **Identify gaps.** Look for areas where additional infrastructure or capabilities are needed. BN discovered that it needed better feedback mechanisms for skills development and stronger analytics for measuring impact. Take these actions at each application level:
   » For pilot initiatives, identify critical barriers to pilot implementation.
   » For the L&D function, map broader capability development needs.
   » For the organization as a whole, address systemic barriers to adoption (for example technology, people, and processes).

3. **Plan strategic growth.** Develop a road map for building additional capabilities over time. For example, BN started with knowledge-based initiatives while developing the infrastructure for more complex approaches. Take these actions at each application level:
   » For pilot initiatives, focus on immediate success factors that you can implement.
   » For the L&D function, prioritize capability development.
   » For the organization as a whole, create cross-functional alignment to ensure the organization's infrastructure allows a stronger integration of microlearning.

From MLR Framework to Change Management

Your MLR Framework assessment provides valuable insights into the changes your organization needs to make to implement different types of microlearning successfully. Table 2-1 highlights examples of how framework findings might indicate areas for change. Your organization's needs will vary based on your specific context.

Table 2-1. MLR Framework Findings and Areas in Need of Change

Area	MLR Framework Findings	What Needs to Change?
Technology	Gaps in learning platform capabilities and integration challenges	Upgrade or integrate platforms to support microlearning, enable mobile access, and improve data tracking.
	Insufficient data collection and analytics capabilities	Implement xAPI, AI-driven insights, and dashboards to track engagement and performance.
Process	Existing evaluation methods don't effectively measure microlearning impact	Shift toward impact-driven metrics, such as behavioral change and application in the workplace.
	Lack of coordination across departments in learning initiatives	Improve cross-functional collaboration among HR, IT, operations, and compliance teams to align learning efforts.
People	Managers not reinforcing learning application	Train managers to support learning goals, provide coaching, and integrate learning discussions into performance reviews.
	Learning not considered in performance evaluation	Embed learning goals into professional development and performance measurement frameworks.

Microlearning represents a *disruptive innovation* in L&D—not because it's negative, but because it requires organizations to rethink their approaches to design, delivery, and measurement. This disruption means that implementing microlearning often requires careful change management.

Managing Change Based on MLR Framework Findings

When implementing microlearning based on your MLR Framework assessment, you'll likely need to manage organizational change. Effective change management for microlearning focuses on six principles:

- **Understand the need for change.** Use your MLR Framework findings to build compelling cases for changing current approaches.
- **Plan thoroughly.** Develop detailed strategies based on your organization's current capabilities, including those of L&D.
- **Engage and communicate strategically.** Focus on the stakeholders and target audiences most affected by your planned microlearning approach.
- **Train and develop capabilities.** Ensure that all stakeholders understand their roles in supporting new learning approaches.
- **Monitor and evaluate progress.** Apply the same rigor to tracking change progress as you do to measuring learning outcomes.
- **Sustain change through reinforcement.** Build mechanisms that support your chosen microlearning approaches for the long term.

🐝 Be Natural's Pilot Initiatives and Principles

When BN initially decided to use microlearning for onboarding, company leaders assumed it would immediately address performance problems. The leadership team believed that simply converting existing onboarding materials into some version of microlearning would solve the two-month competency gap.

However, when the L&D team applied the MLR Framework, it discovered these critical misalignments:
- BN wanted performance-based results but the organization only had knowledge-based assessment capabilities.
- BN leaders expected skills development but the current learning products and departmental onboarding processes lacked practice feedback mechanisms.
- BN's technology for learning initiatives could support basic knowledge delivery but not performance support.

The MLR Framework helped the company understand that it could start with knowledge-based microlearning (product information cards) using minimal technology while building the company's capabilities for more complex approaches. This prevented BN from investing in expensive performance-support technology before having the feedback processes necessary to make it effective.

Rather than abandoning performance goals, BN created a new phased plan:
- **Phase 1.** Knowledge-based product cards with simple pre- and post-assessments
- **Phase 2.** Skills-based practice scenarios once manager feedback capabilities were developed
- **Phase 3.** Performance support tools after workflow integration was better understood

This realistic, capability-based approach allowed the company to make immediate progress while building toward its ultimate performance goals. This example demonstrates how organizational readiness directly affects implementation success. By starting where it had strong capabilities and addressing gaps strategically, BN managed change effectively.

If the prospect of an organization-wide analysis seems too daunting at first, you can work with the MLR Framework exclusively within your L&D function (see chapter 7) or for a specific pilot initiative. Each change management consideration point is still relevant and provides a great way to practice your approach to prepare for when you are ready to involve more of the organization.

This example also demonstrates several of this chapter's key concepts: using the MLR Framework as a diagnostic tool, letting readiness findings guide strategic decisions, and applying change management principles to build capabilities systematically. BN's experience shows how the framework helps organizations start where they are strong while building toward more ambitious microlearning goals.

Chapter Summary

The MLR Framework is a guide to developing effective microlearning initiatives that align with your organization's and L&D's current capabilities while building toward future goals. In this chapter, we've considered:
- The MLR Framework and its six dimensions, organized in relation to intent and execution

- Using the MLR Framework as a diagnostic tool at three different levels (a specific pilot initiative, exclusively with the L&D function, or organization wide)
- How framework findings guide change management efforts

Remember, you don't need perfect readiness to begin. Start where you are, using the framework to guide your growth. Focus on initiatives that match your current capabilities while building toward more ambitious goals. The key is taking that first step in assessing your readiness—everything else builds from there.

The MLR Framework's flexibility allows you to assess readiness at multiple levels—from specific projects or pilot initiatives, to L&D capabilities, to organizational adoption. While subsequent chapters will primarily focus on project-level application focused on a goal of measurement, chapter 7 will explore how L&D capabilities create the foundation for broader implementation.

In the next several chapters, we'll explore each dimension in detail, using Be Natural's microlearning journey to illustrate how the MLR Framework guides strategic decision making. Chapter 3 examines how the Intent dimensions of outcomes, purpose, and potential work together to establish a strong foundation for microlearning success.

Prioritize Your Framework Focus

Purpose
Identify which dimensions of the MLR Framework are most crucial for your specific microlearning initiative and at which level you should begin your assessment. (See the part 1 opening activity as a refresher.) This helps you focus on the dimensions that will most influence your ability to effectively implement knowledge-based, skills-based, or performance-based microlearning.

Strategic Value
By identifying your priority dimensions, you can focus your attention on the areas most critical to success, whether that means improving gaps or leveraging existing strengths. This assessment helps build stakeholder support for targeted capability development.

Instructions
1. Review your proposed microlearning initiative from the part 1 opening activity. (If you haven't yet completed this activity, go back and do that now.)
2. Rate how critical each dimension is for successfully implementing your initiative. Use the following criteria:
   » **Critical.** This dimension is essential for your initiative to succeed.
   » **Important.** This dimension matters but won't make or break your initiative.
   » **Less relevant.** This dimension has minimal effect on your specific initiative.
3. Assess your current readiness for your two highest-rated dimensions. Use the following criteria:
   » **Strong.** You have established capabilities in this area.
   » **Developing.** You have basic capabilities that need strengthening.
   » **Limited.** You have minimal capabilities and significant gaps.
4. Write one to two sentences explaining why these dimensions are critical for addressing the problem or opportunity you identified in the part 1 opening activity.

As you work through the coming chapters, use this prioritization to focus your attention on the areas most critical to your success. The chapters will help you assess your current capabilities in these priority areas and understand what readiness level you can realistically support. Then, you can validate your thinking and develop a more targeted approach to building microlearning readiness.

CHAPTER 3
Outcomes, Purpose, and Potential

By the end of this chapter, you should be able to answer these questions:
- How do outcomes, purpose, and potential work together to create a strategic foundation for microlearning success?
- What questions should you ask to assess your project's readiness in these areas?
- What common challenges might you face when establishing these outcomes, purpose, and potential for a specific microlearning initiative?
- How do outcomes, purpose, and potential affect the types of microlearning your project can realistically support?
- How can you move forward with a focused microlearning project even if your organization lacks a clear strategic direction?

Imagine you're preparing to cook a special meal. Before rushing to the stove, you first consider three essential questions: What specific dish are you creating? Why are you making this particular dish? And what impact do you want it to have on those who eat it? These questions establish the strategic foundation for every decision that follows—from ingredient selection to cooking techniques to presentation.

Creating effective microlearning follows a similar process. In chapters 1 and 2, we explored definitions of microlearning and the MLR Framework as a tool for assessing an organization's readiness to use the three types of microlearning. We established that starting with focused projects or pilots—rather than organization-wide implementation—creates the strongest foundation for success.

This chapter examines the first three dimensions of the MLR Framework: outcomes, purpose, and potential, also called the Intent dimensions. These dimensions appear first in the framework because they establish the foundational starting points that determine microlearning success. Just as those three essential cooking questions work together to guide every decision, these three dimensions work like ingredients in a recipe—individually important but most effective when properly combined. By evaluating how well you've defined your project's goals, reasons for using microlearning, and expected benefits, you'll determine which approaches (knowledge-based, skills-based, or performance-based) are most likely to succeed in your specific context.

Unfortunately, many organizations struggle with these foundational elements. Here's what some of my colleagues have shared:

- "Our stakeholders can't articulate clear outcomes. They just want training fast," a learning architect at an international consulting firm told me.
- "We understand the purpose, but leadership doesn't see the potential beyond cost savings," a training manager in healthcare education said.
- "How can we align our outcomes when the organization's strategy changes every few months?" a chief learning officer in finance asked.

In 2024, LinkedIn's *Workplace Learning Report* noted that the number 1 priority of organizations for a second year in a row was aligning learning programs to business goals. This research also points out that L&D lags in tracking business impact. For example, 36 percent of L&D professionals indicated that they measure the impact of their efforts with performance reviews, and only 30 percent measure business impact! Without clarity around outcomes, purpose, and potential, microlearning initiatives risk becoming just another "quick fix" that fails to deliver real value.

Outcomes, Purpose, and Potential in the MLR Framework

As introduced in chapter 2, outcomes, purpose, and potential form the intent dimensions of the MLR Framework. Together, these three dimensions create a strategic triangle within the six-part framework hexagon—each side supporting and informing the others (Figure 3-1).

Figure 3-1. The Strategic Triangle and the MLR Framework

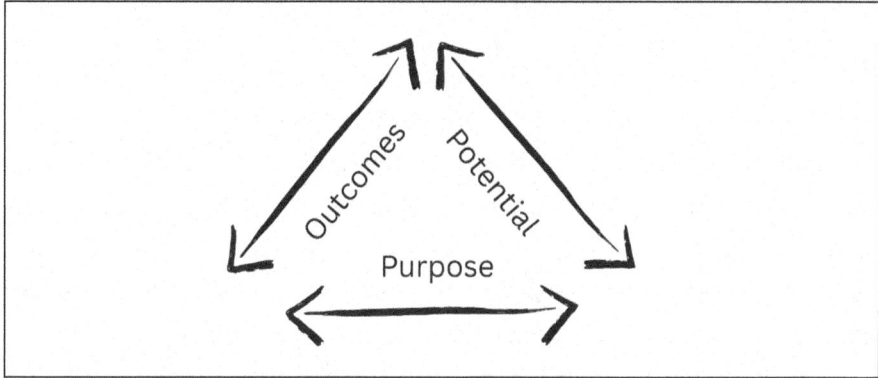

Like a three-legged stool, these three dimensions work in a dynamic relationship, each one informing and strengthening the others. Strong outcomes without clear purpose may lead to activity without impact. Clear purpose without defined outcomes makes it hard to demonstrate success or determine whether investing L&D resources is worthwhile. And without understanding the potential, you risk setting unrealistic outcomes and communicating purpose ineffectively.

Why This Strategic Foundation Matters

Understanding your strategic foundation—how outcomes, purpose, and potential work together—transforms the way you approach your microlearning initiative.

Understanding outcomes, purpose, and potential enables you to guide stakeholders toward solutions that create real business value rather than disconnected training requests. This foundation helps L&D allocate capacity strategically—investing resources in initiatives that align with organizational goals instead of managing one-off content with unclear impact. You can make better decisions about where to focus resources, design targeted microlearning that addresses specific performance gaps, and position L&D as a strategic partner in achieving business priorities.

Assess Your Strategic Foundation

Your strategic foundation builds on the three questions from the part 1 opening activity: What is the problem you're addressing, who is your audience, and what does success look like. Outcomes, purpose, and potential provide the framework for answering these questions strategically and evaluating your readiness.

Outcomes: What Would Success Look Like?

Successful microlearning initiatives start with clarity about what you're trying to achieve. Outcomes represent the specific, measurable results that demonstrate your initiative's value to stakeholders and guide your design decisions. Unlike vague aspirations like "improve knowledge," strong outcomes connect directly to business goals and include mechanisms to track and show results.

The most effective outcomes balance three essential elements:
- They provide clarity through specific, measurable results you aim to achieve rather than general improvement hopes.
- They maintain alignment by connecting to broader business goals, ensuring your microlearning initiative supports organizational priorities.
- They include measurability through established mechanisms to track and demonstrate impact, making success visible to stakeholders.

Many organizations struggle with outcomes because stakeholders focus on activities rather than results, or because competing L&D or organizational priorities dilute focus. Without baseline data to measure against, even well-intentioned initiatives lack the foundation for demonstrating improvement. The key is starting with performance data that connects the use of learning products to business metrics, combined with stakeholder agreement on priority outcomes and clear connection to existing business key performance indicators (KPIs), objectives and key results (OKRs), and knowledge, skills, and abilities (KSAs).

Diagnostic indicators for outcomes are:
- **Strong readiness.** Your project has clearly defined metrics with baseline data, specific targets, and time frames. Stakeholders agree on what success looks like, and you have systems in place to measure results.

- **Limited readiness.** Your project has vague goals like "improve knowledge" without specific metrics. Success criteria are undefined or constantly shifting, and you lack reliable measurement mechanisms.

Purpose: What Opportunity Does Microlearning Address?

Effective purpose requires having a strategic focus on the specific reason for using microlearning, along with a scope definition to provide a clear performance need or opportunity and stakeholder alignment that ensures shared understanding across teams.

Your program will have a weak foundation if you choose microlearning primarily for convenience or because it is trendy. Having an unclear connection to performance needs is another problem. Additionally, stakeholders with competing agendas can derail progress, and a project scope that is too broad or ambiguous makes it difficult to achieve success.

To overcome these barriers, you'll need documented performance gaps and a clear business case for the initiative. Building stakeholder involvement through a well-defined purpose strengthens your approach, especially when combined with a focused scope that addresses specific needs.

Diagnostic indicators for purpose are:
- **Strong readiness.** Your project addresses a specific, documented performance gap with clear business impact. Stakeholders agree that microlearning is the right approach (or part of the right approach) and the scope is well-defined.
- **Limited readiness.** Your project lacks a clear connection to performance needs. Microlearning is chosen primarily for convenience, and stakeholders have different views on what the initiative should accomplish.

Potential: What Impact Do You Anticipate?

Understanding potential requires defining benefits so expected results are clearly articulated. You'll also need a value demonstration to show the benefits to your stakeholders and realistic expectations that align with current capabilities.

Common barriers include overestimating potential benefits to the target audience or organization, which creates unrealistic foundations, as does focusing solely on cost savings and speed of delivery. Additionally, a lack of mechanisms to demonstrate value hampers progress, and misaligned stakeholder expectations about what L&D can deliver or what target audiences will be able to accomplish can derail initiatives.

To strengthen your potential assessment, make sure you're making a realistic assessment of the potential benefits for targeted audiences and organizations, supported by identifying multiple benefit types (not just cost or time). You can enhance your approach by building clear methods for demonstrating value—such as pre- and post-assessments, performance metrics, and stakeholder surveys—especially when combined with stakeholder agreement on expected benefits. This provides clear understanding of what will actually be delivered, ensuring stakeholders don't expect one thing but receive something entirely different.

Diagnostic indicators for potential are:

- **Strong readiness.** Your project has clearly defined benefits that stakeholders and the organization value. You've established mechanisms to demonstrate these benefits, and expectations of what L&D can achieve align with your current capabilities.
- **Limited readiness.** Your project has undefined or constantly shifting benefit expectations. There's no clear plan for demonstrating value, and stakeholders expect results beyond L&D's or the organization's current capabilities.

Assessing Your Current State

Evaluating your project's readiness across outcomes, purpose, and potential involves gathering perspectives from three key groups: the project team, stakeholders, and the L&D function:

- Your project team can help clarify what specific, measurable outcomes the project targets, why microlearning might be the right approach, and what realistic benefits you expect. These conversations often reveal whether your core team shares a common understanding of the initiative's direction.

- Stakeholders bring their own definitions of success, performance expectations, and benefit priorities. Their perspectives often uncover assumptions and expectations that may not align with the project team's vision.
- Your L&D function can identify available measurement capabilities, how this project fits within current strategy, and what resources exist to demonstrate potential benefits. This internal view helps establish what's realistically achievable.

This information gathering informs which type of microlearning strategy matches your current capabilities. Strategic foundation clarity comes from understanding what your project aims to achieve, why it matters, and how you'll demonstrate value.

Your Strategic Foundation and Microlearning Types

Now that you've assessed your strategic foundation across outcomes, purpose, and potential, you can determine which type of microlearning matches your current readiness level. Different types of microlearning require different levels of strategic capability—knowledge-based microlearning has lower requirements than skills-based, which in turn requires less than performance-based approaches. Let's review the bare minimum key indicators for each type:

- **You're ready for knowledge-based microlearning when:**
  - » *Outcomes.* You can track completion and basic knowledge retention.
  - » *Purpose.* Your goal is to build awareness or share information.
  - » *Potential.* You're aiming for improved knowledge retention and consistent messaging.
- **You're ready for skills-based microlearning when:**
  - » *Outcomes.* You can observe and measure skill demonstration.
  - » *Purpose.* Your goal is to develop specific abilities or master procedures.
  - » *Potential.* You're aiming for skill proficiency and standardized performance.

- **You're ready for performance-based microlearning when:**
  - » *Outcomes.* You can measure workplace behavior change and business impact.
  - » *Purpose.* Your goal is to integrate performance support into real work.
  - » *Potential.* You're aiming for measurable business results and business value.

Choose the microlearning type that matches your current readiness level while building toward more advanced capabilities over time. Success with knowledge-based microlearning creates the foundation for skills-based approaches, which in turn build toward performance-based initiatives. However, this doesn't mean you can't try more advanced approaches on a smaller scale to test your capabilities and build experience—just make sure the pilot initiative's scope matches your current infrastructure and support systems.

🐝 Building a Strategic Foundation Through Pilot Programs

Be Natural systematically applied the strategic triangle of outcomes, purpose, and potential across three progressive microlearning pilot initiatives, showing the move from basic knowledge-based to advanced performance-based approaches.

By starting with a focused project, you can establish a strong strategic foundation before expanding to broader implementation. Let's look at how a company like BN might apply an understanding of outcomes, purpose, and potential to improve specific projects.

A Manufacturing Initiative Focused on Safety
BN's first microlearning pilot initiative focused on reducing safety incidents in manufacturing. The company defined:

- Specific outcomes (a 25 percent reduction in incidents within 90 days)
- A clear purpose (addressing the specific procedural gaps identified in safety audits)
- Realistic potential (improved compliance with minimal production disruption)

This focused approach made measuring success straightforward and helped secure leadership support for expansion. By concentrating on just one department with clear metrics, it was possible to directly connect learning to performance improvement. The team also quickly learned that it was much easier to demonstrate value with only three specific outcomes. In previous initiatives, the company had tried to track too many metrics, which prevented it from telling a clear story about impact.

This foundational pilot program established BN's approach to strategic clarity, providing lessons that would inform its subsequent initiatives.

A Sales Training Pilot Initiative to Boost Customer Satisfaction
When BN expanded its offerings to sales training, the L&D team applied lessons learned from the manufacturing pilot program. They established:

- Clear outcomes (a 15 percent increase in product knowledge scores and a 10 percent improvement in customer satisfaction ratings)
- Purpose (to standardize product messaging across regions)
- Potential (reduced customer complaints about inconsistent information)

This solid strategic foundation helped sales managers understand their role in supporting the initiative and set appropriate expectations with sales representatives. Unlike previous attempts, which had promised vague improvements, this focused approach made it easy for everyone to see progress.

BN used this pilot initiative to continue demonstrating how the strategic triangle could be adapted to different departments while maintaining the same disciplined approach to outcomes, purpose, and potential.

A Leadership Development Pilot Initiative to Reduce Turnover
BN was experiencing high turnover among teams with first-time managers. Rather than rolling out another broad leadership program, the L&D team piloted a focused microlearning approach with one newly promoted manager and their team. They established:

- Clear outcomes (reduce turnover on this team within six months)
- Purpose (build critical feedback and coaching skills)
- Potential (improved team performance and reduced turnover costs)

Previous leadership training initiatives had covered numerous topics with vague goals and were designed to demonstrate that they'd been completed, not that they were working. This time, the L&D team targeted specific behavioral changes with measurable business impact. By tracking how the manager's developing skills affected team retention, BN could demonstrate tangible business value before expanding the approach.

BN's progression from basic safety compliance to leadership development illustrates how strong strategic foundations enable organizations to tackle increasingly complex performance challenges through microlearning.

Common Challenges for Projects and Pilot Initiatives

Because outcomes, purpose, and potential work in triadic reciprocity—with each informing and strengthening the others—challenges in one area create ripple effects throughout your strategic foundation. The following issues commonly destabilize this balance:

- **Scope creep.** As stakeholders see potential benefits, they often want to expand the scope beyond what's initially feasible. The solution is to maintain focus on your defined outcomes by explicitly documenting what's in and out of scope.
- **Measurement overreach.** Starting with too many metrics can dilute focus and increase the complexity of assessments. Begin with two to three core measures directly tied to your primary outcome and add more sophisticated metrics as you develop capabilities. For example, trying to measure completion rates, knowledge retention, behavior change, business impact, stakeholder satisfaction, and cost savings all at once requires an overwhelming amount of data collection that most teams can't sustain.
- **Misaligned expectations.** Each stakeholder may have a different idea about purpose and potential. Document alignment discussions to maintain a consistent understanding throughout a pilot initiative or project. Try using Table 1-3 (in chapter 1) during conversations with stakeholders to understand how they are making distinctions

about what they expect microlearning to do. Pay particular attention to how stakeholders frame their expectations. As we discussed in chapter 1, statements like "training will resolve X issue" often reveal assumptions about what microlearning can accomplish, but they may not align with your strategic foundation or current capabilities.

By addressing these challenges proactively, you set the stage for broader implementation. Remember that success doesn't require eliminating all challenges before starting your microlearning initiatives. You just need to understand them and develop pragmatic approaches to working with or around them while steadily building your L&D team's assessment and measurement capabilities.

Chapter Summary

Understanding how outcomes, purpose, and potential work together as a strategic triangle is essential to maximizing your microlearning success, even within complex or unclear organizational contexts. By assessing these elements in your organization, you can make better decisions about microlearning initiatives, align more effectively with business goals, demonstrate clearer value to stakeholders, and build more sustainable solutions.

Even when your organization's strategy is unclear, you can create successful microlearning projects or pilot programs by defining specific, measurable outcomes at the project level. These focused initiatives not only deliver immediate value but also build the foundation for broader implementation as your L&D capabilities grow.

The strategic foundation you establish for your project directly influences which types of microlearning you can effectively implement. Knowledge-based microlearning requires basic outcome clarity, while skills-based and performance-based approaches demand progressively stronger alignment among outcomes, purpose, and potential.

In the next chapter, we'll explore how to evaluate microlearning initiatives effectively, building on this strategic foundation.

Assess Your Strategic Foundation

Purpose
Evaluate your project's strategic foundation in terms of outcomes, purpose, and potential to determine which type of microlearning is most feasible for the project you selected in the part 1 opening activity. This assessment is designed to help you quickly identify current constraints and a realistic starting point—it's not a comprehensive strategic analysis. The key question this activity will help you answer is, "What type of microlearning can you implement effectively given your current strategic foundation?" It should take you 15 to 20 minutes to complete.

Strategic Value
When organizations attempt microlearning approaches that exceed their strategic foundation capabilities, it can lead to failed initiatives and stakeholder skepticism. This constraint-focused assessment helps you make realistic choices that build credibility and demonstrate value, creating a foundation for more advanced approaches over time. Success with appropriate strategic foundation approaches builds organizational confidence in a microlearning investment.

Instructions
In the tables on the next page, rate your current project's strategic foundation using the scale provided. Be honest in your assessment—identifying limitations now prevents overreach later and creates a road map for growth.

Use this rating scale to assess your strategic foundation:
- **Strong**—clearly defined and measurable with a strong organizational connection. You have specific metrics, stakeholder consensus, and organizational support, and you can articulate exactly how this will affect the targeted audience and contribute to organizational goals.
- **Developing**—partially defined with some organizational connection but needs refinement. You have general ideas and some organizational awareness but lack precision or specific measurements that connect directly to your initiative and broader organizational priorities.
- **Limited**—vague or undefined with a weak organizational connection. You may have broad organizational outcomes but haven't translated them to meaningful project-level metrics or a purpose, or your project foundation is clear but doesn't connect to organizational priorities.

Part 1. Determine Your Project's Strategic Foundation

Outcomes	Rating (strong, developing, or limited)
Clarity: Project has specific, measurable results.	
Alignment: Project outcomes connect to business goals.	
Measurability: Data sources for tracking outcomes exist.	

Purpose	Rating (strong, developing, or limited)
Strategic focus: You have a clear reason for using microlearning.	
Scope definition: Performance needs are well-defined.	
Stakeholder alignment: There's a shared understanding of purpose.	

Potential	Rating (strong, developing, or limited)
Benefit definition: Anticipated results are documented.	
Value demonstration: You have methods to show that benefits exist.	
Realistic expectations: Potential aligns with capabilities.	

Part 2. Determine Your Starting Point

What areas did you rate as limited? These are your real constraints for developing a strategic foundation. Instead of asking "What's my total score?" ask "What's preventing me from establishing a stronger strategic foundation?" Your constraints determine the starting point, which then determines the type of microlearning you can effectively implement.

Compare your answers in each category to this list to find your starting point.
- **Knowledge-based microlearning:**
  - » Mostly "developing" or "strong" ratings in outcome clarity and measurability
  - » At least "developing" ratings for purpose
  - » Can measure completion and basic knowledge retention

- **Skills-based microlearning:**
    - » Primarily "strong" ratings across outcomes
    - » At least "developing" ratings in purpose and potential
    - » Can measure skills demonstration and practice effectiveness
- Performance-based microlearning:
    - » "Strong" ratings across most areas
    - » "Strong" alignment across outcomes, purpose, and potential
    - » Can measure workplace behavior change and business impact

It is best to start with a microlearning type that matches your current readiness level while building capabilities for more advanced approaches. Success with focused initiatives creates a foundation for broader implementation.

Next Steps
Based on your assessment, identify:
- Your strongest foundation area: _____
- Your biggest constraint: _____
- One immediate action to address that constraint: _____

Reflection Questions
- What surprised you most about your strategic foundation readiness?
- Which constraint, if addressed, would have the biggest influence on your microlearning success?
- How might your constraint pattern change if you started with a smaller scope?

CHAPTER 4
Evaluation

By the end of this chapter, you should be able to answer these questions:
- How does evaluation function as a strategic dimension of the MLR Framework?
- What are the essential elements of an effective evaluation approach for microlearning?
- How do you assess your organization's current evaluation capabilities for specific microlearning initiatives?
- What common barriers might limit the effectiveness of your evaluations, and what enablers can help you overcome them?
- How can you implement effective evaluation strategies for focused microlearning projects?

In the kitchen, a skilled chef doesn't just follow recipes; they constantly evaluate their progress. They taste a sauce to gauge its flavors, check a roast's internal temperature, and adjust cooking times based on visual cues. Without these evaluation methods, even the most meticulously planned meal might fall short of expectations. The chef who masters evaluation techniques can confidently adapt to different ingredients, kitchens, cooking challenges, and diner preferences.

Similarly, in microlearning, evaluation is not simply a last step; it's a critical strategic element that shapes every aspect of an initiative. Just as cooking without tasting leads to unpredictable results, implementing microlearning without appropriate evaluation methods leaves you unable to demonstrate value or make informed improvements. Consider these concerns shared by learning professionals related directly and indirectly to evaluation:

- "I see that evaluation is important, but we don't even have a strategy for learning in general," an instructional technologist in higher education told me.
- "We can't help align measures because the organization doesn't measure for more than proof that a course was passed," an e-learning supplier complained.
- "Our learning strategy is the LMS," a training director for a small manufacturer said. "It gathers all the measures we need to prove success."

These perspectives highlight a common dilemma: Many organizations recognize the importance of evaluation but struggle to implement meaningful approaches that go beyond basic completion metrics.

In chapter 3, we explored the strategic triangle: How outcomes, purpose, and potential work together to establish your microlearning intent. These three dimensions answer the question, "What do we want to accomplish and why?"

Now we shift to the execution dimension: The three interconnected capabilities that determine how effectively you can deliver on that intent. Evaluation, spaced learning, and implementation don't function as separate sequential steps. Instead, they form an integrated system where decisions in one area directly affect your options and effectiveness in the others.

Think of it this way: You might have strong evaluation methods (chapter 4), but if your spaced learning strategy (chapter 5) requires technology that your implementation infrastructure (chapter 6) can't support, the evaluation data will reveal problems you can't solve. Or you might design spacing approaches that the implementation capabilities can't sustain, making evaluation difficult. These three dimensions need to align for microlearning to succeed.

This chapter focuses on evaluation: your methods for measuring success and demonstrating value. But as you assess evaluation readiness, remember that any choices here will influence (and be influenced by) your spaced learning and implementation capabilities. We'll explore these connections throughout this chapter and the two that follow, culminating in chapter 6 with an integrated readiness assessment across all three execution dimensions.

Find the Right Fit

Not every microlearning effort requires the same evaluation approach. If you're creating standalone awareness content or simple knowledge reinforcement without specific performance goals, basic completion tracking may suffice. This chapter becomes more valuable when you're connecting microlearning to specific outcomes, building skills that need measurement, or demonstrating business impact. The assessment activity at the end of this chapter will help you determine the level of evaluation infrastructure you currently have and what that means for your microlearning approach.

What Is Evaluation in Microlearning?

Evaluation, for the purposes of our efforts, encompasses the full range of measurement activities—including assessments (tests, quizzes, and observations), data analysis, and interpretation of results—to determine effectiveness and impact. It generates actionable insights that inform decisions about content, delivery, and strategy. Rather than simply collecting data to prove value, evaluation can guide improvements and optimization. This means designing measurement approaches that reveal not just what happened, but why it happened and what to do next.

Evaluation influences every aspect of your microlearning initiatives—from initial design through implementation and beyond. It transforms microlearning from an activity-based exercise ("We delivered training") to an outcome-driven strategy ("New hires onboarded and assumed full job responsibilities in less time") that demonstrates specific value—whether reducing compliance infractions, developing internal talent, improving safety outcomes, or enhancing knowledge retention.

Key Elements of Evaluation

Evaluation encompasses two interconnected aspects: measuring whether participants achieved the intended outcomes and assessing whether your microlearning approach is working. These aspects inform each other. When participant outcomes fall short, evaluating your approach helps you determine whether the issue lies with participant readiness, content design, delivery timing, support systems, or infrastructure gaps. For example, if participants aren't retaining information, it could indicate a learning problem or reveal that your spacing intervals are too far apart. If skills aren't improving, participants might need more practice, or managers might not be providing the evaluative feedback your approach requires.

Organizations also vary in their evaluation practices. Some have cultures that dig into what's working and what needs adjustment if initiatives under-perform. Others declare that something "didn't work," but don't examine the specific elements that could be improved. When you're investing in microlearning infrastructure (technology platforms, delivery processes, people development), evaluation helps protect that investment by revealing the components that support success and which ones need refinement.

Effective evaluation requires an infrastructure in three categories: technology, process, and people. These elements don't function independently. Your technology choices create process requirements, your process design determines people needs, and your people capabilities influence what technology and processes are realistic. Understanding how these elements interact helps you assess which types of microlearning you can evaluate today and where to focus infrastructure development. Consider the questions in each section as you complete the assessment activity at the end of this chapter.

Technology

Your technology infrastructure for evaluation determines what you can measure about participant outcomes and your microlearning approach. Organizations with basic LMS tracking can measure completion and quiz scores (participant evaluation) but may struggle to assess whether spacing intervals are effective or content is being accessed at the right moments (approach evaluation). More integrated systems with xAPI or performance analytics can track engagement patterns, identify where participants drop off, and connect learning data to workplace performance metrics.

The technology you have shapes what's realistic. Basic quiz tools require someone to manually review results and identify patterns in participant performance. They also require manual tracking of whether your delivery approach is working. (For example, are people completing on schedule? Are reinforcement products being accessed?) Automated dashboards can flag struggling participants and reveal system-level patterns like low engagement at specific intervals or high drop-off during certain content.

Consider what happens when you lack certain technology. If your systems don't have built-in observation tools, managers evaluating skills application will need checklists and training for manual observation (this becomes a people infrastructure question). If your evaluation approach requires tracking whether managers are actually providing feedback, but your systems don't capture that data, you'll need manual processes for monitoring (this becomes a process infrastructure question). Your technology choices for evaluation also connect to implementation (chapter 6), because some evaluation approaches require workflow integration, which depends on your delivery infrastructure.

Your technology infrastructure determines what you can measure and the amount of manual effort the evaluation will require. Organizations often start with basic systems for participant evaluation (such as completion tracking and simple quizzes) and gradually build toward approach evaluation (such as engagement patterns and system performance) as their technology capabilities grow. Understanding your current technology constraints helps you determine which evaluation approaches are realistic now and where technology investment would reduce manual burden or enable new measurement capabilities.

Process

Your evaluation processes determine when and how you collect data about both participant progress and your microlearning approach effectiveness. Some organizations evaluate once at the end, reviewing participant completion and outcomes. Others build continuous evaluation into their rhythm, checking participant performance weekly or monthly while also monitoring whether delivery systems, spacing strategies, and support mechanisms are functioning as planned.

Process choices depend partly on your technology (for example, automated systems enable frequent review of participant and system data, while manual processes may limit you to periodic checks) and partly on your people (such as who has time to analyze data and act on it?). Consider what happens when evaluation reveals problems. If participant assessments show poor retention, do you have processes for investigating whether the cause is content design, spacing intervals, or delivery timing? If the approach evaluation shows that managers aren't consistently providing feedback, are there processes in place to address that gap?

Organizations with lengthy approval cycles may struggle with evaluation approaches that require rapid adjustments. If the evaluation process requires cross-functional coordination (like connecting learning data to business performance metrics), you'll need clear procedures for data sharing and stakeholder involvement. (Chapter 3 addresses stakeholder alignment on what to measure.) Your evaluation processes also affect implementation because the frequency and method of data collection must align with delivery workflows.

Understanding your current process infrastructure will help determine which evaluation approaches are realistic and where process improvements will enable a more responsive evaluation.

People

People infrastructure determines who's involved in evaluation and whether they can do what your approach requires. This includes your L&D team's assessment design capabilities (one of five core L&D capabilities addressed in chapter 7) and the participation of managers, stakeholders, and subject matter experts in evaluation processes.

If your technology can't automate evaluation tasks, people have to fill the gaps. (And if no one planned to use people, it could also mean that evaluation won't happen.) If you lack automated feedback systems for skills-based microlearning, managers will need to observe participants and provide evaluative feedback. This raises a few questions: Do managers have time for observation? Do they know what performance indicators to look for? Will they provide feedback consistently? If your evaluation approach requires tracking whether managers are fulfilling these responsibilities, you'll need a process (how you monitor this) and potentially technology (systems that capture when feedback occurs).

Organizational evaluation culture affects the types of evaluation stakeholders support and how evaluation data is used. Some organizations view evaluation as providing improvement data to guide refinement. Others see evaluation as a means of compliance checking or proof of completion. This cultural difference shapes what's realistic, regardless of your L&D team's capabilities. If stakeholders only value completion metrics, building people-based performance evaluation may not gain traction until you demonstrate value through simpler measures first.

Understanding your current people infrastructure helps you determine which evaluation approaches are possible and where people development or cultural shifts would enable more comprehensive evaluation.

● ● ●

By now, you should be able to see that your evaluation infrastructure determines which types of microlearning you can effectively measure:

- **Knowledge-based microlearning** typically requires the least complex evaluation infrastructure, so basic assessment tools and completion tracking may suffice.
- **Skills-based microlearning** demands more, such as observation tools, feedback mechanisms, and the ability to track application over time.
- **Performance-based microlearning** requires the most comprehensive infrastructure, including integration between learning and business systems to measure workplace impact.

Be Natural's evaluation journey illustrates how organizations build evaluation infrastructure progressively, starting with what they can support and developing more advanced capabilities over time.

🐝 Building Evaluation Capability Over Time

Be Natural's experience across two microlearning initiatives illustrates how evaluation capabilities can evolve progressively from basic metrics to strategic measurement. Let's take a look at what they did.

Phase 1. Manufacturing Safety—Starting With Limited Capability
BN's first microlearning pilot initiative focused on reducing safety incidents in manufacturing. When the company began, its evaluation capabilities were limited to basic metrics.

The L&D team relied solely on course completion tracking in the company's LMS and simple knowledge checks. It could verify that employees had viewed safety content and passed basic quizzes but couldn't measure whether this knowledge translated to behavior changes on the manufacturing floor.

Without observation tools or performance tracking, the team couldn't connect learning to actual safety improvements. Managers had no structured way to verify skills application, and there was no system for tracking near misses or safety improvements.

Three months in, stakeholders asked whether the pilot was improving actual safety behaviors. The L&D team could report improved quiz scores but couldn't connect learning to workplace changes because their evaluation approach was limited to knowledge metrics. So, the L&D team:

- Added structured observation checklists for supervisors to assess safe behaviors
- Created a system to track safety incidents and near misses by department
- Established regular safety huddles in which teams reviewed incidents and reinforced learning

Building this infrastructure took time. Supervisors needed training on what to observe and how to document consistently. The first month of observation data was inconsistent because managers interpreted the checklist differently. Once the team revised the forms and provided additional coaching, the evaluation process worked more reliably.

This infrastructure investment also revealed a dimension constraint. When the team wanted to implement weekly safety reinforcement (their initial spacing plan), they realized supervisors couldn't conduct weekly observations with their current workload. They adjusted to biweekly spacing to match what supervisors could more realistically evaluate. Six months in, BN's L&D team could demonstrate a connection between microlearning and reduced safety incidents. More importantly, they also understood what evaluation infrastructure future initiatives would require.

Phase 2. Sales Training—Discovering New Gaps

Building on lessons from the company's manufacturing arm, BN expanded its evaluation approach when implementing product knowledge microlearning for its sales team.

The sales team wanted to go beyond knowledge checks to measure actual customer interactions. The company had already gathered some customer feedback through post-sale surveys, but the data wasn't structured to evaluate microlearning effectiveness. Sales managers provided coaching feedback, but their assessment criteria varied widely, which made it difficult to identify patterns or measure improvement consistently.

The L&D team initially planned to have sales managers conduct structured observations, but managers had limited bandwidth for these activities. So, the team chose peer observation protocols instead—sales team members provided feedback to one another using structured scenarios. This worked for skills practice but revealed a limitation: peer observers couldn't access actual customer interaction data to evaluate real-world application of the microlearning content.

This experience showed how people infrastructure constraints shaped evaluation choices. The peer observation approach provided useful feedback on microlearning application, but Be Natural recognized they would need a different infrastructure to evaluate actual on-the-job performance in future initiatives.

Be Natural's experience demonstrates that evaluation capability develops through discovery and adaptation. Organizations may build infrastructure progressively, encounter constraints that require trade-offs, and learn what capabilities they need for future initiatives. Starting with limited evaluation doesn't prevent progress; it can create a foundation for systematic improvement.

Chapter Summary

Evaluation is one of three execution dimensions (along with spaced learning and implementation) that determine what microlearning approaches your organization can realistically support. Understanding your evaluation capabilities helps you make informed decisions about which initiatives to pursue, how to design them, and where to invest in building infrastructure.

In this chapter, we explored how to assess your evaluation readiness across technology, process, and people infrastructures. Different types of microlearning require different evaluation capabilities. Building evaluation capability takes time and reveals constraints that require trade-offs. Sometimes this means adjusting your approach to match current infrastructure rather than attempting to use evaluation methods you can't yet support.

As you move forward with your own microlearning initiatives, remember that understanding your evaluation capabilities isn't about limiting possibilities. It's about making informed choices that set you up for success. The assessment activity at the end of this chapter can help you rate your current evaluation maturity and determine realistic starting points for your initiatives.

In the next chapter, we'll explore spaced learning, which is another execution dimension of the MLR Framework. You'll discover how your current capabilities for distributing learning over time affect the feasibility of different microlearning approaches for your organization.

Assess Your Evaluation Readiness

Purpose
Assess your current evaluation readiness to determine which type of microlearning you can effectively measure and evaluate for the project you selected in the part 1 opening activity. The goal of this assessment is to identify what's limiting you right now and determine your realistic starting point. (See the part 1 opening activity as a refresher.) This activity will help you answer the question, "What type of microlearning can you evaluate effectively given your current constraints?"

Strategic Value
Most organizations attempt microlearning approaches that exceed their evaluation capabilities, which can lead to failed initiatives and stakeholder skepticism. This constraint-focused assessment helps you make realistic choices that build credibility and demonstrate value, creating a foundation for more complex approaches over time. Success with appropriate evaluation approaches builds organizational confidence in the microlearning investment.

Instructions
In the tables on the next page, rate your current project's evaluation capabilities using the scale provided. Be honest in your assessment—identifying limitations now prevents overreach later and creates a road map for growth.

Part 1. Project-Level Assessment
Rate your current project's evaluation capabilities based on technology, people, and process. Each has its own scale.

Use this rating scale to assess your technology infrastructure:
- **Strong.** You have comprehensive measurement capabilities and multiple integrated systems that track, analyze, and report data effectively. For example, you can track completion, measure skill demonstration through observation, and connect learning to business metrics like safety incidents or sales performance.
- **Developing.** You have basic measurement capabilities. Some systems are in place, but they don't connect well or have limited functionality. For example, you can track course completion and quiz scores and gather some feedback, but you struggle to measure actual behavior change or business impact.
- **Limited.** You have minimal measurement capabilities and basic tools that provide little data or insight. For example, you can see who completed training and basic quiz results, but you have little insight into whether learning actually happened or knowledge was applied.

Technology Infrastructure	Rating (strong, developing, or limited)
Measurement tools: Systems are in place to track learning engagement and outcomes.	
Data integration: You have the ability to connect learning data with performance metrics.	
Analytics capabilities: Tools are available to analyze and visualize evaluation data.	
Reporting functionality: Methods are in place to share results with stakeholders.	

Use this rating scale to assess your process infrastructure:
- **Well-established.** You have clear, consistent processes. For example, everyone knows the steps, follows them regularly, and they work reliably.
- **Somewhat defined.** You have basic processes, but they need improvement. For example, some procedures exist but they're inconsistent or people don't always follow them.
- **Unclear or inconsistent.** You have minimal or undefined processes. For example, there aren't any clear procedures or people handle things differently each time.

Process Infrastructure	Rating (well-established, somewhat defined, or unclear or inconsistent)
Evaluation workflows: Defined processes for collecting and analyzing data are in place.	
Quality controls: You have methods to ensure data accuracy and reliability.	
Cross-functional coordination: Processes are in use for sharing data across departments.	
Improvement cycles: You have procedures for using results to enhance learning.	

Use this rating scale to assess your people infrastructure:
- **Strong support.** You have engaged, capable people. For example, team members are skilled and actively participate in this area.
- **Some support.** You have basic capability but need development. For example, people are willing but lack skills, or they're skilled but not fully engaged.
- **Limited support.** You have minimal engagement or capability. For example, people are either unwilling to participate or lack the necessary skills.

People Infrastructure	Rating (strong support, some support, or limited support)
L&D expertise: Your team's measurement and analytics capabilities.	
Manager engagement: Managers support evaluation processes.	
Stakeholder alignment: There's agreement on what to measure and why.	
Data literacy: You have the ability to interpret and apply evaluation findings.	

Part 2. Identify Your Evaluation Readiness

Look at your limited ratings to identify your constraints; these are the areas you rated:

- Limited for technology infrastructure
- Unclear or inconsistent for process infrastructure
- Limited support for people infrastructure

Instead of asking "What's the total score?" ask "What's preventing you from conducting more advanced evaluation?" Your constraints determine the starting point, which determines the type of microlearning you can effectively evaluate.

Compare your answers in each category to this list to find your starting point:

- **If your constraints are mostly related to technology**, start with knowledge-based microlearning. Use your existing systems while building tech capabilities.
- **If your constraints are mostly related to processes,** you can build content but you may struggle with coordination. Focus on simple, standalone microlearning first.
- **If your constraints are mostly related to people,** you have systems but need buy-in and skills. Start with pilot projects to build confidence and expertise.
- **If you have constraints related to technology and processes,** focus on knowledge-based microlearning that leverages your people strengths. Use informal channels and manager support while building systems.
- **If you have constraints related to technology and people,** your processes may work, but you need simpler solutions. Start with basic knowledge-based approaches that don't require high-end tech or extensive buy-in.
- **If you have constraints in processes and people,** you have the tech but lack coordination and support. Begin with very small, contained pilot initiatives to prove value before expanding.

- **If you have constraints across all three areas,** begin with knowledge-based microlearning in small, controlled pilot initiatives to build experience.

Next Steps

Based on your assessment, identify:

Your organization's current strengths

1. _____
2. _____
3. _____

Priority gaps to address

1. _____
2. _____
3. _____

Immediate actions to take

1. _____
2. _____
3. _____

Remember: Start with evaluation approaches that match your current capabilities while strategically building toward more advanced measurement. A focused microlearning project with appropriate evaluation methods will yield more meaningful insights than an ambitious microlearning initiative you can't effectively measure.

CHAPTER 5
Spaced Learning

By the end of this chapter, you should be able to answer these questions:
- How does spaced learning function as a strategic dimension within the MLR Framework?
- What are the essential elements of an effective spacing approach for microlearning initiatives?
- How do you assess your readiness to apply spaced learning strategies within your current organizational conditions?
- What challenges might you face when trying to implement spacing, and how can your project move forward even with limited capability?
- How do spacing considerations differ across knowledge-based, skills-based, and performance-based microlearning?

Last summer, I learned to make sourdough bread after a friend gave me some starter. My first attempts at baking were dense and underwhelming, until an experienced baker taught me that the magic happens during resting periods. The process requires multiple stages of fermenting and proofing, with each rest allowing the dough to develop complexity and strength. When I rushed through these intervals or tried to combine steps, the results were mediocre. But when I respected the timing—allowing proper spacing between each stage—the difference was remarkable.

That's the logic behind spaced learning in microlearning initiatives. It's not just about content. We have to design intentional intervals that give participants the time they need to mentally process, apply, and re-engage with learning. Just as sourdough needs time between stages to develop, effective learning requires strategic spacing to build lasting knowledge and skills. But spacing works only when your project is ready to support it. Consider these experiences shared by learning professionals:

- "We rolled out an elaborate year-round compliance microlearning email campaign, and then discovered our systems couldn't track click-open and click-through data," a pharmaceutical training manager told me.
- "I thought we could manually manage practice scheduling, but it quickly became overwhelming for our small team," a retail L&D director explained.
- "Our managers supported the concept of microlearning but didn't have the tools or processes to effectively reinforce learning," a manufacturing training specialist shared.
- "The stakeholders wanted to personalize practice paths, but both the L&D and business informatics teams lacked the analytics capabilities to make data-driven adjustments," a learning architect at a tech company noted.

These challenges point to the interdependencies within the execution dimension. In chapter 4, we introduced how evaluation, spaced learning, and implementation work as an integrated system rather than separate sequential steps. Evaluation methods determine whether you can measure spacing effectiveness, and implementation infrastructure determines what spacing approaches you can actually deliver. When these dimensions align, spaced learning strengthens your microlearning product. When they don't, you'll discover constraints that require reassessment.

This chapter focuses on spaced learning: your strategy for distributing learning over time to enhance retention and application. But as you consider your spacing readiness, remember that your choices will connect directly to your evaluation capabilities and implementation infrastructure. Chapter 6 will bring all three execution dimensions together for integrated assessment.

What Is Spaced Learning?

Spaced learning and *distributed practice* are used interchangeably to describe learning that occurs over multiple sessions separated by time, as opposed to massed practice (cramming everything into one session). In microlearning, this means intentionally designing intervals between learning moments to enhance retention, application, and performance. These intervals allow participants to process information, attempt retrieval, apply concepts in different contexts, and build stronger neural connections.

Within the MLR Framework, spaced learning influences how effectively your microlearning initiatives deliver lasting impact. Positioned between evaluation and implementation, spaced learning determines when and how frequently participants engage with content. While evaluation focuses on measuring results and implementation addresses delivery mechanics, spaced learning shapes the temporal pattern of the learning experience itself. Within spaced learning, you can use several evidence-based techniques:

- **Spaced repetition** brings back important information at strategic intervals, just when you might be about to forget it. Instead of reviewing the same safety procedure five times in one sitting, for example, you might revisit it briefly after one day, then three days, and then a week. This rhythm helps transfer information from short-term memory to long-term memory.

- **Interleaving** mixes up different topics or skills rather than focusing on just one thing at a time. Instead of spending an entire week on customer greeting procedures before moving to product knowledge, for example, you might alternate between the two topics. This approach helps build schema, which are the connections between different areas that enable more flexible application of the new information. (We explore schema building and mental models in chapter 8.)

- **Varied practice** spreads practice sessions across multiple contexts and conditions rather than repeating the same task in the same way. For example, a sales team learning new techniques might practice for 15 minutes three times a week in different simulated scenarios instead of completing a single 45-minute session with identical repetitions. This variation often leads to better skills transfer than repetitive, identical practice.

These three approaches can be used in conjunction with one another, so you can distribute repeatable practice for one thing while interleaving another topic in between!

Desirable Difficulties vs. Spaced Learning

A note about the term *desirable difficulties*, which can be conflated with *spaced learning* (also known as *distributed practice*). While *spaced learning* focuses on "when and how often" participants engage with content, *desirable difficulties* addresses "how hard" the cognitive challenge should be (Sachdeva 2024). Desirable difficulties are carefully designed learning conditions that temporarily challenge participants in ways that support long-term retention and flexible application—but only when participants have the foundational knowledge to productively engage with the content. (We'll discuss desirable difficulties in more detail in chapter 14).

Spaced learning differs from traditional one-and-done training approaches in fundamental ways. Rather than concentrating all content into single comprehensive events, spacing creates continuous engagement over time. This shift from episodic to ongoing learning helps prevent the forgetting curve that typically follows traditional training. Spacing also enables the opportunity for integration directly into the workflow rather than isolating learning from actual work, which helps participants see immediate relevance and apply concepts in their work environment.

Before we examine your readiness for different spacing approaches, consider how spaced learning intersects with the other dimensions of the MLR Framework. The intervals you design influence what outcomes you can achieve; knowledge retention requires different spacing than skills development or performance improvement (chapter 3). Your evaluation methods (chapter 4) determine whether you can measure the effectiveness of your spacing strategy. Without appropriate assessment tools, you can't tell if your intervals are working. Your implementation infrastructure (chapter 6) determines what spacing approaches you can actually deliver. Some scheduling approaches require technology and processes that not all organizations have in place.

This interdependency means that as you assess your spaced learning readiness, you're also assessing whether your evaluation and implementation capabilities can support your spacing plans. Strong capabilities in one area can compensate for limitations in another, but gaps across multiple dimensions will constrain what types of microlearning you can successfully deploy.

Key Elements of Spaced Learning

Spacing infrastructure involves more than just technology that can schedule content. It depends on aligned capabilities across technology, processes, and people that work together to create sustainable distributed learning. When these elements align, even simple spacing approaches can deliver meaningful retention and application benefits. When they misalign, even advanced scheduling technology may fail to produce lasting results.

The infrastructure you have determines which spacing goals are realistic. Knowledge retention through periodic reviews uses different support than skills development with practice opportunities, which differs again from performance support integrated into the workflow. Organizations often discover that their technology can handle scheduling, but their processes can't coordinate multiple initiatives, or their managers lack time to reinforce learning between sessions. These mismatches between dimensions reveal where to focus infrastructure building.

Your infrastructure also determines how you can tell whether spacing is working. If your technology tracks engagement but can't connect it to performance data, you'll know participants are accessing content but not whether retention improved. If managers observe skills application but you don't have a system to aggregate their feedback, valuable insights will remain siloed. The evaluation methods from chapter 4 and implementation capabilities from chapter 6 directly shape the spacing approaches you can sustain and measure.

Consider these infrastructure elements as you complete the assessment activity at the end of this chapter.

Technology

Technology infrastructure for spacing ranges from simple calendar reminders to adaptive systems that personalize intervals based on performance data. The key isn't advancement level. It's whether your technology supports the spacing approach your organization can actually sustain.

Content Scheduling and Delivery Systems

Content scheduling and delivery systems form the foundation, but "scheduling" looks different across organizations. An LMS with automated release dates provides consistent timing but takes setup time and platform access. Email marketing tools offer flexible scheduling but may not integrate with your learning data. Shared calendars with manual notifications demand coordination but work when automated systems aren't available. Each approach has trade-offs: automation reduces coordination burden but takes technical setup; manual scheduling offers flexibility but depends on consistent execution.

Your scheduling choice connects to your process infrastructure. Automated systems benefit from clear scheduling protocols and content readiness timelines. Manual approaches benefit from coordination workflows and backup plans when key people are unavailable. When technology and process capabilities are misaligned, spacing becomes inconsistent.

Engagement Tracking

Engagement tracking matters because spacing works only when participants actually engage across intervals. Completion tracking shows who accessed content, but engagement patterns reveal when and how people interact with spaced learning. Do they engage immediately when notified, or wait until deadline pressure builds? Do they complete one session but skip the next? Without these insights, you're spacing blindly.

But tracking creates its own challenges. Simple LMS completion data is easy to gather but doesn't show quality of engagement. xAPI provides detailed interaction data but requires implementation expertise and privacy considerations. Manager observation offers rich qualitative insights but doesn't scale easily. Your evaluation capabilities (chapter 4) determine which tracking approaches are feasible.

Notification Systems

Notification systems prompt re-engagement at planned intervals. Yet notifications can feel like either helpful reminders or unwelcome interruptions depending on timing, frequency, and relevance. Email notifications work broadly but may be ignored in busy inboxes. SMS reaches people quickly but feels intrusive if overused. Platform-based notifications work only if participants regularly check the platform. Notification strategy depends on your people infrastructure. Participants benefit from understanding why they're receiving spaced prompts and finding them valuable rather than burdensome.

Adaptive Features

Adaptive features that adjust spacing based on individual performance represent advanced implementation. These systems track mastery and modify intervals accordingly, but they take complex technology infrastructure, strong evaluation methods to assess mastery accurately, and participant trust in algorithmic decision making. Few organizations have the technical and process infrastructure to support truly adaptive spacing, and that's fine. Consistent simple spacing often outperforms inconsistent advanced approaches.

When evaluating your technology infrastructure, the central question isn't "What's possible?" but "What can we actually sustain given our process coordination and people support capabilities?"

Process

Process infrastructure determines whether spacing happens consistently or deteriorates under operational pressures. Even strong technology infrastructure fails without processes to coordinate content delivery, manage competing initiatives, and connect spacing to work application.

Scheduling and Coordination Workflows

Scheduling and coordination workflows become increasingly important with multiple simultaneous initiatives. One microlearning product spaced over time is manageable; however, five products with overlapping participants and competing spacing intervals benefit from explicit coordination. Without scheduling processes, participants face notification overload one week and silence the next.

Some organizations use content calendars that map all learning initiatives, others designate coordination roles, and still others limit simultaneous initiatives to maintain manageable spacing. Each approach involves trade-offs between coverage and coordination burden.

These scheduling processes connect to your technology capabilities. Automated systems can prevent overlapping notifications if programmed correctly, but someone still coordinates content readiness across teams. Manual scheduling offers flexibility but demands more coordination effort. When process and technology capabilities misalign (advanced scheduling technology without coordination workflows or detailed coordination processes without supporting technology) spacing consistency suffers.

Reinforcement Protocols

Reinforcement protocols between formal learning moments bridge the gap between knowledge and application. This might mean manager check-ins after each learning session, peer discussion prompts, or structured practice opportunities. But reinforcement protocols depend on people infrastructure to succeed. Managers benefit from having time, training, and willingness to participate. Participants benefit from seeing value in the reinforcement rather than viewing it as an additional burden. Without aligned people support, even well-designed reinforcement protocols become inconsistent.

Data Collection and Analysis Processes

Data collection and analysis processes inform whether spacing is working and where to adjust. Some organizations review engagement data weekly and adjust intervals based on participation patterns. Others conduct quarterly reviews of spacing effectiveness. Still others lack formal review processes and rely on ad hoc feedback. The right approach depends on your evaluation infrastructure (chapter 4). You benefit from processes to collect and analyze data that your technology can actually track and your people can realistically interpret.

Consider how your current processes would handle scaling. A spacing approach that works for 20 participants may break when scaling to 200 if process infrastructure can't keep pace with coordination demands. This is where implementation infrastructure (chapter 6) becomes particularly relevant. Your ability to scale spacing depends on process infrastructure that can grow without overwhelming your team.

The central process question isn't "What's the ideal workflow?" but "What level of coordination can we maintain consistently over time?"

People

People infrastructure (the human capabilities, support, and buy-in for spacing) ultimately determines whether spacing approaches succeed or fail. Technology and processes enable spacing, but people make it meaningful.

L&D Expertise in Spacing Design

L&D expertise in spacing design matters because effective spacing isn't just about spreading content over time. It involves understanding forgetting curves, retrieval practice, and how to design intervals that challenge participants appropriately without overwhelming them. Some L&D teams have deep spacing expertise; others are learning these principles. Building L&D capability might mean formal training, peer learning, or partnering with experts. The key is recognizing that spacing expertise takes time to develop. Early spacing attempts may be imperfect, and that's expected.

This L&D knowledge connects to process infrastructure. Complex spacing strategies benefit from deep expertise to design and coordinate; simpler approaches work with more basic understanding. When L&D expertise and process complexity misalign (complex spacing strategies without deep expertise, or underutilized expertise with overly simple approaches), spacing effectiveness suffers.

Manager Support and Reinforcement

Manager support and reinforcement transforms spacing from an L&D initiative into workplace-integrated learning. When managers understand spacing value and can reinforce learning between sessions through observation, coaching, or discussion, participants see immediate work relevance. However, manager involvement depends on manager capacity. Managers face competing demands, reinforcement takes time, and some managers are more comfortable with coaching than others. Organizations often discover that their spacing design assumes manager involvement that managers can't actually provide.

Manager infrastructure connects to technology and process. If your technology doesn't make manager reinforcement easy (providing observation guides, feedback templates, or quick progress views), managers struggle to participate consistently. If your processes don't support manager training and coordination, manager involvement becomes haphazard. Aligning technology, process, and people infrastructure around manager support is difficult but powerful.

Participant Understanding

Participant understanding and buy-in grows when participants see how spacing enhances their learning rather than simply extending time to completion. Participants accustomed to one-time training may initially resist extended learning timelines. Building buy-in benefits from clear communication about spacing advantages, visible value from spaced practice, and organizational culture that supports ongoing development rather than just credential completion.

Participant buy-in connects to your evaluation infrastructure (chapter 4). When participants see evidence that spacing improves their retention or performance, buy-in increases. Without visible evaluation data showing spacing value, participant buy-in relies solely on trust, which may not sustain long-term engagement.

Executive Sponsorship and Resource Allocation

Executive sponsorship and resource allocation provides organizational support for sustained learning approaches. Executives comfortable with one-time training events may question why microlearning "takes so long." Building executive understanding benefits from demonstrating spacing value, showing how spacing aligns with organizational goals, and making it clear that extended timelines lead to better retention and application, not slower learning. Executive support determines whether spacing gets adequate resources and organizational patience to prove effectiveness.

When evaluating your people infrastructure, the central question is: "Do we have the human support, understanding, and capacity to sustain this spacing approach over time?" Honest assessment here prevents designing spacing strategies that look good on paper but collapse under real-world people constraints.

● ● ●

These infrastructure elements don't function independently. They work as an interconnected system. Strong technology without process coordination leads to inconsistent spacing. Good processes without people buy-in result in nominal compliance without real engagement. People support without enabling technology places unrealistic demands on manual coordination. The assessment activity at the end of this chapter helps you evaluate your infrastructure across these dimensions and identify alignment gaps that need attention.

The infrastructure you need depends on the type of microlearning you're implementing:

- **Knowledge-based spacing** requires the least infrastructure.
- **Skills-based spacing** needs more coordination and manager involvement.
- **Performance-based spacing** demands the most integration across all three infrastructure types.

Be Natural's journey demonstrates how organizations can build spacing capabilities progressively while matching infrastructure to microlearning type.

Who Controls Spacing?

Spacing approaches exist on a spectrum of control:

- **Organization-controlled spacing** delivers content to all participants on the same schedule. Everyone receives the first reinforcement after three days, the second after a week, and so on. This approach offers consistency and simplifies coordination, but it assumes all participants need the same intervals regardless of prior knowledge, confidence, or learning pace.
- **Participant-controlled spacing** allows individuals to determine their own review timing. Participants might access review content when they

feel ready, request additional practice when confidence is low, or skip reviews when they've already mastered the material. This approach respects individual differences and builds learner agency, but it places responsibility on participants to understand spacing principles and make good timing decisions.

- **Algorithm-controlled spacing** uses performance data to adjust intervals for each person. If someone struggles with a concept, the system shortens the interval to the next review. If someone demonstrates mastery, the system extends the interval. This approach personalizes timing without requiring participant decision making, but it depends on accurate performance assessment and participant trust in algorithmic recommendations.

Some organizations use hybrid approaches. The organization might set the overall spacing structure (weekly touchpoints for six weeks), while participants control whether they engage with optional supplemental reviews. Or an algorithm might recommend review timing while participants can override those recommendations based on their current workload or priorities.

Allowing participants to control their spacing intervals affects all three infrastructure types:

- **Technology infrastructure** benefits from systems that can accommodate individual schedules, track varied engagement patterns, and provide participants with clear information about their progress and recommended timing.
- **Process infrastructure** is more complex when participants are on different timelines. You can't coordinate group discussions or manager check-ins as easily when everyone's at different points.
- **People infrastructure** takes on new dimensions. Participants benefit from understanding why spacing matters and how to judge their own readiness for the next learning moment. Managers may find it harder to support learning when team members are all at different stages.

The question isn't which approach is better. It's which level of participant autonomy aligns with your organizational culture, your participants' capacity for self-directed learning, and your infrastructure capabilities. Organizations with strong participant self-direction cultures and robust tracking systems may find participant-controlled spacing powerful.

Organizations where participants prefer structured guidance or where coordination across teams matters may find organization-controlled spacing more practical.

When assessing your spacing infrastructure, consider: Does your approach to spacing control match your participants' preferences and capabilities? Does your infrastructure support the level of autonomy (or structure) that your spacing design assumes?

🐝 Applying Spaced Learning to Specific Projects

Be Natural's spacing journey demonstrates how an organization can progressively build spaced learning capabilities while discovering infrastructure gaps and dimension constraints along the way. Its experience illustrates practical approaches for knowledge-based, skills-based, and performance-based spacing implementations.

New Hire Onboarding With Manual Spacing

Be Natural's first attempt at spaced learning focused on new-hire onboarding for retail associates. The L&D team wanted to space product knowledge over the first month rather than front-loading everything in the initial training week.

When they began, their spacing capabilities were basic. They didn't have an automated scheduling system or a notification infrastructure and store managers had never been involved in reinforcing learning between sessions. The team created simple product knowledge cards and developed a manual schedule: Managers would distribute one card weekly during morning huddles and ask follow-up questions the next week before introducing new content.

This manual approach worked initially but revealed significant coordination challenges. Managers in different regions were inconsistent in how they implemented the schedule. Some distributed the cards all at once because "it was easier." Others forgot entirely during busy weeks. Without tracking systems, the L&D team couldn't tell who was spacing consistently and who wasn't.

Building process infrastructure took longer than expected. The team created manager guidelines, held training sessions on why spacing mattered, and developed simple paper tracking sheets. But even after training, manager adherence varied. High-performing stores with engaged managers followed the spacing protocol, while stores with overwhelmed managers or high turnover struggled.

Six months in, BN recognized that there was a dimension constraint. Their evaluation infrastructure couldn't provide the information they needed to determine whether spaced onboarding improved product knowledge retention more than the front-loaded approach they'd previously used. They didn't have any baseline data from the old approach, and they hadn't created a consistent way to assess knowledge across regions or a system to connect onboarding completion to sales performance or customer satisfaction.

So, the team made a trade-off decision: Invest in basic evaluation infrastructure before expanding spacing efforts. They couldn't prove spacing was working without better measurement, which meant delaying their next spacing initiative (leadership development) until they built evaluation capabilities that could track learning over time.

Leadership Development With Technology Investment

Building on lessons from onboarding, Be Natural approached leadership development differently. New store managers needed ongoing support, not just initial training. The L&D team envisioned spacing leadership concepts over six months with practice opportunities between formal learning moments.

But they discovered that their manual scheduling approach couldn't scale to this complexity. Managers needed content at different times based on their specific challenges. Some struggled with performance conversations early; others needed help with scheduling or inventory management first. Manual coordination across hundreds of stores was impossible.

BN invested in email marketing automation technology that could schedule content releases and track opens. This investment improved scheduling consistency, but revealed a new gap: While the system could schedule and track, it couldn't adapt intervals based on manager needs or performance.

Every manager received the same spacing intervals whether they needed more or less reinforcement.

Process infrastructure also needed to expand. The L&D team developed content sequencing protocols, created escalation procedures when managers weren't engaging, and established feedback loops with regional directors. But these processes required more coordination than anticipated. Someone had to monitor engagement data weekly, flag managers who were falling behind, and coordinate with regional directors for intervention.

People infrastructure was an unexpected challenge. Senior leaders could identify coaching moments and provide guidance (as originally planned), but they needed training first. They couldn't naturally recognize when spacing reinforcement would help versus when managers needed immediate intensive support. Thus, the L&D team had to spend more time training senior leaders on their role in reinforcing spaced leadership learning.

Even after building this infrastructure, the limitations persisted. The spacing approach worked well for foundational leadership concepts, but struggled with just-in-time performance support. If a manager needed immediate help dealing with a difficult employee situation, weekly spacing intervals weren't responsive enough. The team recognized their spacing strategy and implementation capabilities weren't aligned for true performance support.

Conclusion

Be Natural's experience shows that spacing infrastructure develops through discovery, not predetermined plans. Organizations encounter constraints they didn't anticipate, make trade-off decisions between dimensions, and learn what types of infrastructure future initiatives will need.

The company's onboarding spacing revealed evaluation gaps that delayed expansion. The leadership spacing showed technology limitations that prevented adaptive intervals. Neither initiative failed, but both required infrastructure investment and strategic patience that initial plans hadn't anticipated. Starting with limited spacing capability didn't prevent progress. Instead, it created a foundation for understanding what capabilities mattered most for BN's organizational context.

Chapter Summary

Spaced learning is an important dimension within the MLR Framework. It's one that transforms microlearning from isolated events into ongoing learning experiences. By strategically distributing learning over time, your microlearning initiatives can drive deeper retention, stronger skills development, and more consistent performance growth.

In this chapter, we've explored:

- How spaced learning functions as a strategic element that influences what your microlearning product can achieve
- The infrastructure elements (technology, process, and people) and how they work as an interconnected system
- How spacing connects to your evaluation methods (chapter 4) and implementation capabilities (chapter 6)
- How to assess your project's spacing readiness through the assessment activity at the end of this chapter

Understanding your spaced learning readiness isn't about limiting the possibilities; it's about making informed choices that set your initiatives up for success. Even with limited infrastructure, you can implement effective spaced learning approaches by focusing on what's feasible within your current capabilities and strategically building toward more advanced methods.

BN's journey illustrates how organizations build spacing capabilities progressively. The company started with manual scheduling for new-hire onboarding, discovered coordination and evaluation gaps that required infrastructure investment, and learned that spacing strategy depends on aligned capabilities across all three execution dimensions. Their progression wasn't automatic or smooth. It involved setbacks, trade-off decisions, and discovering constraints they hadn't anticipated. Starting with limited spacing capability didn't prevent progress—it created a foundation for understanding what infrastructure matters most.

Your spacing infrastructure needs will differ based on organizational context, the types of microlearning you're implementing, and how your evaluation and implementation capabilities align. The assessment activity at the end of this chapter helps you identify your spacing infrastructure's strength, as well as any gaps that may limit the approaches you can sustain. Use these insights to make strategic choices about where to start and what infrastructure to build over time.

In the next chapter, we'll explore implementation—the final execution dimension of the MLR Framework. We'll examine how your ability to deliver and sustain microlearning depends on how well technology, process, and people infrastructure work together with your evaluation and spacing capabilities.

Assess Your Spaced Learning Readiness

Purpose
Assess your current spaced learning readiness to determine which type of microlearning you can effectively space and distribute for the project you selected in the part 1 opening activity. The goal of this assessment is to identify what's limiting you right now and determine a realistic starting point. The key question this activity will help you answer is, "What type of microlearning can you space effectively given your current constraints?"

Strategic Value
Most organizations attempt microlearning approaches that exceed their spaced learning capabilities, which can lead to overwhelming coordination demands and participant fatigue. This constraint-focused assessment can help you make realistic choices that build credibility and demonstrate value, creating a foundation for more challenging spacing approaches over time. Success with appropriate spaced learning approaches builds organizational confidence in sustained microlearning investment.

Instructions
In the tables on the next page, rate your current project's spaced learning capabilities using the scales provided. Be honest in your assessment—identifying limitations now prevents overreach later and creates your road map for growth.

Part 1. Project-Level Assessment
Rate your current project's spaced learning readiness based on technology, process, and people. Each has its own scale.

Use this rating scale to assess your technology readiness:
- **Strong.** You have comprehensive spacing capabilities. Multiple integrated systems can schedule, track, and adapt learning distribution effectively. For example, you can automatically schedule content delivery across optimal intervals, track engagement patterns over time, and adjust spacing based on performance data and participant progress.
- **Developing.** You have basic spacing capabilities. Some systems are in place, but they don't connect well or have limited functionality. For example, you can schedule content releases and track basic completion across time, but you struggle to adapt intervals or coordinate complex spacing patterns with people.
- **Limited.** You have minimal spacing capabilities. Your basic tools provide little control over timing or distribution. For example, you can deliver content, but have little ability to control timing, track engagement across intervals, or adapt spacing based on participant needs.

Technology Readiness	Rating (strong, developing, or limited)
Content scheduling: Systems are in place to deliver learning at planned intervals.	
Engagement tracking: You have methods to monitor participation across time.	
Notification capabilities: Tools are available to prompt participation at optimal moments.	
Adaptive features: You have the ability to adjust spacing based on performance.	

Use this rating scale to assess process readiness:
- **Well-established.** You have clear, consistent processes. For example, everyone knows the spacing procedures, follows them regularly, and they work reliably for coordinating learning over time.
- **Somewhat defined.** You have basic processes, but they need improvement. For example, some spacing procedures exist, but they're inconsistent or people don't always follow them reliably.
- **Unclear or inconsistent.** You have minimal or undefined processes. For example, there are no clear procedures for managing spacing or people handle distribution timing differently each time.

Process Readiness	Rating (well-established, somewhat defined, or unclear or inconsistent)
Spacing coordination: Workflows exist for managing learning distribution over time.	
Reinforcement mechanisms: You have processes to support learning between formal moments.	
Maintenance procedures: Methods are in place to sustain spaced learning over time.	
Progress monitoring: You have established approaches for tracking development across intervals.	

Use this rating scale to assess people readiness:
- **Strong support.** You have engaged, capable people. For example, team members are skilled in spacing design and actively participate in coordinating distributed learning approaches. If managers or leaders play a part in the initiative, they understand their role in relation to the spacing.

- **Some support.** You have basic capability, but need development. For example, people are willing but lack spacing expertise, or they're skilled but not fully engaged in coordination efforts.
- **Limited support.** You have minimal engagement or capability. For example, people are either unwilling to participate in extended learning approaches or they lack the necessary spacing design skills.

People Readiness	Rating (strong support, some support, or limited support)
L&D expertise: The team understands spacing principles and design.	
Manager support: Supervisors have the ability to reinforce learning between sessions.	
Participant preparation: Individuals understand the spaced approach.	
Stakeholder alignment: Leadership supports extended learning timelines.	

Part 2. Identify Your Spacing Readiness

Look at your limited ratings and identify your constraint areas; these are the areas you rated:
- Limited for technology readiness
- Unclear or inconsistent for process readiness
- Limited support for people readiness

Instead of asking "What's the total score?" ask "What's preventing you from implementing more advanced spaced learning approaches?" Your constraints determine the starting point, which determines your spaced learning readiness for microlearning.

Compare your answers in each category to this list to find your starting point:
- **If your constraints are mostly related to technology,** start with knowledge-based microlearning using your existing systems while building technology infrastructure like data tracking and analytics capabilities.
- **If your constraints are mostly related to processes,** you can build content but you may struggle with coordination. Focus on simple, standalone microlearning first to minimize evaluation coordination needs.
- **If your constraints are mostly related to people,** you have systems but need buy-in and skills. Start with pilot projects to build confidence and expertise.
- **If you have constraints related to technology and processes,** focus on knowledge-based microlearning that leverages your people strengths. Use

informal channels and manager support while building systems, or start with pilot projects to demonstrate value.

- **If you have constraints related to technology and people,** your processes can work, but you need simpler solutions. Start with basic knowledge-based approaches that don't require high-end tech, data infrastructure, or extensive buy-in.
- **If you have constraints related to processes and people,** you have the tech but lack coordination and support. Begin with very small, contained pilot initiatives to prove value before expanding and prioritize which capabilities to build first.
- **If you have constraints across all three areas,** begin with knowledge-based microlearning in a small, controlled pilot initiatives to build experience and prioritize which capabilities to build first.

Next Steps

Reflect on these questions as you plan your spaced learning approach:

- What type of microlearning (knowledge-based, skills-based, or performance-based) matches your current constraint pattern?
- Which single capability improvement would most expand your spacing options?
- How can you demonstrate the value of spaced learning within your current limitations to build support for capability development?

Remember: Start with the spaced learning approach that matches your current readiness level while building capabilities for more advanced approaches. Success with focused initiatives creates a foundation for broader implementation.

CHAPTER 6
Implementation

> By the end of this chapter, you should be able to answer these questions:
> - Why is implementation the foundation of successful microlearning?
> - What factors should you consider when baselining your implementation capabilities?
> - How can you assess your organization's current implementation capabilities for microlearning initiatives?
> - How do implementation requirements differ across knowledge-based, skills-based, and performance-based microlearning?
> - What types of microlearning can your organization realistically create, deliver, and support?

Imagine a chef who has meticulously selected the finest ingredients and designed a menu for a spectacular dinner. Despite this excellent preparation, however, the meal will fall short if the restaurant lacks the right equipment, efficient processes, or staff with the skills to prepare and deliver the experience. Even the most perfectly conceived dining experience requires proper implementation to succeed.

Similarly, strong implementation in microlearning transforms strategic intent into tangible learning experiences. It encompasses all the methods, systems, and resources required to deliver microlearning effectively to your participants. Without appropriate implementation, even the most well-designed microlearning initiatives will struggle to achieve their intended outcomes.

In previous chapters, we've explored how to establish outcomes, purpose, and potential for microlearning initiatives; considered the systems needed to evaluate microlearning effectiveness; and examined how spaced learning can affect retention and application. We'll now turn to the final dimension of the MLR Framework: implementation. This dimension encompasses all the methods of delivering microlearning experiences to your participants.

Successful implementation requires more than just choosing a delivery platform. Here's what some colleagues have shared about their implementation challenges:

- "We have not been able to implement the microlearning content we created because our client doesn't have the systems in place yet," a learning architect for an international consulting firm told me.
- "Our HR team won't provide access to our employee performance data, claiming it's illegal to share it, so we can't measure impact as requested," a lead training manager in nursing education said.
- "We created a new microlearning curriculum and communicated that it was available, but we keep getting help desk tickets saying that people lost access to the old training content!" a chief learning officer in finance shared.
- "Why don't they understand that the power to learn is in their hands with what we just created for them?" a chief HR officer in the hospitality industry asked.

These quotes highlight the need for organizations to *assess their readiness* to support different types of learning initiatives before they can successfully implement microlearning programs. Understanding your current implementation capabilities will help you determine which microlearning approaches are feasible now, what enhancements you might need for more advanced approaches, and how to create a sustainable path for growth.

This chapter will explore what I think are the essential elements that determine your readiness for different types of microlearning implementation, how implementation connects to the other framework dimensions, and how to assess your current capabilities. We'll explore what implementation looks like for knowledge-based, skills-based, and performance-based initiatives, and use Be Natural's experiences to illustrate common challenges and successful approaches. Once you understand your implementation readiness, you'll be able to make more informed decisions about which microlearning approaches to pursue and how to develop the capabilities necessary for success.

What Is Implementation?

Implementation within the MLR Framework refers to your organization's ability to deliver microlearning experiences effectively to participants. It encompasses all the methods, systems, resources, and processes required to bring microlearning initiatives to life, from initial development through delivery and maintenance.

Implementation is the final execution dimension because it's where everything converges. The outcomes, purpose, and potential you established in chapter 3 define what you're trying to achieve. The evaluation methods you designed in chapter 4 determine how you'll measure success. The spacing strategies you selected in chapter 5 establish when and how frequently participants engage with your content. Implementation is where all these decisions become reality—it determines whether you can actually deliver the learning experiences you've designed, support the evaluation approaches you've planned, and execute the spacing strategies you've chosen.

Unlike traditional L&D approaches that focus primarily on content development and the functionality of LMSs, implementation in the microlearning context requires a more comprehensive ecosystem. Traditional training often involves creating a course, uploading it to an LMS, and tracking completion. Microlearning implementation is more demanding because of its unique characteristics such as shorter experiences that may need to be delivered at specific intervals, potential workflow integration, varied delivery methods across different contexts, and more frequent engagement points that require consistent tracking and support. Your implementation infrastructure must support not only the delivery of content, but also the evaluation mechanisms you need to measure impact and the scheduling systems required for effective spacing.

This interdependency means your implementation capabilities directly determine what's feasible across all other dimensions. You might design an evaluation approach that requires manager observations of behavior change, but if your implementation infrastructure doesn't include manager training and observation tools, that evaluation plan won't work. You might plan spacing intervals that deliver content every three days for two weeks, but if your implementation systems can't reliably schedule and track that frequency, your spacing strategy will fail. Strong implementation readiness expands your options across evaluation and spacing; limited implementation capabilities constrain what you can realistically attempt in those dimensions.

Your implementation assessment reveals which types of microlearning you can realistically support:

- Knowledge-based microlearning requires basic delivery and tracking systems.
- Skills-based microlearning needs interactive platforms and feedback mechanisms.
- Performance-based microlearning demands integration with workflow systems and real-time performance data.

Understanding your implementation readiness helps match your approach to your current capabilities while identifying what infrastructure development would expand your options.

For organizations starting their microlearning journey, an implementation assessment is often most effective when it is focused on a specific pilot initiative, rather than attempting an organization-wide transformation. (Part 3 and chapter 16 speak to the use of pilots.) This focused approach allows you to identify exactly what's necessary for success in a specific context, including which evaluation approaches and spaced learning strategies your current infrastructure can support, and then build capabilities incrementally. Your implementation capabilities rest on three interconnected infrastructure elements—technology, process, and people—which we'll explore next.

Key Elements of Implementation

Most organizations start their microlearning journey by focusing on implementation. "We need to launch microlearning!" becomes the rallying cry, with attention immediately turning to platforms, content formats, and delivery methods. This impulse is understandable. Implementation is visible and tangible. It's where learning actually reaches participants. However, organizations that begin with implementation often discover too late that their readiness was actually determined by decisions and capabilities that should have come earlier. Implementation doesn't create readiness. It reveals what readiness you actually have.

Your implementation success depends heavily on the infrastructure we examined in chapters 4 and 5. The evaluation systems from chapter 4 determine whether you can measure what matters during implementation. The spacing capabilities from chapter 5 determine whether you can deliver learning at the intervals that drive retention and application. Implementation is where these two dimensions must work together, and it's often when you discover which one is your actual constraint. You might plan a spacing strategy that delivers microlearning every three days, only to find during implementation that your evaluation tracking can't handle that frequency. Or, you might design evaluation that requires manager observations, only to discover during implementation that your delivery infrastructure doesn't support the manager involvement your spacing strategy needs.

Beyond the evaluation and spacing infrastructure already discussed, implementation introduces its own considerations. These aren't about technology systems or process workflows, they're about the human and organizational factors that determine whether microlearning actually functions in your environment.

🐝 An Implementation Readiness Evolution

Be Natural initially planned to implement microlearning across all new hire onboarding, regardless of department or role. The L&D team designed evaluation methods to track knowledge retention and early job performance, planned spacing intervals to reinforce key concepts during the first months of employment, and developed content covering company culture, systems access, and role-specific basics. The plan looked solid on paper.

Implementation revealed a different reality. The evaluation approach required managers to observe and provide feedback on new hire progress, but manager preparation varied widely across departments. Some had time and understood their role, while others didn't understand what they were supposed to do or lacked the capacity to participate consistently. The spacing strategy depended on automated delivery through the LMS at set intervals, but new hires started on different schedules across departments, making consistent timing impossible to coordinate. Support requests came from different locations with different technical setups, and the small L&D team couldn't respond quickly enough to keep frustration from building.

Within weeks, the initiative was struggling. Evaluation data was inconsistent because manager participation was uneven. Spacing intervals were missed because the LMS couldn't accommodate rolling start dates without manual intervention, which the team lacked the capacity to provide. New hires in some departments engaged regularly while others barely participated, creating confusion about whether the approach worked or implementation was the problem.

The L&D team made a trade-off decision. Rather than continue struggling with organization-wide implementation, they narrowed focus to new hires in the sales department. They chose sales because the managers in this department were already engaged and prepared to support the effort, new hires started in cohorts rather than continuously, and the sales director had committed resources to help troubleshoot issues. The evaluation approach still required manager observation, but now those managers were ready. The spacing strategy still used the LMS, but coordinating delivery for cohorts was manageable. Support needs were concentrated enough that the L&D team could respond effectively.

The scaled-back approach worked better, although not perfectly. Spacing intervals occasionally required manual adjustments if cohort sizes changed. Evaluation revealed that some managers needed additional coaching on providing useful feedback. Content updates took longer than expected because the approval processes weren't as streamlined as hoped. But the initiative functioned. The L&D team learned what their implementation infrastructure could actually sustain and what they needed to build before expanding to other departments. Not starting at all would have been worse than starting too broadly, but the trade-off to narrow scope allowed them to demonstrate value and identify what capability development would enable broader implementation later.

Chapter Summary

Understanding your implementation readiness is important for determining which microlearning approaches your project can effectively support. Implementation, the final dimension of the MLR Framework, serves as the bridge between your strategic intent and practical execution. By assessing your project's implementation, change management, adoption, engagement, sustainability, and support systems, you can make informed decisions about microlearning initiatives, engage stakeholders more effectively, and optimize your resources.

Throughout this chapter, we've explored how implementation functions as the dimension where evaluation and spacing capabilities converge in actual delivery. We've examined the key elements that determine implementation success beyond infrastructure: the change management needed to prepare organizations and people, the adoption factors that determine whether participants actually use what you deliver, the sustainability considerations that affect long-term viability, and the support systems that help when problems arise. We've also seen through Be Natural's experience how implementation reveals actual constraints and requires trade-off decisions when initial scope exceeds current capabilities.

By understanding your implementation readiness, you can make informed choices that set up your microlearning initiatives for success. The goal is making strategic choices that match your current reality while building capabilities that expand what's possible over time.

A Bridge to Chapter 7: From Projects to Capabilities

Throughout the last four chapters, we've examined each dimension of the MLR Framework from a project perspective—establishing outcomes, purpose, and potential; designing evaluation approaches; implementing spaced learning strategies; and creating effective implementation infrastructure. Each chapter has included tools to assess your readiness for specific microlearning initiatives."

These project-level assessments collectively reveal something larger—your L&D function's overall capabilities and capacity for supporting microlearning. Chapter 7 explores this critical connection, examining how the insights gained from project assessments inform your understanding of broader L&D readiness.

While project assessments help you make immediate decisions about specific initiatives, examining patterns across multiple assessments you can help identify capability gaps that limit the L&D function's ability to scale microlearning successfully. Chapter 7 will help you translate project-level insights into a comprehensive capability development strategy, creating a foundation for organization-wide implementation.

By starting with focused projects and using the MLR Framework to assess readiness across all dimensions, you've already begun building the evidence and expertise needed for broader application. Chapter 7 builds on this foundation to help you develop the L&D capabilities needed to maximize microlearning's potential throughout your organization.

Assess Your Implementation Readiness

Purpose

Assess your project's implementation readiness to determine what factors might limit your ability to launch and sustain microlearning effectively. This assessment builds on the evaluation infrastructure you examined in chapter 4 and the spacing infrastructure you explored in chapter 5, then adds the change management considerations that determine whether microlearning functions in your environment. The key question this activity helps you answer is: "What will constrain your implementation success?"

Strategic Value

Most organizations focus on platforms and content when planning microlearning, overlooking the change management factors that determine implementation success. This assessment helps you identify which elements need attention before launch and which capabilities you need to build for sustainable implementation. Understanding your constraints now prevents failed launches and builds realistic plans for growth.

Instructions

Read each element description, determine the level that best describes your current readiness, and enter that rating into the table on the next page. Be honest in your assessment—identifying limitations now allows you to address them proactively or adjust your approach to work within current constraints.

Part 1. Rate Your Implementation Readiness

Use this rating scale to assess your leadership support:
- **Established:** Leadership is actively supporting the effort, including providing resources, removing barriers, and communicating the importance of the initiative to the organization.
- **Developing:** Leadership is not fully bought in—they may approve the initiative but don't actively champion it or provide the necessary support.
- **Missing:** Leadership support does not exist—leaders are not aware of the initiative, have not approved it, or are resisting it.

Use this rating scale to assess your stakeholder engagement:
- **Established:** All stakeholders are engaged, including managers who oversee participants who will use the microlearning *and* the partner entities L&D needs to deliver the solution (such as IT, HR, operations, and business units).
- **Developing:** Some stakeholders are engaged but not all—L&D may have support from some managers or partner entities, but there are gaps in critical areas.
- **Missing:** Stakeholders are not engaged—managers who oversee participants are unaware or uninvolved, and partner entities have not been brought into the effort.

Use this rating scale to assess your communication strategy:

- **Established:** Communication strategy has been developed, including how the initiative will be announced, what messages will be delivered to different audiences, when communications will occur, and who will deliver them.
- **Developing:** Some communication planning has occurred, but the strategy is incomplete—L&D may know what to communicate but not when or how, or there is a plan for some audiences but not others.
- **Missing:** Communication strategy has not been developed—there is no plan for how to communicate about the initiative to participants, managers, or other stakeholders.

Use this rating scale to assess your feedback mechanisms:

- **Established:** Feedback mechanisms are in place to hear concerns and adjust the approach, including clear channels for participants and stakeholders to share input, processes for reviewing feedback, and ways to make adjustments based on what is learned.
- **Developing:** Some feedback mechanisms exist, but they are incomplete—L&D may have ways to collect feedback but no process for acting on it, or input is gathered from some groups but not others.
- **Missing:** Feedback mechanisms have not been developed—there is no structured way for people to share concerns, questions, or suggestions about the initiative.

Use this rating scale to assess the resistance levels:

- **Established:** Assessment has been done to determine level of resistance, including identifying who might resist the change, understanding their concerns, and developing strategies to address resistance.
- **Developing:** A resistance assessment has not been planned but L&D is aware resistance may exist—L&D has not formally assessed resistance, but recognize it is a potential issue.
- **Missing:** A resistance assessment has not been considered—L&D has not thought about who might resist the change or why, and has no plan for addressing resistance.

Summary: Your Implementation Readiness Ratings

Implementation Element	Rating
Leadership Support	
Stakeholder Engagement	
Communication Strategy	
Feedback Mechanisms	
Resistance Assessment	

Part 2. Identify Your Implementation Constraints

Which elements did you rate as missing? These are your primary implementation constraints. Which elements did you rate as developing? These are the areas that need strengthening.

1. Based on your assessment:
- Your missing elements are: _____
- Your developing elements are: _____

2. Compare your answers in each category to this list.
- **If leadership support is missing or developing:** You risk low engagement, stakeholder resistance, or initiative failure because leaders are not championing the effort. You may need to invest time in building leadership support before launch or scale back your initial implementation to reduce the need for high-level sponsorship.
- **If stakeholder engagement is missing or developing:** Critical partners may not provide the support you need, or managers may not prepare their teams. You need to engage missing stakeholders before launch or adjust your approach to work without their involvement (which may limit what you can accomplish).
- **If communication strategy is missing or developing:** Participants and stakeholders will be confused about the initiative, potentially leading to low adoption or resistance. You need to develop your communication strategy with the appropriate stakeholders or leadership before launch, including clear messages for different audiences and a timeline for delivery.
- **If feedback mechanisms are missing or developing:** You may not hear concerns or problems until they become significant issues. You need to establish clear channels for feedback before launch and commit to reviewing and acting on what you learn to grow from your efforts.
- **If resistance assessment is missing or developing:** You may encounter unanticipated resistance but lack a strategy to address it. You need to assess potential resistance before launch and develop strategies for addressing concerns or accept that you will have to address resistance reactively as it emerges.

3. Does the evaluation or spacing infrastructure create additional constraints? Any gaps in evaluation infrastructure (chapter 4) or spacing infrastructure (chapter 5) will also limit what you can implement. Implementation reveals whether those foundational elements are adequate.
- **If evaluation infrastructure is limited,** you may not be able to measure impact as planned.
- **If spacing infrastructure is limited,** you may not be able to deliver at planned intervals.

4. What is your strongest element?
Which elements did you rate as established? Can they help compensate for other limitations? For example:

- Strong leadership support can help overcome some stakeholder engagement gaps by directing people to participate.
- A strong communication strategy can help address some resistance by proactively explaining the change.
- Strong feedback mechanisms can compensate for incomplete resistance assessment by allowing you to identify and address concerns as they emerge.

Next Steps
Based on your assessment:

- **If you have one or two missing elements:** Address them before launch, or adjust your implementation approach to work within those limitations. Chapter 7 will help you identify which L&D capacities to develop to strengthen these areas.
- **If you have multiple missing elements:** Consider starting with a smaller pilot that requires less developed change management infrastructure. Build evidence and capabilities before expanding.
- **If evaluation or spacing infrastructure is limiting:** Return to chapters 4 and 5 to identify what infrastructure is missing and what you need to build.
- **If all elements are developing or missing:** You are probably not ready to launch. Focus on building the most critical elements first, then develop the others before moving forward.

Remember: Implementation reveals your actual readiness. Understanding your constraints now and planning accordingly builds stakeholder confidence and sets you up for sustainable success rather than failed launches that damage credibility.

CHAPTER 7
L&D Capacity and Scaling

By the end of this chapter, you should be able to answer these questions:
- What's the difference between L&D capability and capacity?
- Why does capacity matter when scaling from pilots?
- What infrastructure factors constrain L&D's ability to scale microlearning?
- How do you move from successful pilot to L&D function readiness?

In previous chapters, we've explored the MLR Framework through the lens of particular pilot (or project) initiatives, examining how outcomes, purpose, potential, evaluation, spaced learning, and implementation shape your readiness for microlearning. Now, we'll shift our focus to the L&D function level.

Just as a restaurant kitchen team must consider not only their culinary skills but also their bandwidth to serve more customers, your L&D function must understand both what you can do and how much you can sustain before attempting to scale microlearning across your organization. You might have successfully completed a pilot initiative using the assessments from previous chapters. This chapter will help you understand what it takes to move from one successful pilot to multiple sustained initiatives.

Think of your L&D function as the kitchen team in a restaurant. Even with excellent ingredients (content), advanced equipment (technology), and an appreciative audience (engaged participants), your success ultimately depends on your team's culinary skills (capabilities) and their available time and resources (capacity). A skilled chef with limited ingredients can still create remarkable dishes, but a novice with premium ingredients might struggle to produce even basic meals. Consider these experiences shared by learning professionals:

- "We launched a successful sales training pilot, but scaling it meant we needed IT to help with system integration and operations to adjust schedules. Those relationships took months to build, and we hadn't planned for that," shared a learning architect.
- "The organization wants us to scale microlearning across all departments, but we barely have the capacity to support our current projects. We need to be realistic about what we can effectively maintain," a learning architect shared.
- "Our team knew how to create traditional courses, but microlearning required us to think differently about chunking content and designing for shorter attention spans. The learning curve was steeper than we expected," an L&D manager explained.
- "We can handle one or two microlearning initiatives, but when the organization asked for five more, we realized we'd need manager support for reinforcement and HR's help with performance data. Building those partnerships takes time and capacity we hadn't accounted for," a training director noted.

These stories highlight why understanding capacity is crucial for scaling microlearning. Your organization might be perfectly aligned on outcomes and purpose and the pilot might have been a success, but if your L&D team lacks the bandwidth to maintain multiple initiatives simultaneously, scaling will fail. The difference between capability (what you can do) and capacity (how much you can sustain) becomes critical as you move beyond individual pilot initiatives.

This chapter will help you understand the distinction between L&D capability and capacity, recognize the infrastructure constraints that limit how much your team can sustain, and make realistic decisions about scaling from successful pilots to broader implementation. By understanding your capacity constraints, you can set appropriate expectations and build a sustainable path for microlearning growth in your organization.

How Scaling Reveals Capacity Constraints

A successful pilot demonstrates that microlearning can work in your organization. But moving from one successful initiative to multiple sustained efforts requires a different kind of readiness. The shift from pilot to function level reveals capacity constraints that weren't apparent when you were focused on a single project.

When you're running one pilot, your team can often absorb the extra work without formal process changes. Someone coordinates with IT as needed. Another person handles stakeholder questions. Content updates happen when there's time. Support requests get answered promptly because volume is manageable. This informal approach works because the scope is limited and the team can adjust on the fly.

Scaling reveals what happens when the informal approach breaks down. Multiple initiatives mean multiple stakeholder relationships to maintain, more content to keep current, competing priorities for IT support, and support requests that exceed what your team can handle responsively. The person who could coordinate everything for one pilot can't sustain that level of involvement across five departments. The ad hoc processes that worked for a single initiative create bottlenecks when applied to multiple projects simultaneously.

This is where capacity becomes the limiting factor, not capability. Your team might have the skills to design excellent microlearning, but lack the bandwidth to maintain quality across multiple initiatives. You might understand how to implement spaced learning effectively, but not have the capacity to manually coordinate scheduling for six different audiences. You might know what evaluation data would be valuable, but not have time to pull, analyze, and report on it for every active project.

Organizations often respond to this constraint in one of three ways. Some try to maintain the same quality across multiple initiatives, which leads to team burnout and declining quality despite best intentions. Others lower their quality standards to handle the volume, which damages credibility and reduces impact. The third approach recognizes capacity as a real constraint and makes deliberate choices about how many initiatives to support and at what level of quality, while identifying which infrastructure improvements would be needed to expand capacity.

Understanding your capacity constraints before attempting to scale helps you set realistic expectations with stakeholders, make informed decisions about which initiatives to pursue, and identify what infrastructure or resource investments would enable sustainable growth. The goal isn't to delay scaling indefinitely, but to scale in ways your L&D function can actually sustain.

What About Capacity?

Capacity and capability are distinct but interconnected concepts. *Capability* is your team's ability to perform tasks effectively. *Capacity*, on the other hand, is your team's bandwidth to execute and maintain initiatives.

We can return to our restaurant analogy here. A chef might have the skills (capability) to prepare 40 different dishes, but if the kitchen team can produce only 15 dishes simultaneously (capacity), the restaurant must limit its menu accordingly. While capability determines what your L&D function can do, capacity determines what it can sustain. Even the most skilled L&D team faces capacity constraints that limit how many microlearning initiatives it can effectively support, especially if the team is asked to keep original, long-form training content during a conversion.

Capacity, Constraints, and the Need for Balance

When planning microlearning initiatives, consider these capacity dimensions:

- **Development capacity** includes the resources available for creating microlearning, whether new, conversions, or updates.
- **Maintenance capacity** refers to the bandwidth for keeping content current, relevant, and scheduled for participants. Some organizations may need to do manual work to enact spaced learning, for example.
- **Support capacity** includes the resources needed for ongoing assistance and troubleshooting. This includes pulling data, analyzing it, and sharing reports with stakeholders.

As you plan your microlearning strategy, acknowledge that capacity constraints will affect both the number and complexity of initiatives you can support. Obviously, you also need to recognize current projects and efforts that are more traditional to what your organization has been doing. By understanding these realities, you can set appropriate expectations with stakeholders and make informed decisions about where to invest your limited resources.

Remember that capacity, unlike capability, can't always be increased through training or development. It often requires additional resources or strategic trade-offs. Recognizing these constraints isn't a limitation, however. It's a prerequisite for sustainable success.

How Infrastructure Context Shapes L&D Capabilities

Your L&D capabilities don't exist in isolation—they develop and operate within your organization's broader infrastructure. While previous chapters explored infrastructure for particular initiatives, here we'll focus specifically on how your organizational infrastructure shapes your L&D capabilities.

Four key infrastructure areas directly influence the capabilities your L&D function can develop and apply:

- **Cultural infrastructure** sets expectations and values around learning that either support or constrain capability development. Organizations with strong learning cultures enable coaching and feedback capabilities, while compliance-focused cultures may limit experiential design approaches.
- **Technology infrastructure** enables or constrains what you can create and deliver by determining the tools and platforms available for your work. Basic authoring tools support knowledge-based development, while limited analytics capabilities prevent complex skill and performance assessment.
- **Process infrastructure** determines how efficiently you can work, and which approaches are feasible within your organizational workflows. Streamlined development processes enable rapid content creation, while lengthy approval cycles limit agile updates for performance-based solutions.
- **People infrastructure** provides the human resources and expertise needed to execute capability development plans. Teams with strong foundational design skills can build knowledge-based capabilities

quickly, but they may need additional development for scenario design and skills-based approaches.

Infrastructure Gaps

Understanding how your infrastructure shapes L&D capabilities enables you to plan strategically for capability development. You can identify which capabilities are most affected by infrastructure constraints and focus your improvement efforts where they'll have the greatest impact. This insight also helps you target infrastructure improvements to enable critical capabilities rather than making random technology or process changes. When infrastructure improvements aren't immediately feasible, it's possible to develop work-arounds for infrastructure limitations to maintain progress on priority initiatives. Most importantly, this understanding helps you set realistic expectations for capability development timelines because infrastructure changes often take longer than skill development.

Remember that capability development often requires corresponding infrastructure development, particularly for microlearning approaches that are skills- or performance-based.

Chapter Summary

This chapter has examined how capacity constraints shape your ability to scale from successful pilot initiatives to sustained microlearning implementation across the L&D function. Understanding the distinction between capability and capacity helps you make realistic decisions about what your team can sustain.

The key insights from this chapter include:

- Capability is what your team can do; capacity is how much your team can sustain
- Three dimensions of capacity affect scaling: development, maintenance, and support
- Infrastructure constraints (cultural, technology, process, and people) limit what's possible regardless of team skills
- Scaling from one pilot to multiple initiatives requires different approaches than informal coordination

- Recognizing capacity constraints enables strategic choices about sustainable growth.

Moving from a successful pilot to broader implementation requires honest assessment of your team's bandwidth and the infrastructure context that shapes what's feasible. Informal processes that work for one initiative create bottlenecks when applied to multiple projects. Quality and quantity trade-offs become necessary when capacity is limited.

Remember that recognizing capacity constraints isn't about limiting possibilities. It's about making strategic choices that set up your microlearning initiatives for sustainable success. By understanding what your L&D function can realistically maintain, you can set appropriate expectations with stakeholders, identify where infrastructure improvements would expand capacity, and build a foundation for long-term impact rather than short-term burnout.

A Bridge to Part 2

As you transition to part 2, understanding your capacity constraints will inform how you apply the design principles. The assessment work you completed in chapters 3 to 6 revealed your readiness for specific initiatives. Now, as you consider scaling microlearning across your organization, capacity becomes the key constraint to manage. The learning science foundations in chapter 8 and the design principles that follow will help you create effective microlearning experiences that work within your L&D function's capacity while demonstrating value that can justify resource investments for growth.

Design Principles

In part 2, we'll explore design principles that build on the foundation of the MLR Framework to ensure that your microlearning solutions match your L&D capabilities and support effective learning. The journey from organizational readiness to effective design starts with understanding how people learn, so we will discuss how to apply learning science within your current design capabilities and then build toward more sophisticated approaches.

Learning science directly connects your organizational readiness with effective design in several ways:

- Memory and cognitive processes inform content structure.
- Learning domains guide assessment approaches.
- Motivation principles shape engagement strategies.
- Learning theory influences delivery methods.
- Behavioral science supports performance change.

In the chapters that follow, we'll focus on how a few mainstays of learning science—cognitive load theory, Robert Gagné's Conditions of Learning (also known as the Five Categories of Learning Outcomes), and Gagné's Nine Events of Instruction—can inform your microlearning initiatives so they will align with how people actually learn and retain information.

Connecting Capabilities to Design Principles

Your and your L&D team's capabilities will influence how effectively you can implement each of the seven design principles:

- **Principle 1, Know Your Tools' Capacity,** requires technical capabilities to evaluate and leverage tools effectively. Teams with strong technical skills can maximize existing platforms, while those with gaps may need to focus on simpler implementations or build technical capabilities first.
- **Principle 2, Craft an Appropriate Context,** depends on instructional design acumen to create relevant learning situations. Without strong contextual design capabilities, your microlearning initiatives may struggle to connect with employees' real-world experiences.
- **Principle 3, Ensure Global Equity,** requires capabilities in inclusive design and cultural awareness. L&D teams that lack these capabilities

may inadvertently create solutions that work well for some audiences but exclude others.

- **Principle 4, Design With Concision,** relies on content curation and prioritization skills. Without these capabilities, your microlearning initiative may become overcrowded or miss critical elements that your participants need. Leveraging Gagné's frameworks in a modified fashion can assist in managing the cognitive load put upon the individual participant.
- **Principle 5, Make Media Meaningful,** depends on media selection and production capabilities. Teams with limited multimedia skills may default to text-heavy approaches, missing opportunities for engagement through varied media.
- **Principle 6, Elicit Action,** requires skill in activity design and application. Without these capabilities, your microlearning initiative may become passive knowledge transfer rather than active acquisition and development that aids performance.
- **Principle 7, Avoid Overuse,** depends on integration and design capabilities along with understanding cognitive load. Teams lacking these skills may desensitize participants with too many microlearning products or the same design approaches and engagement techniques within the microlearning campaigns.

Chapter 8 explores cognitive load theory and Gagné's framework—understanding these foundations represents another critical capability. Teams with stronger learning science knowledge can better apply the design principles to create effective microlearning experiences.

Be Natural, our illustrative company, began with principles that matched its strongest capabilities while systematically developing expertise in more challenging areas. This progressive approach to capability development ensures that your microlearning initiatives build on your strengths while systematically addressing gaps.

Part 2 is not a prescriptive manual, but a critical exploration of design principles that illuminate the complex landscape of microlearning. These chapters will challenge you to consider how organizational context, technological capabilities, learning goals, and human cognitive processes intersect. You'll discover that effective microlearning design is less about finding rule-based solutions and more about developing an adaptive approach that responds to your organization's unique ecosystem.

Before diving into the design principles that will guide your microlearning development, take a moment to identify a specific opportunity in your organization or with a client. This activity will help you apply each principle to a real project (or even one you envision creating that has yet to come to life!) as you progress through this section. Whether you've completed the MLR Framework assessments from part 1 or you're starting here, this approach will help you apply the seven design principles to your microlearning project using the current tools you have available, your current capability level, and within the current known environment for your target audience.

Identify and Plan Your Project

In chapters 9 through 15, you will have a chance to check in and reflect on your project in light of what you've read. Prepare now by considering the project you will explore.

Step 1. Select Your Focus

Choose one of the following to work with throughout part 2, and then briefly describe your selected focus:

- Improve a current microlearning product that needs enhancement.
- Convert an existing training program you want to transform into microlearning.
- Create a new performance need that could benefit from a microlearning approach.

My focus will be: _____

Step 2. Define Your Essential Parameters

Which microlearning type best describes your intended solution?

- Knowledge-based. Helping people learn and remember information
- Skills-based. Helping people practice and develop specific abilities
- Performance-based. Supporting people directly in their workflow

Consider your target audience:

- Who will use this solution?
- What is their current knowledge or skill level?
- What is their work context (such as their environment, tools, systems, and constraints)?
- Can you think of or do you know any challenges they currently face?

Consider your desired outcome:

- What specific, measurable result should this solution achieve?
- What should people be able to do after engaging with your microlearning?

Step 3. Identify Initial Constraints and Opportunities

Now, it's time to consider your available tools, constraints, and opportunities.

Answer the following questions:

- What technological and environmental tools can you leverage?
- What limitations must you work within (think of yours for developing and implementing, not just your target audience)?
- What unique advantages can you capitalize on?

Step 4. Create Your VISR Lens

As you read each chapter about microlearning principles (chapters 9–15), use the VISR reflection framework to evaluate how the principle applies to your project. This has been one of the best ways I've found for L&D folks to stymie their desire to have rules and ready-made answers so they can see the potential of microlearning through their unique lens and maximize its power.

The VISR framework allows you to ask targeted questions to help sharpen your focus on how each principle applies to your project. You don't have to answer these now, but at the end of each chapter, you'll find a VISR Check-In.

Validate
- Does this principle validate my current approach or challenge assumptions?
- What aspects of my design align with this principle?
- What assumptions should I reconsider based on this principle?

Innovate
- How might this principle help me innovate my solution?
- What new approaches does this principle suggest?
- How could I apply this principle in unexpected ways?

Spark
- What new ideas does this principle spark for my project?
- What creative possibilities emerge when applying this principle?
- How might this principle lead to breakthrough solutions?

Refine
- How can I refine my design based on this principle?
- What specific improvements can I make to my current design?
- How might I better align my approach with this principle?

The VISR check-in activity combines reflection and planning. As you progress through the next chapters, you'll develop a deeper understanding of how people create and retain memories, the critical role of cognitive load in learning, and how microlearning design principles can support more effective microlearning experiences.

CHAPTER 8
Learning Science and Microlearning Design

By the end of this chapter, you should be able to answer these questions:
- How do cognitive load and learning conditions influence microlearning design decisions?
- What practical impact do cognitive load theory (CLT) and Robert Gagné's Conditions of Learning have on knowledge-based, skills-based, and performance-based microlearning?
- How do schemas and mental models affect how people interpret and apply microlearning?
- How can you apply learning science and instructional design theories to strengthen your microlearning solutions?
- How do these foundations connect to the design principles in the upcoming chapters?

By now, you realize that creating microlearning isn't just about making content shorter! As we begin looking at the design of our microlearning products, we need a learning science foundation. *Learning science* is the interdisciplinary study of how people learn—including how they process, store, retrieve, and apply information—and how instructional environments can be designed to support effective learning. In this chapter, we draw on key insights from cognitive science, instructional psychology, and educational theory to inform the microlearning design principles that shape the rest of part 2. Without this foundation, even the most carefully designed microlearning programs may fall short of delivering meaningful results. Consider these challenges shared by colleagues:

- "We shortened our training into bite-sized pieces, but people still aren't retaining the information like the stakeholders had hoped," a training manager reported.
- "Our microlearning looks great, but we're not seeing the performance improvements we expected," an L&D director said.
- "People complete the modules quickly, but managers are indicating that their employees struggle to apply what they've learned on the job," a learning specialist noted.

These challenges stem from a fundamental gap between design choices and how people actually learn. Just as a chef who doesn't understand food science might create visually appealing dishes that lack flavor or proper texture, L&D professionals who skip learning science may create microlearning that looks good but doesn't produce the envisioned potential.

This chapter introduces two essential theories that will inform the microlearning principles in chapters 9 through 15: cognitive load theory (CLT) and Gagné's Conditions of Learning. These theories help us design more effective solutions for all three types of microlearning. Whether you've completed the MLR Framework assessment from part 1 or you're starting here with design principles, understanding these learning foundations will help you create microlearning that works with—rather than against—how people naturally process, store, and retrieve information.

To do that well, designers must understand two cognitive structures: schemas and mental models. *Schemas*—how we organize knowledge in memory—are groupings of related concepts that help us recognize, interpret, and respond quickly. *Mental models*, on the other hand, represent how we think a system works. Both influence how we perceive, remember, and apply new information, and both will appear throughout the rest of the book.

In this chapter, we'll explore how CLT and Gagné's framework can transform your microlearning from merely short training bursts to genuinely effective content that drives knowledge retention, skills development, and performance improvement. (Remember, this isn't just about fixing problems!)

Learning Science Foundations

Just as a chef needs to understand how heat transforms ingredients, L&D professionals need to understand how memory processes transform information into knowledge and skills.

Three Memory Processes and What They Do

Our memory includes three main processes: encoding, storage, and retrieval. Each process has significant implications for how we design effective microlearning experiences.

- **Encoding** transforms incoming information into a form our memory can handle. Our brains can encode information visually through images, acoustically through sound, or through the meaning of words. The stronger and more varied the encoding, the more likely the information will be remembered (Dirksen 2015).
- **Retrieval** is how we access stored information when we need it. Short-term memory retrieval works sequentially, like searching through a brief list, while long-term memory retrieval works through associations, following connected pathways. The more pathways that lead to a memory, the easier it is to retrieve—which is why creating multiple connections to information is so valuable in microlearning design. It reinforces the ideas behind spaced repetition, interleaving, and desirable difficulties (proactive challenges that strengthen retention).

Each of these memory processes—encoding, storage, and retrieval—can be directly supported through targeted microlearning strategies.

🐝 Be Natural's Memory-Driven Microlearning

Be Natural's L&D team applied their understanding of memory processes in their sales training using a microlearning product called a "product feature card." Each card in the collection was focused on a different BN product and featured a clear product image, a concise text description, and a brief audio pronunciation of each ingredient name. Sales representatives accessed these cards via their tablets during morning preparation or as needed between sales visits. By simultaneously engaging the user's visual, verbal, and auditory encoding, this microlearning product used multiple encoding paths to strengthen memory formation. The product feature cards were part of a broader sales enablement campaign that included several complementary microlearning products designed to reinforce product knowledge at different points in the sales cycle.

BN's L&D team also created a microlearning product for manufacturing safety training called "safety spot checks." This product consisted of brief, targeted safety verification interactions that supervisors conducted during their shifts. Rather than reviewing all 12 safety protocol points at once, the safety spot checks focused on one logical group of four related items at a time, and provided distinct visual cues for each group.

Supervisors carried small, durable prompt cards that guided them through 30-to-60-second verification questions for a single protocol group. The manufacturing team then rotated through three groups over the course of a week, which helped ensure regular reinforcement without overwhelming the operators' working memory. This chunking approach respects short-term memory limitations while building stronger connections for long-term retention through spaced learning practices.

The safety spot checks were part of a broader microlearning campaign that included several complementary products delivered at different points in the workflow, all reinforcing the same chunked safety information.

Retrieval

BN creates strong retrieval paths for sales representatives through its "customer challenge simulator." This interactive digital microlearning product presents brief, realistic customer scenarios in which various customer personas ask different questions about the same product. Sales representatives must quickly respond to these inquiries by retrieving relevant information through multiple contextual pathways. Each simulation takes two to three minutes to complete, so sales representatives can access them between customer visits on their mobile devices.

The customer challenge simulator is part of a larger microlearning campaign that reinforces product knowledge and customer selling skills in different contexts throughout the sales cycle. Sales managers report that representatives who regularly engage with this microlearning product demonstrate more confident and accurate product knowledge during actual customer interactions compared with those who complete only the initial product training.

From Memory to Learning

While understanding memory processes gives us important insights, we need comprehensive theories to guide our microlearning design. Just as a chef moves beyond understanding individual ingredients to mastering how to combine them, we need to understand how these memory processes work together in learning. Two complementary explanations of how learning works can help us create optimal learning experiences:

- **Cognitive load theory** (CLT) addresses how we manage mental resources during learning. It helps us understand how much information people can process at once and how to avoid overwhelming their working memory. Our goal in this part of the book is to ensure that our designs don't create memory noise (irrelevant or competing information that interferes with learning).

- **Gagné's Conditions of Learning** framework shows us how to structure learning experiences for different types of outcomes in the flow of learning. It helps us create the right conditions for knowledge acquisition, skills development, and attitude formation. It also guides the design of experiences that can shape behaviors and reinforce the attitudes needed for sustained performance.

Together, these two theories provide a comprehensive foundation for microlearning design that respects both the capacity of memory and the conditions necessary for effective learning. Let's explore each in more depth and see how they apply to different types of microlearning.

Cognitive Load Theory

Understanding CLT is essential for effective microlearning design. Just as a chef must be mindful of how many flavors can harmoniously combine in a single dish, microlearning designers need to understand how much information people can process at once.

CLT, initially developed by John Sweller, explains how our working memory manages information during learning. Working memory has limited capacity—it can process only a certain amount of information simultaneously. When this capacity is exceeded, learning becomes difficult or impossible (van Merriënboer and Sweller 2005).

This theory is particularly relevant for microlearning because we need to make the most of brief learning experiences. By understanding how cognitive load works, we can design microlearning products that optimize mental processing rather than overwhelming it.

Three Types of Cognitive Load

CLT identifies three distinct types of cognitive load that affect learning. Each has different implications for microlearning design.

- **Intrinsic load: The challenge of content itself.** Intrinsic load represents the inherent complexity or difficulty of what's being learned. It's determined by the number of elements that must be processed simultaneously and the relationships between them.
  - » *Microlearning implications:* While we can't eliminate intrinsic load, we can manage it through sequencing, chunking, and scaffolding.
- **Extraneous load: The burden of poor design.** Extraneous load is unnecessary mental effort that doesn't contribute to learning. This includes confusing instructions, irrelevant information, and poorly designed interfaces. While other factors like the learning environment and multitasking can contribute to distraction, our focus here is on design-driven extraneous load: the elements a designer can manage within the microlearning product itself. (We'll explore context and environment more fully in chapter 10.)
  - » *Microlearning implications:* Our goal is to minimize extraneous load, freeing cognitive resources for actual learning.
- **Germane load: The effort that builds understanding.** Germane load represents the mental effort that contributes directly to learning by creating and automating schemas or mental models. This is the good cognitive load we want to optimize.

» *Microlearning implications:* We should design activities that promote schema development while effectively managing overall cognitive demand.

🐝 Be Natural's Microlearning Solutions and the Three Types of Cognitive Load

Be Natural's approach to designing a variety of microlearning solutions illustrates how managing intrinsic, extraneous, and germane load in practice creates more effective learning experiences.

When introducing a new customer relationship management (CRM) system, the L&D team's initial training attempt included a comprehensive digital manual with screenshots of every feature. This approach overwhelmed sales representatives with information that wasn't immediately relevant to their roles. The L&D team replaced this with a set of on-demand microlearning products. These digital guides appeared directly in the CRM interface when a representative accessed specific features, providing only the essential information needed for the immediate task. Each guide used consistent formatting, plain language, and minimal text with supporting visuals. By eliminating extraneous information and presenting guidance exactly when needed, these microlearning products reduced the mental effort sales reps spent figuring out the system.

To help HR onboarding specialists develop effective interview techniques, BN created "interview scenario cards" to use during weekly team huddles. Each card presented a brief hiring scenario that specialists might encounter, with candidate background information on one side and potential follow-up questions on the reverse.

During 15-minute practice sessions, the specialists worked in pairs—one played the candidate and the other the interviewer. After each scenario, they spent two to three minutes discussing which follow-up questions were most effective and why. This face-to-face microlearning product was deliberately designed to promote germane load through:

- Comparison of similar cases with subtle differences (cards were grouped by scenario type)

- Progressive difficulty levels (marked by different-colored borders)
- Guided reflection questions
- A final activity in which specialists contribute their own real scenarios to create new cards

This approach encouraged specialists to develop robust mental models about effective interviewing rather than just memorizing question lists. The product was part of a broader microlearning campaign integrated into regular team meetings, creating brief but consistent learning touchpoints throughout the onboarding specialists' work week.

Understanding Schemas and Mental Models

The Be Natural case study demonstrates how cognitive load principles work in practice. Now let's examine how understanding schemas and mental models can guide your design decisions when creating microlearning products. Schemas and mental models play a critical role in how microlearning supports meaningful learning. While closely related, they serve distinct cognitive purposes that influence how information is processed and applied.

A *schema* is an organized structure of related concepts stored in memory. Schemas help participants recognize patterns, group information efficiently, and retrieve knowledge with less cognitive strain. When microlearning supports schema development—through consistent language, examples, and cues—it strengthens long-term retention and recall.

A *mental model* reflects how we think something works. It includes our assumptions, past experiences, and expectations about processes or systems. Two people may share the same schema for a procedure, but they'll have different interpretations or applications if they have different mental models for how the content fits into their job.

Microlearning can strengthen or challenge both structures. When well aligned with the audience's existing schemas and mental models, learning feels fluid and intuitive. When misaligned, on the other hand, even well-designed content could be misunderstood or resisted. Designers don't need to correct every mental model, but they must be aware of how existing beliefs and expectations shape interpretation.

Managing Cognitive Load in Microlearning Design

Effective microlearning design requires a balanced, three-part approach to cognitive load:

- **Analyze the intrinsic load** of your content and break complex topics into smaller, manageable microlearning products.
- **Minimize extraneous load** through clear, focused design that eliminates distractions.
- **Optimize germane load** by creating meaningful connections and practice opportunities.

When cognitive load is managed effectively, microlearning products can deliver significant benefits within their brief formats. By respecting the limitations of working memory while supporting schema development, we can create experiences that truly enhance learning and performance.

Cognitive Load Across Microlearning Types

Understanding the three types of cognitive load helps us make better design decisions for different types of microlearning solutions, as explained in Table 8-1.

Table 8-1. How Cognitive Load Is Managed in Three Types of Microlearning

	Knowledge-Based Microlearning	Skills-Based Microlearning	Performance-Based Microlearning
Focused on:	Information presentation and retention	Practice and application	Real-time support during actual work
Manages cognitive load by:	Breaking information into logical chunks	Breaking complex skills into component parts	Providing just enough information at the moment of need
	Removing distracting elements	Managing the complexity of practice scenarios	Creating clear decision support tools
	Creating clear organizational structures	Providing appropriate guidance that fades as skills develop	Eliminating nonessential information during task execution
	Using visual frameworks to support understanding	Creating realistic but simplified practice environments	Supporting recall without requiring extensive working memory

Table 8-1. How Cognitive Load Is Managed in Three Types of Microlearning (cont.)

	Knowledge-Based Microlearning	Skills-Based Microlearning	Performance-Based Microlearning
Design characteristics:	Consistent information architecture	Focused scenarios targeting specific skills	Context-sensitive support
	Progressive information disclosure	Graduated difficulty levels	Clear, actionable guidance
	Strong visual organization	Immediate, targeted feedback	Minimal steps to access support
	Multiple encoding opportunities	Simplified but authentic practice	Visual rather than text-heavy format

Gagné's Framework

Just as a chef creates ideal conditions for different cooking techniques—gentle heat for simmering and high heat for searing—effective microlearning requires creating the right conditions for different types of learning. This is why Robert Gagné's work provides valuable guidance for our microlearning design. His Conditions of Learning framework (also known as the Five Categories of Learning Outcomes) helps us understand what types of learning outcomes we might target and what conditions support them. Let's explore this framework and see how it applies to microlearning design.

Learning Outcomes

Gagné identified five major categories of learning outcomes that your microlearning solutions could target—verbal information, intellectual skills, cognitive strategies, attitudes, and motor skills.

- **Verbal information:** This category focuses on declarative knowledge—facts, principles, and concepts that individuals can state or explain. In microlearning, this often involves helping participants remember specific information.
  - » *Microlearning implications:* Many knowledge-based microlearning products target verbal information outcomes, which need clear organization, meaningful context, and systematic recall opportunities.
- **Intellectual skills:** This category involves applying rules, concepts, and procedures to solve problems or complete tasks. These skills build

on one another hierarchically, from simple comparisons to complex problem solving.

» *Microlearning implications:* Skills-based microlearning targeting intellectual skills requires clear examples, guided practice, and progressive skills building.

- **Cognitive strategies:** These are higher-order skills that govern how individuals manage their own thinking, learning, and problem-solving processes. They involve developing approaches to tackle unfamiliar problems.

  » *Microlearning implications:* Microlearning targeting cognitive strategies requires varied challenges and opportunities to develop personal approaches. All three microlearning types can apply cognitive strategies.

- **Attitudes:** Attitudes involve choices, preferences, and emotional responses that influence behavior. They combine cognitive, affective, and behavioral components.

  » *Microlearning implications:* Microlearning targeting attitudes requires credible models, positive experiences, and demonstrated values.

- **Motor skills:** Motor skills involve physical movements and coordination. While less common in corporate learning, they remain important in some contexts.

  » *Microlearning implications:* Microlearning targeting motor skills requires clear demonstrations, regular practice, and immediate feedback.

Gagné's Learning Outcomes and Microlearning Types

Gagné's learning outcomes and microlearning types operate in different but complementary dimensions. Learning outcomes describe what we want participants to achieve, while microlearning types describe the context and approach to learning.

- **Knowledge-based microlearning can effectively target:**

  » Verbal information, through concise presentations of facts and concepts

  » Attitudes, by presenting credible information that shapes perspectives

» Cognitive strategies, by introducing thinking frameworks and approaches
- **Skills-based microlearning can effectively target:**
  » Intellectual skills, through guided practice of procedures and rules
  » Motor skills, through demonstration and structured rehearsal
  » Cognitive strategies, by providing practice with self-reflective techniques
- **Performance-based microlearning can effectively target:**
  » Intellectual skills, by supporting real-time application of procedures
  » Motor skills, by guiding physical actions during actual work
  » Cognitive strategies, by providing decision frameworks at critical moments
  » Attitudes, by reinforcing values during authentic situations

The key is designing with Gagné's framework in mind—understanding which learning outcome you're targeting and which microlearning context is appropriate (knowledge, skills, or performance).

Gagné's Conditions of Learning

While the five categories tell us which learning outcomes we might target, Gagné's Conditions of Learning explain what can optimize learning. Gagné identified two types of conditions: internal and external.

- **Internal conditions** are what the participant brings to the experience, including cognitive capabilities, existing skills, and attitudes. These factors influence not only how new information is processed, but also how behaviors and attitudes can be shaped through the learning experience. Remember that performance is not simply improvement, but the advancement of one's ability to apply knowledge and skills in ways that produce desired outcomes. This includes the learner's existing mental models, which shape how they interpret and apply new information. If these mental models are misaligned with what the microlearning content is attempting to convey, even accurate schemas may not result in shared understanding or effective application.

» *Microlearning implications:* Effective microlearning must account for participants' existing internal conditions, either by ensuring that prerequisites are in place or by activating relevant prior knowledge. It should also acknowledge that behaviors and attitudes may require intentional shaping over time, not just knowledge transfer.

- **External conditions** are what the learning environment or instruction provides to support learning. These include how content is presented, what practice opportunities exist, what feedback is provided, and how transfer is supported.
  » *Microlearning implications:* Microlearning design focuses primarily on creating optimal external conditions within brief learning experiences. This ensures that content, practice, feedback, and transfer supports are aligned to the desired knowledge, skills, behaviors, and attitudes.

Gagné's Nine Events of Instruction

Gagné also developed the Nine Events of Instruction, which provides a specific instructional sequence for implementing these external conditions. While applying all nine events in their full form often leads to long-form learning rather than microlearning, it's possible to streamline these events for microlearning applications while maintaining instructional integrity. (Chapter 12 explores how to adapt Gagné's Nine Events into a concise framework for microlearning design.)

Gagné's Conditions of Learning and Microlearning Types

Gagné's framework can help us design more effective microlearning by guiding us to create the optimal conditions for our targeted learning outcomes.

- **Knowledge-based microlearning** typically targets verbal information outcomes and requires external conditions such as:
  » Clear organization of information
  » Meaningful context for new knowledge
  » Connections to existing knowledge
  » Opportunities for systematic recall
  » Varied use of encoding channels (such as visuals and sounds)

- **Skills-based microlearning** typically targets intellectual skills or cognitive strategies and requires external conditions such as:
  » Clear examples and demonstrations
  » Guided practice opportunities
  » Immediate, specific feedback
  » Progressive complexity
  » Application in varied contexts
- **Performance-based microlearning** typically targets the application of multiple skill types in real contexts and requires external conditions such as:
  » Support at the moment of need
  » Clear decision frameworks
  » Contextual triggers
  » Integration with actual workflow
  » Reinforcement of key behaviors

Connecting Function and Flow

Now we can see how Gagné's framework complements CLT to create more effective microlearning.

CLT (*function*, or how learning happens) helps us manage mental resources effectively. We can monitor how much information people can process and how to avoid overwhelming them. CLT addresses the mental-processing capacity of participants—how much information they can handle at once, what creates unnecessary burden, and how to support meaningful processing.

Gagné's framework (*flow*, or when learning happens) helps us create the right conditions for different types of learning. We can determine what needs to be in place for knowledge acquisition, skills development, or performance development. Gagné's framework addresses the sequence and structure of learning experiences, or what conditions must be in place for different types of learning and how to organize instructional elements.

Together, these theories provide a comprehensive foundation for designing microlearning that respects both the capacity of memory and the conditions necessary for effective learning. Understanding CLT and Gagné's framework will give us a more complete picture of how to design effective microlearning.

Microlearning's brief nature makes both function and flow critical. With limited time available, we must optimize how information is processed (function) as well as how learning experiences are structured (flow).

How Learning Science Informs Our Design Principles

With the foundations of CLT and Gagné's framework established, let's see how these learning science concepts inform the microlearning design principles we'll explore in chapters 9–15. Each principle addresses specific aspects of learning and performance, building on the foundations we've established in this chapter. Understanding these connections will help you apply the principles more effectively to your microlearning designs. Just as a chef applies food science to create exceptional dishes, you'll ensure you are addressing function and flow through these seven principles to create more effective microlearning:

- **Principle 1, Know Your Tools' Capacity,** builds on cognitive load theory by helping us manage mental resources through appropriate technology choices. Your tools' capabilities and constraints directly affect all three types of cognitive load and influence how effectively you can create the conditions for learning that Gagné identified.

- **Principle 2, Craft an Appropriate Context,** applies our understanding of how memory and schemas work in different environments. This principle helps you create conditions that support effective encoding, storage, and retrieval while managing cognitive load in real-world settings.

- **Principle 3, Ensure Global Equity,** extends our understanding of learning conditions to diverse audiences with different needs, preferences, and capabilities. This principle ensures we create inclusive microlearning that works for everyone by addressing variations in prior knowledge, learning preferences, cultural backgrounds, and accessibility needs.

- **Principle 4, Design With Concision,** directly addresses cognitive load management by helping you focus content for maximum impact. This principle shows you how to reduce extraneous load, manage intrinsic load, and optimize germane load through strategic decisions about what to include and exclude. I'll also introduce an abbreviated version of Gagné's Nine Events of Instruction.

- **Principle 5, Make Media Meaningful,** leverages our understanding of encoding pathways and memory processes. This principle helps you select or create media that enhances comprehension and retention while supporting appropriate cognitive processing for different learning outcomes.
- **Principle 6, Elicit Action,** creates conditions for effective practice and transfer based on Gagné's framework. This principle shows you how to design activities that promote schema development and strengthen retrieval pathways while managing cognitive load appropriately.
- **Principle 7, Avoid Overuse,** targets cognitive fatigue while supporting long-term retention through distributed practice (also known as spaced learning). This principle helps you design sustainable microlearning approaches that respect cognitive limitations while maximizing learning impact.

Microlearning Principles and Gagné's Nine Events of Instruction

As I noted earlier, Gagné's Nine Events of Instruction provide a specific instructional sequence for implementing the external conditions that support learning. Each of my seven microlearning design principles can help you implement specific events in this sequence. Table 8-2 shows which of Gagné's Nine Events of Instruction are most strongly influenced by each microlearning design principle. It also illustrates how the principles work together to implement effective learning experiences. For example, while Design With Concision primarily affects how we inform our target audience of objectives, present content, and provide guidance, Elicit Action focuses on performance, feedback, assessment, and transfer.

Function and Flow Working Together

As we explore these principles in the upcoming chapters, you'll see how they can help you address both function (cognitive processing) and flow (learning sequence) in your microlearning design:

- **Know Your Tools' Capacity, Design With Concision, and Make Media Meaningful** principles primarily help you manage cognitive function—how information is processed.
- **Craft an Appropriate Context, Elicit Action, and Avoid Overuse** primarily help you manage learning flow—how experiences are structured.
- **Ensure Global Equity** ensures both function and flow work for all participants regardless of background or needs.

By understanding these connections between learning science foundations and design principles, you'll be better equipped to create microlearning that respects cognitive limits while providing optimal conditions for learning and performance.

In the next seven chapters, we'll explore each principle in detail, discussing how to apply it effectively across different types of microlearning. As we begin with Principle 1, Know Your Tools' Capacity, in chapter 9, keep these learning science foundations in mind. They'll help you understand not just what to do, but why certain approaches work better than others.

Connecting Learning Science to the MLR Framework

The theories we've explored in this chapter also help explain why some types of microlearning are easier for your organization to implement than others.

If you completed the MLR Framework activities in part 1, you likely gained insight into where your organization stands. You may have learned that you're well positioned to support knowledge-based microlearning, but not yet equipped for skills- or performance-based solutions. That's not a shortcoming—it's a reality many teams face.

Learning science helps make sense of those differences. Knowledge-based microlearning often places fewer demands on infrastructure and working memory. Skills-based microlearning requires support for practice and feedback, while performance-based solutions must work in real time—demanding contextual alignment, minimal friction, and stronger behavioral reinforcement.

Even if you haven't used the MLR Framework, the distinctions between these microlearning types matter. The design principles we discuss in the next seven chapters are more than generic advice—they're tools that help you tailor

Table 8-2. Microlearning Principles and Gagné's Nine Events of Instruction

Design Principle	Gaining Attention	Informing of Objectives	Stimulating Recall	Presenting Content	Providing Guidance	Eliciting Performance	Providing Feedback	Assessing Performance	Enhancing Retention and Transfer
1. Know Your Tools' Capacity	✓	✓	✓	✓	✓	✓	✓	✓	✓
2. Craft an Appropriate Context	✓	✓	✓	✓	✓				✓
3. Ensure Global Equity	✓	✓	✓	✓	✓	✓	✓	✓	✓
4. Design With Concision		✓		✓	✓				
5. Make Media Meaningful	✓		✓	✓	✓				
6. Elicit Action	✓				✓	✓	✓	✓	✓
7. Avoid Overuse	✓	✓	✓	✓	✓	✓	✓	✓	✓

your designs to the type of microlearning you're building and the realities of your organizational environment.

Chapter Summary

This chapter introduced the science of learning foundations that inform the microlearning design principles we'll discuss in chapters 9–15. We explored how CLT helps us manage mental resources effectively and how Gagné's Conditions of Learning guide us in creating optimal learning experiences.

Understanding memory processes—encoding, storage, and retrieval—provides the foundation for effective microlearning design. By respecting how memory works, we can create microlearning products that facilitate better knowledge retention, skills development, and performance improvement.

CLT helps us understand how to manage mental resources through three types of load: intrinsic (the inherent complexity of content), extraneous (unnecessary mental effort), and germane (effort that builds understanding). Each microlearning type requires different approaches to cognitive load management, from organizing knowledge-based content into logical chunks to creating realistic but simplified practice environments for skills-based microlearning. Performance-based microlearning relies on real-time, contextualized support that helps individuals apply knowledge and skills in the moment of need. By managing both cognitive demands and instructional flow, you can enable performance execution without overwhelming the participant's mental bandwidth.

Gagné's framework complements CLT by helping us understand which types of learning outcomes to target (verbal information, intellectual skills, cognitive strategies, attitudes, or motor skills) and what conditions must be present for learning to occur. We also explored how schemas and mental models influence how people interpret and apply what they learn. While schemas help participants recognize and retrieve knowledge, mental models shape how they make sense of broader systems or processes. Microlearning that respects both structures enhances clarity, reduces resistance, and supports better transfer to real-world contexts. However, when schemas and mental models are misaligned, even accurate knowledge recall may not translate into effective application. Thoughtful design can help close that gap. Understanding function and flow ensures that microlearning addresses both how information is processed and how learning experiences are structured.

Looking Ahead

Each of the seven principles in the following chapters builds on these foundations in specific ways, from managing cognitive load through appropriate tool choices to creating effective conditions for practice and application. Each chapter has a VISR Project Check-In to help you further determine which principles to target to benefit your work.

In the next chapter, we'll explore our first design principle, Know Your Tools' Capacity, which shows how your technology choices fundamentally shape cognitive processing and learning conditions.

VISR Project Check-In

Let's put this information together before moving on. Revisit the project you chose for the part 2 opening activity and use the VISR reflection framework to consider these questions around CLT and Gagné's framework prior to diving into the next chapter.

Validate

- Does your understanding of CLT confirm or challenge your current approach to your project?
- Are there aspects of your project that might create excessive cognitive load for participants?
- How do Gagné's Conditions of Learning apply to your current design approach?

Innovate

- How might understanding memory processes improve your solution?
- Could you apply different approaches to managing cognitive load in your project?
- How could you structure your project to create optimal conditions for learning?

Spark

- What new ideas about chunking or sequencing emerge from CLT for your project?
- How might applying Gagné's learning outcome categories spark new approaches for your project?
- What possibilities emerge when you consider both function (cognitive load) and flow (learning conditions)?

Refine

- Where could your project be adjusted based on memory processes?
- What specific changes to your design could assist with managing cognitive load?
- How might you adjust your approach to align conditions for learning?

As you work through the design principles in the following chapters, return to these reflections to identify which principles will have the greatest influence on your project.

CHAPTER 9
Principle 1: Know Your Tools' Capacity

By the end of this chapter, you should be able to answer these questions:
- How do your tools' capacity affect microlearning design decisions?
- How do your tools' capacity affect cognitive load management in different microlearning contexts?
- What strategic considerations should guide your tool selection for different types of microlearning?
- How can you design effectively within technological and organizational constraints?
- What approaches can help you maximize tool effectiveness across knowledge-, skills-, and performance-based solutions?

Have you ever watched competitive cooking shows where contestants face unexpected constraints? Imagine a chef who suddenly learns they can't use knives—despite having them available—for an entire challenge. The most successful chef doesn't panic; instead, they strategically select dishes that can be prepared using alternative tools, such as mandolines, graters, food processors, and even the flat edge of a spatula. Their success depends not on having the perfect tools, but on understanding their available tools' features and limitations, and then making strategic decisions based on these constraints.

Similarly, in microlearning design, understanding your tool capacity means recognizing constraints and working creatively within them. Sometimes, you'll want more advanced tools that your organization can't afford, or you'll need to work with previously purchased tools and platforms that limit your options. At other times, you'll need to repurpose existing tools in innovative ways to accomplish your learning objectives.

This constraint-driven approach applies differently across microlearning types. For knowledge-based microlearning, you might use simpler presentation tools when more advanced interactive platforms aren't available—just as our chef might use a food processor instead of knives. For skills-based solutions, you might create video demonstrations with follow-up activities when simulation software isn't accessible—similar to using a mandoline for precise cutting. And for performance-based microlearning, you might develop quick-reference guides or QR-linked resources when ideal performance support tools aren't feasible—much like using the edge of a spatula to smash garlic or grind spices if you don't have a mortar and pestle. In each case, understanding your tool's capacity isn't about limitations; it's about making strategic decisions that still achieve your learning objectives.

In this chapter, we'll explore the first principle of microlearning design: Know Your Tools' Capacity. This principle serves as our foundation because it establishes the practical boundaries within which all other design decisions must operate. Before you can craft appropriate contexts, ensure global equity, or use media in a meaningful way, you need to understand what's actually possible given your technological and organizational constraints.

Think of tool capacity as the canvas on which all other principles will be painted—its size, texture, and properties determine what artistic techniques will work. Starting with a clear understanding of your tools prevents you from designing elegant solutions that can't be implemented or maintained within your organization's ecosystem.

This first principle focuses on identifying the limitations and opportunities of your microlearning tools—including authoring platforms, delivery systems, and analytical tools—to make strategic design decisions that maximize effectiveness while working within organizational constraints. Understanding your tool capacity allows you to create solutions that are not only engaging and effective, but also feasible and sustainable.

If you worked through part 1 of this book and used the MLR Framework, you have a good sense of what microlearning types your organization can currently design, develop, implement, and sustain. If you haven't, this principle, along with the project you selected in part 2's opening activity, will guide your application. If your microlearning project requires tools and technology that your L&D function doesn't have, this chapter can assist you in thinking through what to do when your vision collides with reality. Tool capacity depends on your L&D team's technical capabilities. (If you haven't assessed your team's overall capabilities yet, review chapter 7.)

Your tool choices directly affect how participants process information and the conditions that support different types of learning outcomes. Whether you're developing knowledge-based tutorials, creating skills practice activities, or implementing adaptive performance support tools, your tools' capacity shapes what's possible and practical for your organization. By assessing this capacity early, you can design microlearning solutions that work within your constraints while still achieving your learning outcomes.

Knowing your tools' capacity also helps you have more informed conversations within your L&D team and with your partnered stakeholders to set realistic expectations. You can't promise performance-based microlearning if your tools and platforms are geared for knowledge-based microlearning. Most important, this principle will help you avoid stopping to question if you have to scrap what you are working on or undo hours' worth of work because you have the wrong tools for your needs. We've all been there, and we do *not* like going back!

Understanding the Principle

Tool capacity isn't just about what tools you own; it's also about truly understanding what those tools can and can't do. This means recognizing the capabilities and limitations of everything from your digital-authoring platforms to your physical training spaces. This chapter is about taking stock and:

- Recognizing the full potential—and constraints—of your toolkit
- Making informed decisions about which tools suit different microlearning types

- Adapting your design decisions to work within technical realities
- Leveraging every bit of functionality that your available tools offer

The Science of Learning and Tool Capacity

Your tools directly influence all three types of cognitive load—intrinsic load, extraneous load, and germane load.

- **Intrinsic load management**. Your tools can help organize complex content into manageable segments or make it more confusing. Tools with clear structuring capabilities, progressive disclosure features, or layered information design can help your target audiences navigate inherent complexity. When your tools restrict how you organize content, intrinsic load often increases—like trying to serve soup on a plate. The content doesn't fit the container, and your participants end up in a mess when trying to consume it!

- **Extraneous load reduction.** Have you ever tried to learn something on a platform with a frustrating interface? The mental effort spent figuring out how to navigate it becomes extraneous load that steals cognitive resources from actual learning. Your choice of tools directly affects how much mental energy participants spend on figuring out your solution versus engaging with the content and activities. Slow loading times, confusing navigation, and media constraints that force suboptimal presentation formats all increase extraneous load. That's just an interface; interface navigation is hard enough in isolation, but imagine how much worse it becomes when people are trying to navigate while juggling shifting work priorities and customer demands!

- **Germane load support**. The right tools can create meaningful engagement to support the development of schema (the organized knowledge structures that help us understand and categorize information). Interactive capabilities, feedback mechanisms, and authentic scenario builders help participants process content in ways that are meaningful to their mental models (the internal frameworks people use to interpret and predict how things work). Limited tools might restrict these opportunities for deeper processing. It's like trying to teach someone to bake using a toy oven. You might get a cookie at the end, but has your aspiring baker really developed the schema for actual baking?

Understanding how your tools affect these three types of cognitive load is just the beginning.

Learning Conditions and Tool Capacity

While CLT helps us understand how tools affect mental processing (the function of learning), Robert Gagné's Conditions of Learning framework helps us see how tools support different learning experiences (the flow of learning). Your tool choices directly influence what kinds of learning experiences you can create.

- **Knowledge-based microlearning.** Your presentation tools determine how effectively you can communicate information, organize content, and create recall opportunities. Limited media capabilities might restrict how you present complex information, while robust organization tools can help create clear knowledge and conceptual structures.

- **Skills-based microlearning.** Practice and feedback features shape skills development opportunities. Without interactive capabilities for guided practice, realistic scenarios, or immediate feedback, developing procedural skills becomes more challenging. Your tools' simulation capabilities directly affect how authentically participants can practice.

- **Performance-based microlearning.** Tools that integrate with workflow determine how effectively you can support real-time performance. Features such as contextual triggers, access at the moment of need, and environmental integration create conditions where performance support can happen when someone requires it. Without contextual integration, performance support is like giving someone cooking instructions that they have to memorize before entering the kitchen. The guidance isn't available at the moment of need.

When tool capacity is optimized for both function (cognitive processing) and flow (learning experience), microlearning becomes not just technically feasible but truly effective. Think of it like a chef who selects not only the right ingredients but also the proper cooking equipment to prepare them—both elements are essential for a successful meal.

Application by Microlearning Type

Let's explore how tool capacity affects your microlearning ecosystem holistically, paying attention to common constraints and their impact on the three types of microlearning.

Common Tool Constraints

Rather than examining each microlearning type in isolation, let's look at common tool constraints and how they affect all three types of microlearning (knowledge-based, skills-based, and performance-based), highlighting the challenges and some creative solutions.

When Your Authoring Tools Have Limited Interactive Capabilities

Many organizations face significant constraints in the types of interactions their authoring tools support.

> ### 🐝 How Be Natural Worked Around Limited Authoring Tool Capabilities
>
> When Be Natural's L&D team faced this challenge, they looked for creative solutions across all three types of microlearning. Instead of creating three completely different work-arounds, they kept the interactions simple (mostly multiple choice and basic clicks) and changed the surrounding content to fit each purpose. Here's how this approach worked across each type of microlearning:
>
> - **Knowledge-based microlearning.** BN's L&D team initially planned to use complex drag-and-drop knowledge checks for the sales product information training, but realized that the authoring tool couldn't support this. Instead, they created simple image-based comparisons with multiple-choice questions that achieved similar cognitive-processing goals.

- **Skills-based microlearning.** When creating products for the manufacturing team's microlearning campaign, BN's L&D team had to work around their lack of access to simulation software. Their solution was to create simple step-by-step guides with embedded links to short demonstration videos on the company intranet. Team leads would walk new operators through these guides during morning huddles, combining digital resources with in-person coaching.
- **Performance-based microlearning.** BN's onboarding program needed moment-of-need performance support, but the platform didn't have a contextual trigger feature. The L&D team's solution was to create location-based QR codes that new employees could scan to access relevant guidance exactly when needed.

When Your LMS Lacks Mobile Accessibility

Mobile access is an increasingly popular choice for microlearning, but many organizations work with learning management systems (LMSs) that offer limited or frustrating mobile experiences. This leads to the belief that the organization is not ready for microlearning, but that's not true. When BN faced this challenge, it discovered that LMS limitations could actually spark innovative solutions.

🐝 How Be Natural Overcame LMS Mobile Limitations

Be Natural's L&D team took a people-first, systems-second approach to the mobile challenge. Instead of forcing everything through its limited LMS, the team asked, "What's the easiest way for people to access what they need?"

Here's how this approach worked across each type of microlearning:

- **Knowledge-based microlearning.** BN's sales team needed to be able to access product knowledge on mobile devices. When the L&D team discovered the LMS's poor mobile experience, it exported key product information as downloadable PDF infographics that representatives could access offline on their phones.
- **Skills-based microlearning.** For customer-service skills development, BN's L&D team created a simple email campaign that delivered text-based scenarios with short video demonstrations. Representatives could

practice during their downtime, responding directly to the emails with their solutions to receive manager feedback.

- **Performance-based microlearning.** When BN's manufacturing team needed mobile-accessible performance support, the L&D team bypassed the LMS entirely. Instead, it created waterproof reference cards with simple decision trees that could be stored at each workstation. A buddy system was established with experienced operators for navigating complex situations.

When Budget Constraints Limit Media Production Resources

Budgets can also constrain investments in microlearning, but this doesn't have to be the case. For example, high-quality media can improve microlearning experiences, but budget limitations may not allow for professional production services. BN discovered that budget limitations could actually lead to more authentic and effective solutions.

🐝 How Be Natural Overcame Budget Constraints for Media Production

Be Natural's L&D team realized that fancy production quality was less important than helpful content. So, instead of spending money it didn't have on professional videos, the team found simple, low-cost alternatives for each situation.

Here's how this approach worked across each type of microlearning:

- **Knowledge-based microlearning.** Instead of professionally produced overview videos for its sustainability initiatives, BN's L&D team created narrated slideshows using existing product photography and simple screen-recording software.
- **Skills-based microlearning.** For sales conversation skills, the L&D team used smartphone cameras to record peer-to-peer role-play sessions with top performers. These authentic demonstrations resonated better with the sales team while costing a fraction of professional production.

- **Performance-based microlearning.** For quality checkpoint decisions, the L&D team created brief tablet-based prompts organized by equipment and process step. When operators reached critical decision points, they could quickly access 30-second reminders showing what to look for and what actions to take. Rather than expensive interactive modules, the team used simple text with photos, making the guidance accessible at the exact moment operators needed it without sophisticated production costs.

Many of these DIY solutions worked better than more professionally produced ones because employees thought they were more authentic and relatable.

Work With What You Have

The examples we've just explored demonstrate a fundamental truth about microlearning design: Effective solutions require you to make strategic decisions with the tools you have. BN's experience reveals three successful approaches that apply, regardless of your specific constraints:

- **Start with learning objectives, not tool features.** Notice that in each scenario, BN began by clarifying what it needed to accomplish, and then found creative ways to achieve that goal within its constraints.
- **Look for patterns across microlearning types.** Rather than solving each challenge in isolation, consider how similar constraints affect knowledge, skills, and performance solutions, and look for unified approaches when possible.
- **Embrace constraints as creativity drivers.** Some of BN's most effective solutions emerged because it couldn't use the ideal tools. The limitations forced creative thinking that often led to more accessible, practical approaches.

As you assess your own tools' capacity, remember that constraints aren't only obstacles; they're also design parameters that can focus your thinking and lead to more pragmatic solutions. The most effective microlearning designers aren't those with the most advanced tools; they're the pros who thoroughly understand their tools' capabilities and limitations, then design strategically within those boundaries.

Common Challenges and How to Overcome Them

We have explored how technological constraints affect microlearning design across knowledge-based, skills-based, and performance-based solutions. Another critical dimension of tool capacity that is equally important but often goes unaddressed is your team's ability to leverage available tools effectively. Sometimes, the most significant constraint isn't the technology itself, but the human expertise needed to unlock its potential.

When Team Skills Don't Match Tool Capabilities

Many organizations invest in tools only to discover that their teams can't fully utilize them. BN faced this exact challenge when implementing its onboarding microlearning initiative and developed a systematic approach to build team capabilities over time.

> #### 🐝 How Be Natural Addressed the Team Skills vs. Tool Capabilities Mismatch
>
> Rather than abandon a tool or delay microlearning implementation, BN developed a three-part strategy: Identify core features, build progressive expertise, and create a sustainable knowledge transfer process. Let's discuss how this approach evolved over time.
>
> **The Situation**
> BN purchased an authoring platform with advanced simulation capabilities, but the L&D team had limited experience with the tool. Initial attempts to use it resulted in delays, frustration, and underutilization of features the organization had paid for.
>
> **Short-Term Solution**
> BN identified the essential tool features that would deliver the majority of its immediate needs. (Think 80/20 here: 20 percent of the features for 80 percent of their need.) The team focused first on mastering just these features and creating a small library of templates they could adapt for various

content. This allowed them to launch their initial microlearning products while still developing deeper tool expertise.

Medium-Term Development
The L&D team identified tool champions—individuals responsible for gaining the necessary training to become proficient. It was their responsibility to create simple reference guides documenting what they learned for the rest of the team. This built internal capacity while providing immediate support for ongoing projects.

Long-Term Sustainability
BN's L&D team created a microlearning campaign about the tool itself. They developed a series of short tutorials on key features the department was using. Each was followed by a practical challenge to use the feature. A new hire to the L&D team could take this training course to become competent in building assets, and current employees used it to revisit old projects and current project needs. This built progressive expertise while immediately applying new skills.

BN's approach highlights the fact that tool capacity is more about what your team can do with technology than it is about what the technology can do. By recognizing the human component of tool capacity, BN avoided the common trap of investing in feature-rich tools that are underused.

When You Need to Evaluate Your Tools' Capacity
When assessing your tools' capacity, consider these often-overlooked elements:

- **Conduct honest skill assessments.** Before purchasing new tools or planning ambitious microlearning initiatives, inventory your team's current technical capabilities. Create a simple matrix that maps tool features against team member expertise to identify gaps.
- **Test tools against complex scenarios.** Don't evaluate tools based solely on supplier demonstrations or simple use cases. Create a prototype that tackles your most challenging microlearning needs. BN learned this lesson when its authoring tool handled basic knowledge content beautifully but struggled with the complex branching scenarios that its sales training required.

- **Factor adoption time frames into planning.** New tools typically require several months before teams achieve proficiency. BN discovered this when its initial three-month implementation timeline proved inadequate, creating pressure that led to rushed, lower-quality microlearning products. Its revised timeline incorporated dedicated skills-building phases, resulting in better outcomes despite the delayed launch.
- **Create skills development pathways.** Just as you design learning pathways for your audience, develop skills-building journeys for your team. BN's L&D director realized that the team needed to apply its own microlearning principles to its tool proficiency. The director concluded that focused mastery of a feature with immediate application worked better than comprehensive training that overwhelmed everyone.

When Your Resources Are Limited

Even with limited resources, you can expand your tools' capacity in several ways:
- **Leverage peer-learning networks.** Connect with other organizations using the same tools to share knowledge and templates.
- **Prioritize strategic tool investments.** Rather than purchasing comprehensive platforms with features you won't use, invest in targeted tools aligned with your high-priority microlearning needs.
- **Create a tool portfolio.** BN discovered that combining a few specialized tools often provided more flexibility than a single all-in-one solution, while requiring less comprehensive expertise from any individual team member.
- **Build external partnerships.** For specialized microlearning needs, consider partnering with external experts who already possess the necessary tool proficiency rather than developing all capabilities in-house.

By addressing these human elements of tool capacity, you create more realistic assessments of what's possible and develop strategies that leverage both your technological and human resources effectively.

Chapter Summary

Tool capacity forms the foundation of effective microlearning design by establishing what's realistically possible given your technological and human resources. Throughout this chapter, we've explored how understanding the capabilities and limitations of your tools shapes every aspect of microlearning development:

- **Tool capacity encompasses both technological and human dimensions.** Your tools' features matter, but so does your team's ability to leverage them effectively. Understanding both aspects prevents the frustration of designing solutions that can't be implemented or maintained. This isn't a bad thing. It is just a reality—and one that should be acknowledged to manage stakeholder expectations and avoid team burnout.
- **Tools directly affect cognitive load management.** They influence how you organize content (intrinsic load), how participants navigate your solutions (extraneous load), and how effectively participants can engage in meaningful processing (germane load).
- **Different microlearning types require different tool capabilities.** Knowledge-based microlearning needs effective presentation tools, skills-based microlearning requires practice and feedback mechanisms, and performance-based microlearning depends on workflow integration.
- **Constraints can drive innovation.** As BN demonstrated, working within tool limitations often leads to creative solutions that are more accessible, authentic, and effective than what might have emerged with unlimited resources. This should lend confidence to those with limited tools and lean budgets, because there is always a way!
- **Strategic assessment should precede design decisions.** Rather than designing first and discovering tool limitations later, start by honestly evaluating your tools' capacity, and then design within these realistic boundaries.

Practical next steps include conducting a thorough inventory of your existing tools, assessing your team's proficiency with those tools, identifying critical gaps in your tool ecosystem, and establishing skills development pathways to maximize your tools' capacity over time.

Looking Ahead

The next chapter explores Principle 2, Craft an Appropriate Context. It builds directly on what we've learned about tool capacity. While tool capacity establishes what's technically possible, understanding context will determine how your solutions fit into participants' real-world environments.

VISR Project Check-In

Take a moment to connect this principle to the microlearning project you selected for the part 2 opening activity. Use the VISR reflection framework to evaluate how the principle of knowing your tools' capacity applies specifically to your project.

Validate
- How does your current approach align with the principle of knowing your tools' capacity?
- Have you assessed the technological and human dimensions of your tools' capacity?
- Are your design decisions grounded in what your tools can realistically deliver?
- Are you trying to build solutions that exceed your team's current capabilities?
- Do your tool choices align with the type of microlearning you're creating (knowledge-, skills-, or performance-based microlearning)?

Innovate
- What unexplored features of your existing tools could enhance your content?
- Could constraints in one area lead to creative solutions for your design?
- Are there simpler approaches that might be more effective than complex solutions requiring advanced tools (and potentially more of your time)?
- What capacity-building approaches could help your team gradually unlock more features of your existing tools?

Spark
- How might you leverage nondigital tools or human elements to complement your technical solutions?
- How might you combine different tools in your ecosystem to overcome individual limitations?
- Could you create templates or frameworks that maximize efficiency while working within constraints?
- Is there an opportunity to develop progressive expertise in parallel with your microlearning implementation?

Refine
- What trade-offs are necessary between ideal design and practical implementation?
- What elements of your current design could be adjusted to work within your tools' capacity?

- How can you design this project to be maintained and updated by your team given their current tools' proficiency?
- How might you create a more sustainable approach that balances innovation with reliable execution?

By considering these questions, you'll create a microlearning approach that not only respects tool constraints but strategically leverages your available resources for maximum impact.

CHAPTER 10

Principle 2: Craft an Appropriate Context

By the end of this chapter, you should be able to answer these questions:
- What are the five dimensions of context and how do they influence effective microlearning design?
- How can you systematically analyze context to identify different patterns and barriers that affect microlearning success?
- How do CLT and Gagné's framework shape our understanding of context in microlearning?
- What practical tools can help you craft appropriate context for your solutions?
- How can context analysis improve your microlearning personas and enhance learning outcomes?

One of the easiest ways to understand the value of context is to watch a cooking show competition. For example, on one high-stakes show, a renowned chef was critiquing a contestant's dish, praising the flavors and how perfectly the dish fit the challenge's context—a summer picnic for two. While the same dish might seem light or overly simplistic in a different setting, it worked beautifully for casual outdoor dining. The contestant had considered not just the recipe, but the complete experience of eating the food in its intended environment.

As you know by now, a food-related comparison often helps me get to the heart of complex topics. The comparison of a meal's setting and microlearning design's context frequently helps L&D professionals think differently. Microlearning must work within its organizational context, just as a dish needs to work in its dining context. As you will read in the two BN case studies in this chapter, these insights were valuable because the L&D team hadn't fully considered how context would shape engagement and outcomes.

Crafting an appropriate context means designing microlearning that fits seamlessly into the real conditions where it will be used, considering the physical environment, mental and emotional states, organizational culture, social dynamics, and technological realities. When a microlearning design fails to account for these contextual elements, even excellent content can go unused. Organizations then report on those failures, saying things like, "We created these great microlearning products, but people aren't accessing them" or "Our completion rates are disappointing despite the investment in revamping the curriculum to be solely microlearning."

Principle 2 builds directly on Principle 1. While understanding your tool capacity (Principle 1) helps you identify what's technically *possible*, crafting appropriate context ensures that your solutions are practically viable within your audience's real-world circumstances. Together, these principles will help you create microlearning that's not only well designed but also well positioned for actual use and impact.

In this chapter, we'll explore how to analyze context using a framework developed by Martin Tessmer and Rita Richey, create realistic personas (detailed profiles that represent distinct groups within your target audience based on their contextual realities rather than just demographics) that guide design decisions, and implement strategies that align microlearning with the way people actually work and learn. By mastering this principle, you'll be able to design microlearning solutions that integrate naturally into your audience's environment, enhancing learning outcomes while managing cognitive load effectively.

Understanding the Principle

Context is everything—or at least it feels that way when you're trying to learn something new. Have you ever tried to learn a complex task while surrounded by distractions? Or attempted to follow instructions that don't match your actual work environment? The frustrations that inevitably occur in those situations highlight why context matters so much in microlearning design.

Crafting appropriate context means designing microlearning that fits into the real conditions in which it will be used. It's about aligning your solutions with the multidimensional world in which your participants live and work. When I say "multidimensional," I'm referring to physical spaces, mental states, organizational cultures, social relationships, and technological environments— all of which shape how effectively people can learn. As Tessmer and Richey (1997) so aptly describe it, *context* is "a multilevel body of factors in which learning and performance are embedded." Picture context as the water in which your microlearning fish swim. The quality of the water determines whether your fish thrive or struggle.

When we ignore context, we create solutions that look great on paper but stumble in execution. I've seen this play out countless times in organizations that rush to create "snackable content" without considering where, when, and how it will actually be consumed. The result? Beautiful microlearning products that no one completes, skills practice that doesn't translate to real work, and performance support tools that are designed for knowledge acquisition.

In contrast, context-aware microlearning feels intuitive to participants. The key is understanding the real context first, and then creating solutions that fit that reality.

Five Dimensions of Context

As demand for in-the-flow of work training opportunities continues to rise, we need to get our bearings on what that means and how it influences participation in a learning or skill development moment. This means we need to understand the work context of our target audiences. To help us analyze context more systematically, let's explore five dimensions drawn from the work of Tessmer and Richey. When combined, these dimensions create a complete contextual experience.

Physical Environment: Set the Stage

The physical environment encompasses both where learning occurs and where skills will be applied. When analyzing your physical context, examine the spaces where participants work and learn, considering environmental factors such as noise, lighting, and movement patterns. Pay attention to time constraints and scheduling realities that affect when learning can actually occur and assess the physical accessibility of learning resources across different work locations.

Here are some questions to guide your environmental analysis:

- Does your frontline staff have the physical space and time to engage with learning content?
- Do noise levels, lighting conditions, or movement requirements affect your target audience's ability to interact with microlearning effectively?
- Are there any physical barriers that might prevent access to digital resources?
- What natural breaks in the workflow could realistically fit microlearning without disrupting productivity (but potentially increase it)?

Mental and Emotional States: Understand Your Audience

The mental and emotional contexts encompass the cognitive and emotional conditions that affect learning readiness. Our mental and emotional states directly affect our ability to pay attention. When participants are stressed, overwhelmed, or emotionally taxed, their ability to focus diminishes significantly. Environmental distractions compete with already limited attentional capacity, further undermining learning effectiveness.

Focus your analysis on cognitive load from competing work demands and how participants manage attentional capacity amid workplace distractions. Remember from chapter 8 that cognitive load management is crucial for effective microlearning. When your audience is already experiencing high extraneous load from environmental factors, they have less capacity available for germane load (meaningful processing). Examine stress patterns throughout the workday to identify when cognitive resources are most available and consider motivation and engagement levels that vary by role and individual circumstances. Understanding energy patterns and attention spans helps you time microlearning for maximum effectiveness.

Here are some questions to consider during your context analysis:

- When during the day or week are your participants most mentally receptive to learning? (Low intrinsic load potential.)
- What competing cognitive demands affect their ability to engage meaningfully with new information? (High intrinsic load potential.)
- How do stress cycles affect their capacity for processing and retaining new information? (Cognitive load management opportunity.)
- What motivational factors might enhance or diminish their engagement with learning opportunities? (Target audience attitude factors for engagement.)
- How does attention vary across different roles and work environments within your organization? (Extraneous load potential.)

Organizational Culture: Create Supportive Systems

Cultural context determines how learning initiatives are perceived and supported within the organization. Examine your organization's values and norms around professional development, assessing whether continuous learning is genuinely valued or viewed as an interruption to "real work." Consider how leadership demonstrates support for learning initiatives through actions, resource allocation, and communication. In addition, analyze whether time for improvement is protected organizationally or routinely sacrificed for immediate operational demands.

Pay special attention to how growth and application are recognized and reinforced within your culture so you can better understand existing cultural attitudes and design microlearning that aligns with those cultural realities. Some organizations embrace bite-sized learning as efficient and practical, while others may view it as insufficient or superficial compared with traditional training approaches.

Here are some questions I suggest you ask during your cultural assessment:

- What cultural expectations exist about where and when learning happens, and how might these expectations support or hinder microlearning adoption?
- Does your culture genuinely value continuous learning, or is development viewed as an interruption to productivity?

- How do leaders demonstrate authentic support for learning initiatives beyond stated policies?
- Do managers actively encourage learning, or do they subtly discourage time away from immediate tasks?
- How does your organization acknowledge and reward employees who successfully apply new learning to their work?

Social Dynamics: Leverage Relationships

The social context shapes knowledge sharing and application through interpersonal connections with your colleagues, leadership, and peers. Analyze your team structures and relationships to understand how information flows naturally within your organization. Examine collaboration patterns that reveal how people currently share knowledge and solve problems together. Also, consider peer influence on adoption, recognizing that informal leaders often drive acceptance of new learning approaches more effectively than formal mandates.

You'll want to assess communication channels and social learning preferences to ensure you're designing microlearning that leverages existing relationship structures. Understanding how people prefer to learn from one another—whether through formal mentoring, casual conversations, or collaborative problem-solving—will help you integrate microlearning into natural social patterns.

Here are some questions you can ask to explore your organization's key social dynamics:

- How might peer-to-peer learning enhance your microlearning approach by building on existing social structures?
- How do current team structures affect knowledge sharing and collaborative learning?
- What social factors might encourage genuine engagement with microlearning versus resistance or superficial compliance?
- Who are the influential adopters who could authentically champion microlearning initiatives?
- What communication patterns could support implementation, and which might create barriers?

Technology Environment: Enable Access

The tech context enables or constrains how microlearning can be delivered and accessed. Focus on device availability and preferences, understanding what technology participants actually use during their workflow rather than what's theoretically available. Assess whether system access and permissions might create barriers and consider varying technical literacy levels across your audience. You should also examine connectivity and bandwidth limitations that could affect content delivery, especially for remote or mobile workers.

Make sure to consider how well microlearning can integrate with existing work systems to create seamless experiences, rather than additional technological burdens. The goal is to leverage technology that enhances rather than complicates the learning experience.

Here are some technology questions to consider:

- How well can microlearning integrate with existing work systems to create seamless rather than disruptive experiences?
- What devices do participants actually use during their workflow, and how comfortable are they with different interfaces?
- Are there system-access barriers or permission restrictions that might prevent engagement with learning content?
- How comfortable are participants with different technologies, and what support might be needed for successful adoption?
- Are there connectivity issues that might affect delivery options, particularly for mobile or remote workers?

The Interplay of Contextual Dimensions

In reality, the five dimensions constantly interact, overlap, and influence one another. The physical environment affects mental states, cultural expectations shape social dynamics, and technological capabilities affect physical accessibility. All the dimensions form a web, and the relative importance of each dimension varies depending on the situation. For some microlearning initiatives, physical context might be the dominant consideration, while cultural factors might prove decisive for others. At times, all five dimensions will exert equal influence, creating a contextual tapestry that requires careful analysis.

This variability is why cookie-cutter approaches to microlearning often fail. When organizations attempt to implement solutions that worked elsewhere without understanding their own unique context, they risk creating a mismatch between design and reality. Effective contextual design requires recognizing these interactions and adapting your approach accordingly.

🐝 Be Natural's Marketing Team—When All Five Context Dimensions Intersect

BN's marketing team needed to learn innovative approaches and skills for global product launches. The L&D team wanted to provide microlearning products as part of their overarching strategy to help the marketing team master its new global strategy. However, they encountered challenges when designing these microlearning solutions, and a context analysis revealed multiple interconnected dimensions.

How the Five Dimensions Created Complexity
Let's look closer at each dimension:

- **Complexity of physical context.** Team members worked across three time zones, alternating among open-plan offices with varying noise levels, home offices, and client meeting spaces. Some had reliable Wi-Fi; others relied on spotty hotel connections.
- **Mental and emotional variance.** Marketing campaign launch periods created intense stress spikes with unpredictable schedules. Cognitive load fluctuated dramatically between hurry-up-and-wait periods and crisis management moments. Some team members juggled multiple campaigns simultaneously, while others focused deeply on single projects.
- **Cultural contradictions.** The marketing culture valued creative risk taking and meticulous brand consistency. This tension meant microlearning couldn't simply present black-and-white guidelines; the L&D team needed to help navigate gray areas while respecting both cultural imperatives.
- **Challenging social dynamics.** Collaboration patterns shifted constantly. Sometimes, the marketing team worked in isolation; other times, it partnered intensely with the research and development or legal team, or external agencies. Power dynamics varied by project, with different team members taking lead roles based on a campaign's focus.

- **Inconsistencies in the technology environment.** While some had access to advanced tools, such as augmented reality product visualization platforms, others used basic presentation software. File-sharing systems varied by region due to different subscription levels and IT approval processes, creating technical barriers to unified microlearning delivery.

The Multi-Faceted Solutions

This contextual complexity meant that no single solution would work. Instead, BN's L&D team developed a multifaceted approach:

- Learning content was designed to accommodate these variances through universal access features, including captioning for audio content, volume controls for noisy environments, and downloadable scripts for offline access.
- The content used adaptive design to optimize the device experience and leveraged assessment tools to recommend microlearning products based on individual needs and context.
- Different formats were provided for different contexts: quick-reference guides for limited internet access, explanatory videos for office settings, and practice activities during dedicated learning time.
- Content was tailored to job roles. Different microlearning products were provided for team members leading marketing campaigns versus those supporting roles.
- Microlearning content acknowledged and directly addressed the tensions and challenges around balancing creativity with brand consistency.

Key Insight

This example demonstrates that context isn't only about the physical environment or timing; context is an intricate web of factors that influence learning effectiveness. Microlearning design must respect this complexity rather than oversimplifying it.

Understanding how the five contextual dimensions interact helps you move beyond generic solutions toward more targeted approaches. This analysis became the foundation for developing context-based personas at Be Natural, ultimately guiding microlearning design decisions. We will discuss the use of personas later in this chapter. Before we get there, let's ground our understanding of context in learning science.

Context and Cognitive Load Theory

Let's try first to understand how context interacts with cognitive science. Context directly influences all three types of cognitive load. It can make inherently difficult content more manageable or more overwhelming. When microlearning connects to familiar contexts, participants can leverage existing schemas and mental models, reducing extraneous load. For example, BN's sales team found that product information presented in the context of customer conversations was processed more efficiently than the same information presented in isolation.

Designs void of context increase unnecessary mental effort (extraneous load). Imagine a factory worker trying to follow detailed instructions on a smartphone screen while wearing protective gloves in a noisy environment. The contextual mismatch creates extraneous load, which steals cognitive resources from actual learning.

The right context supports germane load, or meaningful processing. When microlearning occurs in environments that mirror application settings, the contextual cues strengthen schema development. For example, BN's manufacturing team realized that safety procedures learned at workstations were better incorporated into the workflow than those learned in training rooms.

In practice, you need to assess how multiple contextual factors can compound cognitive load challenges. Environmental distractions, emotional stress, cultural expectations, social pressure, and technical friction can all contribute to cognitive overload. This is especially important when stakeholders think that microlearning is the answer for addressing things like limited time to gain professional development, or that it's a solution that fits all job roles.

Effective microlearning design must account for these contextual realities to manage cognitive load successfully. For example, a perfectly designed knowledge check that requires quiet concentration won't work for someone surrounded by warehouse noise and frequent interruptions. Context-aware design responds to these challenges by adjusting the format, timing, or delivery method to match the actual work environment rather than forcing workers to adapt to inappropriate learning designs.

Context and Gagné's Conditions of Learning

As we've discussed, Gagné's Conditions of Learning framework helps us see how context supports different learning experiences, or the flow of learning. Gagné emphasizes that varied types of learning—verbal information, intellectual skills, cognitive strategies, motor skills, and attitudes—require specific conditions to succeed. Context shapes these conditions.

For knowledge-based microlearning (verbal information), context influences how easily information is encoded and retrieved. Physical environments, emotional states, and organizational culture all affect attention and memory formation. BN discovered that important product facts presented in the context of brand storytelling were remembered better than isolated fact lists.

For skills-based microlearning (intellectual and motor skills), context determines whether practice conditions mirror performance conditions. Social dynamics and technological environments particularly affect skills development. When BN's onboarding team redesigned its customer service training to include realistic background noises and interruptions in progressively challenging content in the microlearning products, skills transfer improved significantly because those changes helped the new customer service rep comprehend the work environment from early on.

For performance-based microlearning (cognitive strategies and attitudes), context is everything. The right contextual triggers, environmental cues, and cultural support determine whether performance support tools actually get used. BN's sales team embedded decision support tools directly into its CRM system, making them available precisely when needed.

Contextual Challenges and Solutions

Context requirements evolve as organizations move from knowledge acquisition to skills development to performance support. Each type faces different contextual challenges requiring different solutions:

- **Knowledge-based microlearning** typically faces challenges around attention, timing, and information overload. Solutions focus on when and how information is delivered to respect cognitive limitations and cultural expectations.

- **Skills-based microlearning** encounters practice limitations, feedback needs, and confidence building. Solutions emphasize structured practice opportunities, peer support, and safe learning environments that build competence progressively.
- **Performance-based microlearning** deals with real-time pressure, variable conditions, and application gaps. Solutions embed support directly in workflow through visual aids, decision trees, and environmental cues that provide guidance exactly when needed.

BN's transition to organic ingredients illustrates this evolution perfectly. Its pre-shift knowledge sessions worked well for teaching ingredient properties, but it needed hands-on practice stations for skills development and waterproof reference cards at workstations for performance support. Each phase required different contextual accommodations, from quiet learning spaces to real-time workflow integration.

This evolution demonstrates that effective microlearning doesn't just respect context; it adapts as contextual needs change throughout the learning journey.

Considerations in Assessing Context

As you assess the five dimensions of context, keep a few things in mind. These are especially important if members of your organization don't quite agree on a definition of microlearning or don't understand the impact of cognitive load on learning.

Context is never static. It evolves as organizations change, technologies advance, and participants develop. Regular context assessments help your microlearning content remain relevant. The frequency of reassessment depends on your organization's pace of change; for example, it could be annually for relatively stable environments, quarterly for rapidly evolving ones, or whenever significant organizational shifts occur.

Even within the same organization, different teams experience different contexts. Resist the temptation to create one-size-fits-all solutions. Be Natural discovered that while its corporate team had reliable Wi-Fi and quiet spaces for learning, its retail associates had spotty connectivity and constant customer interruptions. These contextual differences required completely different approaches to microlearning design.

Now that you understand why context matters and what dimensions to consider, let's explore some practical frameworks for analyzing context and developing solutions that can thrive in your organization's unique environment.

Context "In the Flow of Work"

A common misconception worth addressing is the conflation of *contextual design* with *in the flow of work* microlearning. These are two distinct concepts:

- **In the flow of work** refers specifically to when and where learning happens, typically during regular work activities rather than in dedicated training time. Simply making microlearning available during work hours doesn't automatically make it contextually appropriate or performance based.
- **Contextual design** is a broader idea, encompassing all five dimensions we've discussed. A solution might be available in the flow of work but still fail contextually if it doesn't account for mental states, social dynamics, or cultural factors.

Performance-based microlearning supports real-time task execution during actual work moments. While it's always in the flow, it's defined by its purpose (supporting immediate performance) rather than just its timing. For example, a three-minute video about customer objections that a sales rep watches between calls is available in the flow of work but is still knowledge-based microlearning. In contrast, a quick-reference tool the rep consults during a live customer conversation is both in the flow and performance-based. Understanding these distinctions helps you design solutions that are truly contextual across all microlearning types.

Context Within Content

One of the most powerful ways context shapes microlearning effectiveness is through the content itself. When your microlearning content reflects familiar context, you dramatically reduce the cognitive burden of transfer.

When we fail to incorporate realistic context into our content, we create what is called the "learning-doing gap" (Lowenthal 2025). This gap forces participants to mentally translate abstract concepts into their real-world application—a process that consumes valuable cognitive resources (extraneous load) and often leads to implementation failure.

The problem manifests when training content uses generic principles and abstract examples that don't reflect participants' actual work environments. Service representatives, for instance, may receive customer service training built around theoretical best practices and hypothetical scenarios. While they can understand these concepts intellectually, they will struggle to apply them during real customer interactions because the training hasn't prepared them for the specific language, objections, and contextual pressures they'll actually encounter.

Effective microlearning design eliminates this translation burden by embedding authentic workplace context directly into the content. Rather than teaching abstract principles that participants must later adapt, context-rich microlearning presents concepts within the familiar environments, language, and scenarios where they'll be applied. This approach transforms each customer objection into a specific learning module, uses industry-specific terminology throughout, and features authentic scenarios that reflect the actual conversations, pressures, and constraints participants face in their roles.

To incorporate context directly into your microlearning content, focus on authenticity across multiple dimensions:

- **Language authenticity.** Use terminology, phrases, and communication patterns that mirror actual workplace interactions rather than formal training language.
- **Scenario authenticity.** Feature realistic situations that reflect genuine job challenges, complete with the interruptions, time pressures, and competing priorities participants actually experience.
- **Environmental authenticity.** Include visual and procedural contexts that match the physical spaces, tools, and systems where learning will be applied.
- **Cultural authenticity.** Reflect organizational values, unwritten rules, and cultural expectations that shape how work actually gets done.
- **Constraint authenticity.** Acknowledge and work within the real limitations participants face, from time constraints to resource availability to regulatory requirements.

Contextual alignment like this is fundamentally a cognitive load management strategy. By embedding familiar contexts within your content, you're essentially prepackaging the transfer process, making it easier for participants to apply learning without the mental overhead of translation. This is like a recipe that's written specifically for your kitchen, using ingredients you already have and tools you own. You don't have to mentally adapt a generic recipe, freeing up mental resources to focus on the actual cooking.

This approach is particularly powerful in skills-based and performance-based microlearning, when application is the primary goal. But it's also valuable in knowledge-based microlearning, when familiar contexts help anchor new information to existing mental frameworks.

Tools for Context Analysis

Effective context analysis requires a systematic approach that moves from data collection to actionable design guidance. This section presents two complementary frameworks that work in sequence: The context analysis framework helps you systematically gather and interpret contextual information across the five dimensions, while the persona development framework transforms those insights into detailed profiles that guide specific design decisions. Used together, these frameworks ensure your microlearning design decisions are grounded in contextual understanding rather than assumptions or ideals (especially those of your stakeholders).

A Context Analysis Framework

Context analysis provides the foundation for developing effective *personas*—representations of distinct subpopulations within your target audience that guide design decisions. While traditional personas often focus on demographics or job titles, context-based personas incorporate the five dimensions to create richer, more actionable profiles.

Always start by understanding the contexts in which your microlearning will be used. Your context analysis might reveal that in-the-flow learning isn't appropriate in some situations because of safety concerns, excessive distractions, or other factors. Or it might show that dedicated learning time outside the workflow is necessary. The contextual analysis should determine these decisions, not preconceived notions about where microlearning should happen. Let's review some starting points for approaching a context analysis:

- **Conduct your analysis systematically across all five contextual dimensions.** Start with the physical environment by observing where participants actually work and when they have access to learning opportunities. For the mental and emotional dimension, identify stress patterns, cognitive demands, and motivational factors that are specific to each role. Examine organizational culture by understanding how learning is perceived and supported, and explore social dynamics by mapping communication patterns and relationship structures. Finally, assess the technology environment by documenting actual device usage, technical comfort levels, and connectivity constraints.

- **For each dimension, ask targeted questions that reveal design implications.** Rather than collecting abstract information, focus on factors that directly affect learning design. For example, instead of simply noting that someone works in a noisy environment, determine specifically how noise levels affect their ability to process audio content or concentrate on text-heavy materials. Connect environmental factors to cognitive load implications and practical design constraints.

- **Link your contextual findings to your organizational readiness insights from the MLR Framework assessment.** Your context analysis should build on what you already know about your organization's technical infrastructure, process capabilities, and people readiness. When contextual needs conflict with organizational constraints, prioritize solutions that work within your current capabilities while addressing the most critical contextual barriers.

- **Look for patterns that reveal distinct contextual profiles within your audience.** Group people not by job titles or departments, but by shared contextual realities. For example, Be Natural discovered that sales representatives split into two distinct contextual groups—field-based and office-based—despite having identical job titles. These contextual patterns become the foundation for developing targeted personas that guide specific design decisions rather than generic, one-size-fits-all approaches.

Remember that not all contextual dimensions will carry equal weight. As you review your context analysis, identify which dimensions have the most significant impact on your specific audience and prioritize these in your persona development. For example, the physical environment and mental and emotional dimensions critically affected the manufacturing team's learning opportunities at Be Natural, while the technology environment was less influential because of existing constraints. Trust what your contextual analysis reveals rather than assuming any single dimension is universally most important.

A Persona Development Framework

The persona development process helps you transform collected information into actionable design guidance. For example, rather than creating a single solution for all sales representatives, you can adapt your design for different contextual needs. The same content about product features might be delivered as audio briefings (for field-based reps working from their cars) and interactive modules with embedded resources (for office-based reps). Both formats could be accessible to all sales reps, allowing them to choose based on their current context, or you might prioritize specific formats for specific personas.

Effective microlearning personas capture how people actually experience their work environments rather than just who they are. A persona development framework helps you transform contextual insights into comprehensive personas. The framework consists of four components:

- **Contextual environment.** How the five dimensions shape this persona's daily experience
- **Learning access patterns.** When, where, and how this persona can engage with microlearning
- **Contextual barriers.** What factors limit or prevent learning for this persona
- **Design implications.** What approaches will work best given these contextual realities

Rather than creating generic user profiles (sales representative with five years of experience who is tech-savvy and goal-oriented, for example), context-based personas capture the multidimensional reality of work environments (mobile field rep who works primarily from their car between client visits, experiences high cognitive load during customer interactions, values peer success stories over formal training, and relies on spotty cellular connectivity, for example).

For example, Be Natural followed this process when developing their new hire personas (Table 10-1). They analyzed all five contextual dimensions for new employees, identified three distinct patterns based on work environment and learning access, created personas for each pattern, and designed different microlearning approaches—progressive system learning for corporate professionals, visual job aids for production operators, and mobile-first scenarios for field representatives.

Table 10-1. Be Natural's New Hire Personas

Persona	Contextual Environment	Learning Access Patterns	Contextual Barriers	Design Implications
Entry-level professional (corporate)	Has scheduled learning blocks, dedicated workspace, and strong Wi-Fi	Can engage for 15–30 minutes during designated development time	• Information overload • Unclear priorities • Limited organizational knowledge	• Progressive system learning • Cohort activities • Dedicated reflection time
Production line operator (manufacturing)	Has limited device access, a noisy environment, and safety priorities	Preshift availability or limited opportunities during shifts	• Physical constraints • Divided attention • Varying technical comfort	• Visual job aids • Peer mentoring • Hands-on skills building
Regional account representative (sales)	Has a mobile workspace, client-focused attention, and varied connectivity	Early-morning preparation, between appointments, or an evening recap	• Unpredictable schedule • Customer interruptions • Performance pressure	• Mobile-first design • Offline access • Scenario-based practice

These rich, context-aware personas provide far more design guidance than traditional demographic profiles. They tell you not just who your participants are, but how their environments shape their ability to engage with microlearning.

Using the Frameworks Together

The most effective approach combines both frameworks in sequence:
1. Use context analysis to analyze the five dimensions.
2. Identify patterns and variations within your audience.
3. Develop context-based personas that represent these patterns.
4. Design microlearning solutions customized to each persona's contextual realities and your tools' capacity.

This process ensures that your microlearning design decisions are grounded in contextual understanding rather than assumptions or ideals. As we'll see when we discuss contextual challenges by microlearning type, this foundation directly informs how you approach different types of solutions.

Chapter Summary

Context fundamentally shapes how microlearning initiatives will succeed or struggle. By understanding and designing with all five dimensions of context in mind—physical environment, mental and emotional state, organizational culture, social dynamics, and technology environment—you'll create more effective solutions that align with real-world conditions.

I hope you're now thinking about microlearning not just as isolated content pieces, but as experiences that must be crafted with appropriate context in mind. When you embrace contextual design, you're able to:

- Reduce unnecessary mental burden by aligning content with everyday realities.
- Support meaningful learning by creating connections to familiar environments.
- Design solutions that integrate naturally with workflow.
- Create more realistic audience profiles (or personas) that drive stronger design decisions for your microlearning campaigns and products.
- Optimize your approaches across different learning outcomes.

The context analysis worksheet and persona development framework give you practical ways to systematically analyze your learning environment. If you're new to microlearning, these frameworks will help you build a solid foundation; if you're experienced, they may help you refine your approach. Remember, even excellent content won't be effective if the context isn't right—but when you align with context, even simple solutions can drive remarkable results.

Looking Ahead

The next chapter explores Principle 3, Ensure Global Equity, which extends our thinking about context to ensure that microlearning works for everyone, regardless of their background, abilities, or preferences. As you'll discover, creating truly inclusive microlearning requires us to consider how diverse contexts influence learning experiences and how we can design with accessibility in mind from the start.

VISR Project Check-In

Let's return to your project from the part 2 opening activity and use the VISR reflection framework to evaluate how the principle of crafting appropriate context applies.

Validate

- How does the principle of crafting appropriate context validate or challenge your current approach?
- Does your current or planned design account for all five contextual dimensions?
- Have you observed situations in which context affected learning outcomes?
- What assumptions about your audience's environment might need reconsideration?

Innovate

- Could you repurpose existing environmental elements as contextual triggers?
- How might this principle help you innovate your solution?
- What contextual barriers could become opportunities with creative design?
- How might you leverage social context in new ways to enhance the microlearning experience?

Spark

- How might developing audience profiles improve your microlearning design decisions?
- What new ideas does this principle spark for your project?
- What untapped contextual resources exist in your organization?
- What environmental observations could provide fresh microlearning design insights?

Refine

- Which contextual dimensions need more attention in your current approach?
- How can you refine your microlearning design based on this principle?
- How might you adjust your solution to ensure alignment with mental and emotional context?
- What technical contexts should you reconsider to reduce barriers to use?

CHAPTER 11

Principle 3: Ensure Global Equity

By the end of this chapter, you should be able to answer these questions:
- How does global equity in microlearning design affect engagement, comprehension, and application for diverse participants?
- What are the four dimensions of global equity, and how do they shape inclusive microlearning experiences?
- How can you apply global equity considerations differently across knowledge-based, skills-based, and performance-based microlearning?
- What is Universal Design for Learning and how can it be applied to microlearning?
- What are common challenges you might face in addressing global equity?

A couple years ago, a dear friend gave me a six-liter bottle (yes, it's huge!) of Beaujolais à l'Ancienne wine, and I decided I needed to create a fete fit for serving it. I opted for a bougie spring brunch. I usually host friends in the evening, and I quickly discovered that coming up with a morning menu that took into account everyone's dietary needs (diabetes, lactose intolerance, vegetarianism, and veganism) was tough. Despite my careful planning, I failed to adequately accommodate one friend's needs because I made the incorrect assumption that her dietary restrictions were similar to a vegan's. Boy, was I wrong. Luckily, the smoked salmon and artichoke salad were safe!

Although she insisted everything was fine, I wanted to do better. For her next visit, I invited her to join me in the kitchen and we collaborated on menu planning and cooking. This shared experience not only resulted in delicious meals that met her needs but also enhanced my understanding of inclusive food preparation.

This culinary experience mirrors a challenge that many learning designers face: creating microlearning that truly works for everyone. Just as I discovered that even thoughtfully curated menus can keep a guest from dining, many organizations find that standard approaches to microlearning leave some participants unable to fully engage or benefit. When microlearning isn't designed with global equity in mind, organizations often see uneven results across different employee groups, confused international team members, or accessibility complaints that require costly retrofitting.

Global equity in microlearning isn't about creating special accommodations as afterthoughts. Rather, we should be designing experiences from the ground up that are accessible, inclusive, and effective for all participants, regardless of their backgrounds, abilities, or preferences. Global equity is the difference between a brunch where some guests can eat only side dishes versus one where everyone enjoys a complete and satisfying meal.

Understanding the Principle

Global equity builds directly on the first two principles we've explored. In chapter 9, we examined how understanding your tools' capacity requires identifying the limitations and opportunities within your existing authoring platforms, delivery systems, and analytical tools. Global equity extends this concept by ensuring that those tools can work effectively for everyone, not just those with typical abilities or backgrounds. Whether you're working with advanced technology or simple environmental supports, understanding your tools' capacity helps you maximize the inclusive potential of the resources available.

Chapter 10's focus on appropriate context emphasized understanding your audience's environment, mental state, and social dynamics. Global equity deepens this contextual awareness by helping you recognize the diversity within your audience. While context helps you design for your target audience's general situation, equity ensures that you account for the varied needs, abilities, and perspectives of every individual within that audience.

Together, these three principles—Know Your Tools' Capacity, Craft an Appropriate Context, and Ensure Global Equity—create the foundation for microlearning experiences that are not only technically feasible and contextually relevant but also truly inclusive for all participants. As we'll see throughout this chapter, designing with equity in mind doesn't just benefit those with specific needs—it creates better learning experiences for everyone.

Unlike traditional approaches that might create separate accommodations for different groups, ensuring global equity in microlearning design means creating flexible, adaptable solutions that work well for everyone from the start.

This principle extends beyond basic compliance with accessibility standards. At its core, global equity acknowledges that:

- Individuals bring diverse abilities, backgrounds, and needs to every learning experience.
- These differences significantly affect how people process, engage with, and apply information.
- Effective microlearning accommodates this diversity without creating separate or inferior experiences.

The Four Dimensions of Global Equity

In this chapter, we'll explore four dimensions of global equity that create inclusive microlearning experiences: accessibility; language inclusivity; diversity, equity, and inclusion (DEI); and neurodiversity accommodation.

Accessibility

Accessibility ensures that all participants—including those with disabilities or situational limitations—can effectively perceive, understand, navigate, and interact with microlearning content. You will need to consider:

- **Visual accessibility** (color contrast, screen reader compatibility, and text sizing)
- **Auditory accessibility** (captions, transcripts, and audio quality)

- **Motor accessibility** (touch targets and keyboard navigation)
- **Cognitive accessibility** (clear language and consistent navigation)

Language Inclusivity

Language choices in microlearning significantly affect comprehension, engagement, and a sense of belonging among diverse audiences. You will need to strive for:

- Clear, concise language that avoids unnecessary jargon
- Cultural sensitivity in examples and references
- Translation and localization when needed, even addressing regional colloquialisms
- Inclusive terminology that respects diverse identities

Diversity, Equity, and Inclusion

The goal of DEI measures is to ensure that microlearning content reflects, respects, and engages diverse identities, experiences, and perspectives. This means you will need to consider:

- Diverse representation in examples, scenarios, and visuals
- Recognition of different cultural perspectives and experiences
- Equitable portrayal of different groups
- Content that acknowledges diverse socioeconomic realities

Neurodiversity Accommodation

Recognizing and designing for cognitive diversity ensures that microlearning is effective for people with different information-processing styles and needs. You will need to accommodate:

- Multiple ways to engage with content
- Options for pacing and sequencing
- Minimizing unnecessary cognitive load
- Clear structure and organization

🐝 Be Natural's Four Dimensions of Global Equity

Be Natural applied all four equity dimensions across the organization, demonstrating how each addresses different inclusion challenges.

Accessibility

BN realized that its series of microlearning campaigns were difficult for the manufacturing team to follow in their noisy factory environment. This was especially true for employees with hearing impairments caused by prolonged exposure to loud machinery, as well as for those who did not speak English as their first language.

To address these challenges, the L&D team added clear captioning, translated subtitles, and visual cues such as on-screen symbols and process diagrams. These changes not only supported auditory accessibility but also improved cognitive clarity because they simplified language and ensured consistency across videos. Comprehension improved for all employees (regardless of language fluency or hearing ability) after the changes were implemented.

Additionally, because the training was provided on tablets, the microlearning product's interface had larger touch targets and simple navigation so the team members could easily interact with the content while wearing gloves on the production floor.

Language Inclusivity

The terminology used to describe BN's products in marketing materials was causing confusion among international team members and, in some cases, ran afoul of local regulations. For instance, in Korea, *lotion* refers to a lightweight toner, rather than a body moisturizer. In the European Union, the term *anti-aging* can't be used without providing scientific proof, and more compliant phrases are necessary for describing some products.

To improve clarity and alignment across regions, the L&D team worked with SMEs to develop a standardized product vocabulary with accompanying visuals. It also encouraged regional teams to localize content, ensuring cultural sensitivity and compliance with local guidelines. This approach boosted comprehension and confidence among sales representatives across markets, regardless of language or location.

Diversity, Equity, and Inclusion

When BN created onboarding experiences about company culture, it intentionally included visuals, voice-overs, and scenarios featuring employees from diverse backgrounds, age groups, roles, and life experiences. It also revised any examples to reflect a variety of cultural norms and work styles to better resonate with a broader range of new hires.

As a result, new hires reported feeling more welcome and better able to see themselves succeeding within the organization. By actively representing its workforce's diversity, the company reinforced inclusion from day 1.

Neurodiversity Accommodation

BN's company-wide safety team recognized that all safety-based microlearning products needed to serve vastly different work environments—from the fast-paced manufacturing floor to sales reps on the road, as well as employees in home offices and international branches. By redesigning the content to break down procedures into clearly delineated steps with consistent visual cues and modular sequencing, BN reduced cognitive overload across the board. These changes supported individuals with attention differences and processing challenges, while improving clarity and performance for everyone.

The team also provided multiple content formats—step-by-step checklists, short explainer videos, and printable summaries—to support different information-processing preferences, pacing needs, and working conditions.

This approach demonstrates how the four dimensions of global equity reinforce one another, creating microlearning experiences that work effectively for all participants while addressing the specific challenges each dimension presents.

The Science of Learning and Global Equity

The principle of global equity is firmly grounded in what we know about how people learn. Let's examine it using CLT (which examines how mental effort affects learning) and Gagné's Conditions of Learning framework (elements that designers can create or control to facilitate effective learning), which we discussed in chapter 8.

Cognitive Load Theory and Inclusive Design

When microlearning fails to incorporate global equity considerations, it often unintentionally increases extraneous cognitive load, or mental effort that doesn't contribute to learning. This affects learning outcomes in measurable ways. Table 11-1 highlights each of the four dimensions of equity in relation to cognitive load and some relevant design considerations.

Table 11-1. Dimensions of Global Equity and Cognitive Load

Equity Dimension	Impact on Cognitive Load	Design Implication
Accessibility	Inaccessible content forces individuals to expend mental resources to overcome barriers rather than process content.	Clear, perceivable content reduces extraneous load.
Language inclusivity	Complex or unfamiliar language requires translation effort, which competes with learning.	Plain language optimizes cognitive resources for understanding concepts.
DEI	Mental effort is required to translate noninclusive examples to personal context.	Diverse representation reduces cognitive barriers to engagement.
Neurodiversity accommodation	Inflexible presentation formats of the content overloads some cognitive processes.	Multiple formats support different cognitive processing strengths.

Gagné's Conditions of Learning and Inclusive Design

Gagné's framework emphasizes that different types of learning require specific external conditions—elements that designers can create or control to facilitate effective learning. Global equity helps ensure that these optimal conditions are available to all participants, regardless of their individual needs or backgrounds. We can achieve this by designing multiple pathways for participants to access, engage with, and demonstrate their understanding of content. This approach allows us to adapt external conditions to support diverse individuals across all three microlearning types—knowledge-based, skills-based, and performance-based.

Application by Microlearning Type

Global equity applies across all types of microlearning, but how it applies and what it influences most will vary depending on the type of learning outcome you're targeting. Knowledge-based solutions need to prioritize clear, accessible language and visual design; skills-based products require flexibility in how individuals observe and practice; and performance-based microlearning must respect real-world conditions, cultural differences, and neurodiverse ways of performing.

Designers can't assume that one set of equity checks will cover all learning contexts. Instead, aligning global equity considerations to the type of microlearning ensures that content is not only inclusive but actionable for every individual. This alignment strengthens both reach and impact, especially in distributed or diverse workplaces. Table 11-2 summarizes which dimensions of global equity you should consider for each type of microlearning.

Table 11-2. Types of Microlearning and the Application of Global Equity

Dimensions of Global Equity	Knowledge-Based	Skills-Based	Performance-Based
Accessibility	Crucial for text, audio, and video content delivery	Vital for interactive tools and demo replication	Important, but also includes accessibility of real-world contexts
Language inclusivity	Needs high clarity and localization	Precise instructional language is vital	Tone and nuance matter in context-sensitive content
DEI	Ensures representation in examples	Critical for fair skill framing and practice contexts	Central to framing success and competence without bias
Neurodiversity accommodation	Must support alternate formats and pacing	Allow error-tolerant, flexible, or chunked practice	Needs adaptive design for planning, reacting, and decision making

Knowledge-Based Microlearning

Knowledge is comprised of concepts, facts, terminology, compliance, and processes. Gagné tells us this requires clear presentation, meaningful context, and opportunities for retrieval.

These global equity considerations are important:

- **Accessibility.** Knowledge-based content often relies heavily on text, graphics, and video explanations. Ensure you have captions for instructional videos, alt text for diagrams explaining concepts, and screen-reader compatibility for terminology definitions. Multiple format options (text, audio, visual) help individuals access the same conceptual information through their preferred or necessary modality.

- **Language inclusivity.** Clear terminology and precise definitions are essential. Misinterpretation of key terms or concepts due to translation gaps or cultural framing can create foundational misunderstandings that compound throughout learning. Use plain language for explanations and provide glossaries for technical terms.

- **Diversity, equity, and inclusion.** Examples and case studies used to illustrate concepts should reflect diverse contexts and perspectives. Avoid framing knowledge as if there's only one cultural lens through which to understand it, for instance, leadership concepts, business practices, and communication norms vary across cultures. Ensure that explanatory examples don't inadvertently center one group's experience as universal.

- **Neurodiversity accommodation.** Dense text blocks and complex visual hierarchies can create cognitive overload when presenting new concepts. Break information into smaller chunks, use a consistent visual structure, and provide processing time between concepts to support different information-processing needs.

Equity in knowledge-based microlearning centers on ensuring clear, accessible entry points for understanding. It's about interpretation, cognitive load, and inclusion in the framing of facts and explanations.

Skills-Based Microlearning

Skills-based microlearning commonly focuses on application, demonstration, procedural accuracy, and repetition for mastery. Gagné emphasizes that intellectual and motor skills development requires demonstration, guided practice, and feedback. With this in mind, your approach to global equity may need to consider:

- **Accessibility.** Skills-based microlearning requires accessible practice opportunities, not just observation. Interactive simulations must work with assistive technologies, keyboard navigation for those who can't use a mouse, alternative input methods for motor skill practice, and tactile or verbal alternatives when visual-motor coordination is required. Provide multiple practice modalities—such as digital simulations, physical manipulatives, verbal rehearsal, or peer practice sessions—to accommodate different physical and sensory abilities.

- **Language inclusivity.** Instructional clarity is key. Verb-based commands and directions must not be ambiguous, especially across cultures. Procedural steps need precise language that translates clearly across languages and cultural contexts to ensure consistent skill execution.

- **Diversity, equity, and inclusion.** Scenarios, tasks, and practice contexts that reflect diverse cultural perspectives help all learners see relevance. Demonstrations showing diverse practitioners successfully performing skills avoid the implication that only certain people can master particular abilities. Ensure feedback doesn't reflect cultural bias about what "correct" technique looks like when multiple approaches can achieve the same result.

- **Neurodiversity accommodation.** Many skills require practice and feedback loops. Designs that accommodate varied pacing, high tolerance for error during learning, and clear instruction support different processing needs. Provide a variety of practice opportunities, such as digital simulations, physical practice stations, and verbal role plays. Allow learners to repeat practice without penalty and adjust feedback timing to individual processing needs.

Equity in skills-based microlearning focuses on providing accessible practice opportunities and feedback, as well as the ability to safely repeat and refine skills without penalty or exclusion due to design.

Performance-Based Microlearning

Performance-based microlearning supports real-world execution, decision making, or adaptive behavior change, often aligned with a competency. Gagné notes that applying cognitive strategies in real settings requires appropriate challenges and opportunities for transfer. This brings the following considerations to the forefront:

- **Accessibility.** Performance support must be accessible at the moment of need, in actual work environments. This means mobile access for field workers, voice-activated tools for hands-busy situations, and quick-reference formats viewable in challenging conditions (such as bright sunlight, low lighting, or noisy environments). Performance tools must also accommodate different regional norms and organizational settings. Keep in mind that what works in one context may need to be adapted for another.

- **Language inclusivity.** Nuances matter significantly in performance contexts. A tone considered assertive in one culture may be seen as aggressive in another. Performance guidance that uses culturally specific idioms or communication styles may create confusion or inappropriate behavior. Avoid defaulting to a single cultural model of "correct" performance.

- **Diversity, equity, and inclusion.** When simulating leadership decisions, customer interactions, or communication styles, avoid bias in how success is framed. Show a variety of performers with different body types, speech patterns, and cultural expressions successfully achieving (or not) performance goals. Ensure that performance criteria doesn't inadvertently privilege one cultural approach over equally effective alternatives. Multiple pathways to solving problems—including decision trees, expert tips, and adaptive approaches—recognize that diverse work styles can achieve the same results.

- **Neurodiversity accommodation.** Performance situations often require quick decision making under pressure, which can overwhelm some cognitive processing styles. Provide performance support that accommodates different planning and reaction patterns, some individuals need step-by-step guidance, while others prefer high-level frameworks. Allow for different response times when possible, and design feedback systems that support varied reflection and adjustment processes.

Equity in performance-based microlearning emphasizes representation and cultural fairness in how success is defined and assessed, while ensuring support tools are accessible across diverse work contexts and cognitive approaches.

Universal Design for Learning: A Framework for Implementation

Universal Design for Learning (UDL) is a science-based approach to implementing global equity in microlearning design, rather than creating separate accommodations. It provides:

- **Multiple means of representation,** including content in different formats (such as text, audio, visual, and interactive) so all participants can access information in ways that work for them
- **Multiple means of action and expression,** offering various ways for participants to navigate content and demonstrate understanding so you can accommodate different physical abilities and communication preferences
- **Multiple means of engagement,** creating several pathways to motivation and engagement that respect diverse interests, backgrounds, and learning preferences

While these three principles provide the foundation for UDL, their application varies depending on the type of microlearning you're creating. Knowledge-based, skills-based, and performance-based microlearning each require different approaches to representation, action, and engagement. Table 11-3 provides ideas of how to apply UDL principles across all three microlearning types.

These UDL applications aren't mutually exclusive—you can combine approaches within a single microlearning initiative. The key is ensuring that learners have genuine options for how they access, engage with, and demonstrate their learning, rather than forcing everyone through identical experiences.

Table 11-3. UDL Principles in Microlearning: Examples

UDL Principle	Knowledge-Based Example	Skills-Based Example	Performance-Based Example
Multiple means of representation	Compliance training offers a video with captions, a downloadable transcript, and an audio-only version for different learning contexts	Customer service skills are demonstrated through silent video with annotations, a narrated video, and in-person observation options	A safety checklist is available as a laminated card, a mobile app with a voice reader, and a wall-mounted visual guide
Multiple means of action and expression	Product knowledge is assessed through a quiz, a verbal explanation to manager, or a written summary	A sales technique is practiced through role play, a recorded pitch review, or a written scenario response	A quality control decision is documented using a touchscreen checklist, a voice memo, or a photo with annotation
Multiple means of engagement	Leadership concepts are explored through self-selected case studies from different industries or regions	Conflict resolution is practiced using scenarios chosen by participants based on their actual challenges	Troubleshooting support offers a step-by-step guide, expert tips, or a decision tree, based on worker preference

When Implementing This Principle

Implementing the global equity principle in microlearning design can seem daunting, but you can apply it in a managed and measured way. Be sure to:

- **Address access before you design.** Understand your audience's diverse needs before creating content. The MLR Framework is an invaluable tool because it can help you find opportunities and challenges for each audience with more certainty. Using this information, in addition to the resources you have access to, can help you determine the level of global equity you can accommodate in your microlearning solutions.
- **Implement progressively.** Start with foundational accessibility and build toward comprehensive inclusion. However, if your

organization can't be comprehensively inclusive, you can still create microlearning. Start where you are, and plan how to reach the desired state over time.

- **Balance other principles.** Find the right balance of equity, concision, and other design principles. Avoid assuming that one design choice supports all individuals equally; because equity requires intentional layering across principles.
- **Improve continuously.** Aside from planning improvements through progressive implementation, use feedback and data to refine your approach as necessary.

UDL provides an excellent foundation, but effective implementation requires thoughtful application that accounts for your specific organizational context, available tools, and learning objectives.

Common Challenges and How to Overcome Them

Implementing global equity in microlearning design is an ideal worth pursuing, but many L&D professionals face practical obstacles. We'll now explore common barriers to creating equitable microlearning experiences and some practical strategies for overcoming them.

Resource and Technical Limitations

Perhaps the most frequent concern about global equity is the perception that it requires significant additional resources—time, budget, and specialized expertise that many organizations simply don't have. You've probably heard these concerns:

- "We don't have the budget for translations."
- "Our team doesn't include accessibility experts."
- "Creating multiple versions will take too much time."

While they are valid, they needn't prevent progress toward more equitable microlearning. There are practical solutions to these concerns:

- **Prioritize high-impact elements.** Start with improvements that benefit the widest audience. For example, ensuring good color contrast and readable font sizes benefits nearly everyone, not just those with visual impairments.

- **Use progressive implementation.** Organizations can begin with simple accommodations and gradually add more advanced features as resources become available. For example, providing a microlearning product in both its original format and as a PDF offers basic accessibility and learning preference options. Many organizations start with a minimum viable product and prioritize improvements based on audience analysis and addressing the most common needs first.
- **Leverage existing tools.** Many authoring platforms already include accessibility features that are underutilized. Before requesting budget for new tools, thoroughly explore the capabilities of your current technology (which leads us back to Principle 1, Know Your Tools' Capacity) so you can maximize what you have or get innovative with a work-around.
- **Build skills incrementally.** Instead of trying to become experts in all aspects of accessibility at once, have team members develop expertise in different areas, and then share knowledge through internal training sessions, a central repository, and tools, templates, and techniques.
- **Document your constraints.** When complete accessibility isn't possible because of technical limitations, document these gaps in your design. This transparency helps you set appropriate expectations and identify priorities for future improvements.

Start with what you can implement today rather than what you wish you could do someday. This mindset shift makes equity achievable rather than overwhelming.

Organizational Resistance

Sometimes, the barrier isn't technical or financial but organizational: Stakeholders don't always understand the importance of equity or may view it as unnecessary extra work. There are practical solutions to this concern:
- **Focus on business benefits.** L&D teams can build support for equity initiatives by highlighting how inclusive design improves performance metrics for all employees. Data often shows that teams

with accessible training materials have fewer incidents and better performance outcomes than those without.

- **Start with small wins.** Rather than attempting organization-wide transformation, begin with pilot projects that demonstrate value. Build momentum by starting with the training materials for a single product line or department, and then use those results to determine when to expand to other areas.
- **Leverage compliance requirements.** While global equity goes beyond compliance, legal requirements can provide leverage for initial approvals. Once stakeholders see the benefits beyond compliance, buy-in typically increases.
- **Educate stakeholders.** Short demonstrations showing how different users experience microlearning can be eye-opening. Show executives what a screen reader user experiences when accessing training, which often shifts their perspectives and builds support for accessibility improvements

🐝 Be Natural's Progressive Approach to Global Equity

Be Natural demonstrates how organizations can overcome these challenges using a progressive, pragmatic approach to global equity. When the company began its journey toward more equitable microlearning, leaders faced typical constraints: limited budget, outdated technology, and stakeholders who viewed accessibility as a "nice to have" rather than a necessity. Rather than abandoning their efforts, the L&D team developed a three-phase strategy.

Phase 1: Foundation (Year 1)

- Added captions to all videos
- Improved color contrast in visual materials
- Created simple alternatives for complex visual content
- Developed style standards for clear, inclusive language

Phase 2: Expansion (Years 2 to 3)

- Incorporated multiple learning paths in new microlearning products
- Trained the L&D team on accessibility best practices
- Added alternative navigation options for complex interactions
- Collected feedback from diverse user groups

Phase 3: Integration (Years 1 to 3)

- Updated the design process to include equity considerations from the start
- Developed an equity assessment checklist
- Created success metrics tied to equitable outcomes
- Established an ongoing feedback loop with users representing different needs

This phased approach allowed BN to make steady progress without overwhelming its team or budget. Although it took time, BN had transformed its microlearning approach and could demonstrate concrete benefits that included broader engagement, improved performance metrics, and positive feedback from previously underserved employee groups.

The L&D director noted, "The key was starting where we were, not where we thought we should be. Each small improvement built our confidence and capabilities, eventually leading to much more significant changes than we initially thought possible."

By approaching global equity as a journey rather than a destination, you can make meaningful progress regardless of your starting point or available resources. The goal isn't perfection but continuous improvement toward more inclusive, effective microlearning for everyone.

Chapter Summary

This chapter focused on the importance of global equity in designing microlearning. We explored four dimensions of global equity and the diverse needs of individuals in our target audiences. We highlighted the importance of UDL as a design approach to support diverse learning needs and foster an equitable learning environment.

We know that if we are building knowledge-based microlearning, we have to make the content comprehensible and accessible for diverse audiences. For skills-based microlearning, we have to ensure inclusive practice and learning by doing. And for performance-based microlearning, we can't bake bias into what good performance looks like; we have to allow room for diverse paths to success.

It can seem impossible to make content meaningful and accessible to all who need to take it. However, that doesn't mean we don't make an effort. Global equity should always be part of solution development, not an afterthought. It also reinforces the need and value of determining readiness using the MLR Framework, which aids in discovering the unique needs of the various audiences within your organization.

Looking Ahead
The next chapter explores Principle 4, Design With Concision, and how to focus content for maximum impact. Now that we've established the importance of inclusive design through global equity, we'll now dive into how to craft microlearning experiences that are not just accessible, but also streamlined and purposeful.

VISR Project Check-In

It's time for you to consider the four dimensions of global equity and UDL within the context of your target audience. As you work through your selected microlearning initiative from the part 2 opening activity, use this VISR reflection framework to consider how the global equity principle applies to your project. Take a few minutes to reflect on each element.

Validate
- Which aspects of your current design already support accessibility, language inclusivity, cultural diversity, or neurodiversity?
- Where might your assumptions about your audience create unintentional barriers?
- How well does your solution work for participants with diverse abilities, backgrounds, and preferences?

Innovate
- How might you incorporate multiple means of representation beyond what you've already planned?
- What alternative ways of engagement could you introduce to support different learning preferences?
- How could you adapt your assessment or feedback mechanisms to accommodate diverse expression styles?

Spark
- What possibilities emerge if you design for flexibility from the start rather than adding accommodations later?
- How might embracing neurodiversity lead to better microlearning for everyone?
- What creative solutions come to mind for addressing equity with limited resources?

Refine
- What adjustments to your design process would ensure that equity is considered from the beginning?
- What concrete changes will you make to increase accessibility in your microlearning solution?
- How can you incorporate inclusive language and examples that reflect diverse experiences?

Based on your reflections, list two to three specific actions you'll take to enhance global equity in your microlearning project.

CHAPTER 12
Principle 4: Design With Concision

By the end of this chapter, you should be able to answer these questions:
- What does designing with concision mean in microlearning, and how does it differ from simply making content shorter?
- How does concision in microlearning design help manage cognitive load and enhance information processing?
- What strategies can you use to identify essential content while eliminating the extraneous?
- How do concision techniques differ across the different types of microlearning?
- What techniques can you apply to write concisely without sacrificing clarity or engagement?

The first time I heard the word *edit* in the context of cooking was when a food critic mentioned it on *Top Chef*. The critic said a dish was not "refined enough" in taste and presentation and had too many elements, which had led to a lack of harmony in flavor and presentation. The dish under discussion was a stir-fry with multiple vegetables, steak, and shrimp. I initially thought it sounded delicious—until the judges pointed out that all the ingredients and heavy seasonings meant that flavors were competing rather than complementing one another. They suggested editing, or simplifying, the dish by focusing on just three vegetables, one protein, and a sauce that highlighted the core flavors.

I've often thought about this example when giving feedback on learning products. Just as a skilled chef must carefully select ingredients to create a harmonious dish, learning designers must thoughtfully choose what to include and exclude in microlearning. When we fail to edit our work carefully, or design with concision, we create experiences that overwhelm participants with too much information, competing visuals, or unnecessary interactions. This leads to cognitive overload, reduced comprehension, and learning products that fail to achieve their outcomes despite the quality of individual elements.

Designing with concision means making intentional decisions about content and design to deliver cohesive, focused microlearning that serves a clear purpose while eliminating anything that doesn't contribute directly to the objective. It's not about brevity for brevity's sake, but about ensuring that every element—whether text, media, or interaction—plays a necessary role in achieving the desired outcome.

This fourth principle builds on the foundation established in the previous chapters. Our understanding of tool capacity (Principle 1) helps us determine how to structure content efficiently within our available platforms. Appropriate context (Principle 2) guides us in identifying which contextual elements are essential and which can be streamlined. Global equity (Principle 3) ensures that concise design serves diverse audiences by providing accessible core content while offering optional depth for those who need it. Designing with concision helps us refine these considerations into focused, effective microlearning experiences that respect participants' cognitive limitations and time constraints.

In this chapter, we'll explore practical approaches to identifying essential content, techniques for concise writing across different formats, and strategies for maintaining engagement while eliminating extraneous material. We'll also examine how this principle applies differently to knowledge-based, skills-based, and performance-based microlearning, with examples from Be Natural.

Understanding the Principle

Concision means communicating only what is necessary in the clearest and most meaningful way possible, without losing instructional integrity. In the microlearning context, it's the intentional practice of delivering cohesive, focused microlearning products and campaigns in which every element serves a clear purpose in achieving learning outcomes. This principle applies to all aspects of microlearning, including:

- **Content.** Present only information necessary for understanding or performing a specific task, avoiding tangential or excessive details (such as including an additional comment in parentheses).
- **Design.** Structure layout, interactions, and media to support focus and clarity and minimize distractions and unnecessary complexity.
- **Narrative elements.** Focus on the most relevant aspects of scenarios or examples that directly drive learning outcomes.

Designing with concision doesn't mean stripping away all context or depth, as if you are creating instructions for putting together an IKEA table. Rather, it means carefully evaluating each element against its contribution to learning outcomes. The goal is to ensure that everything included serves an essential purpose while removing anything that might create cognitive barriers to understanding.

The Science of Learning and Concision

Designing with concision in mind directly supports cognitive load management (which we explored in chapter 8). When we understand how cognitive load affects learning, the importance of concision becomes clear.

- **Intrinsic cognitive load** represents the inherent complexity of what's being learned. While we can't eliminate this complexity, concise presentation helps participants focus on essential elements without unnecessary distractions.
- **Extraneous cognitive load** comes from how material is presented. Concision directly reduces extraneous load by eliminating unnecessary information, poor organization, and distracting design elements that don't contribute to learning.
- **Germane cognitive load** involves mental effort dedicated to creating lasting mental schemas. By focusing content on what truly matters, concision helps direct participants' cognitive resources toward this productive mental effort.

When we fail to design with concision, unnecessary content increases extraneous load, distracting from learning and reducing efficiency. Concise content helps focus attention, improve retention, and promote cognitive efficiency.

Concision Through the Lens of Gagné's Frameworks

Gagné's Conditions of Learning (or Five Categories of Learning Outcomes) and Nine Events of Instruction provide complementary support for concision in microlearning design.

Different types of learning outcomes require different approaches to concision. For intellectual skills, concision means focusing on critical relationships and principles. For verbal information, it means prioritizing essential facts. For motor skills, it means highlighting key movements without unnecessary detail. Recognizing which outcome category you're targeting helps determine the appropriate level of concision.

The Nine Events of Instruction provide a natural framework for determining what's essential versus what's extraneous. In microlearning, these events can be efficiently streamlined into four parts (Hook and Objective, Recall and Content, Try It and Feedback, and Reinforce and Apply) without losing instructional integrity. This streamlined approach ensures that we include all essential elements while maintaining concision. We'll discuss this a bit more later in this chapter.

This approach to concision emphasizes meaningful reduction guided by what we know of how people learn. By understanding the essential requirements for different learning outcomes (Gagné's Conditions of Learning), we can make informed decisions about what to include and exclude (Gagné's Nine Events of Instruction).

The Case for Keeping It Concise

I hope that I've provided a compelling case for concision, but it has been conceptual. Let's look at a few real-world examples of how microlearning can go off the rails when we ignore the need to be concise:

- **Stakeholder pressure.** "How will they know if we don't put it in there?" Stakeholders often push for including more information out of fear something essential might be missed. This is just their perspective. It's not proof.

- **Design complexity.** Learning designers sometimes struggle with concise writing when taking technical, pensive, or creative approaches to their designs. The average modern advertisement on TV or YouTube is well under 30 seconds. If a company can get your attention, share a memorable message, and maybe even convince you to take action as a consumer in such a short time, we can all make our learning messages a little shorter.

- **SME relationship challenges.** Many L&D professionals lack the confidence to edit subject matter experts' (SMEs) work. SMEs are experts, but that doesn't mean that they are experts in how people learn. SMEs appreciate knowing their contributions will matter to the target audience when delivered with accuracy and concision.

- **Expert bias.** When an L&D professional is the expert, they may find it difficult not to share all their experience and knowledge on a topic they're passionate about. I will put myself in that position with respect to this book. My first draft was too long because I wanted to be exhaustive to ensure I covered *everything* for *every reader*. Then, I attempted to abbreviate my ideas, which led to large gaps and confusion. Like Goldilocks, my editor and I worked to develop what I hope is now a "just right" balance.

Frameworks and Microlearning Types

Concision begins with decision making, not with implementation. Before you can write, draw, or record with concision, you need a framework for deciding what deserves inclusion and what should be eliminated. Concision isn't about saying things in fewer words—it's about saying fewer things, but saying the right ones!

This section introduces two decision frameworks, followed by content element techniques, and then explains how these apply across different microlearning types.

A Streamlined Nine Events Framework

Gagné's Nine Events of Instruction (gaining attention, informing learners of objectives, stimulating recall, presenting content, providing guidance, eliciting performance, providing feedback, assessing performance, and enhancing retention and transfer) provide a comprehensive structure for learning that we looked at in chapter 8. Applying all nine events in their full form often leads to long-form learning, not microlearning; however, we can make some adjustments and still use this effective framework to guide our efforts in concision.

Table 12-1 consolidates these nine events into four components, helping you maintain instructional integrity while achieving concision.

Why This Framework Works for Microlearning

This streamlined approach is particularly powerful for microlearning design for several reasons:

- **It's domain-flexible.** The framework adapts seamlessly across knowledge-, skills-, and performance-based microlearning, making it versatile for different learning needs.
- **It's structured.** While it provides clear organization, it doesn't constrain creative design choices, allowing you to adapt each component to your specific context and tools.
- **It's memory friendly.** The paired components (hook and objective, recall and content, try it and feedback, reinforce and apply) create a natural flow that's easy for designers to remember and implement.
- **It respects time constraints.** Each component can be sized appropriately for brief microlearning experiences—whether that's a single three-to-five-minute product or components spread across a microlearning campaign.

This framework compresses instructional intent without sacrificing instructional integrity, allowing you to quickly identify what your participants need to do and the best way to structure it, regardless of whether your goal is to inform, instruct, or build capability.

This framework provides a solid structure for all other decisions, helping you identify which instructional elements must be present while eliminating

Table 12-1. Streamlined Nine Events Framework

Streamlined Component	Original Events	Concise Implementation	What to Emphasize	What to Minimize
Hook and objective	1. Gain attention 2. Inform learners of objectives	Brief scenario or question that immediately establishes relevance and a clear statement of what each participant will learn or do	• Direct connection to job performance • Specific, measurable objective	• Background information • Theoretical foundations • Multiple objectives
Recall and content	3. Stimulate recall 4. Present content 5. Provide guidance	• Brief activation of prior knowledge • Essential content focused on objective • Clear guidance	• Key concepts and critical steps • Visual organization • Concrete examples	• Comprehensive coverage • Tangential information • Theoretical explanations
Try It and feedback	6. Elicit performance 7. Provide feedback	Focused practice opportunity and specific, concise feedback	• Essential skills • Immediate application • Specific feedback	• Multiple practice scenarios • Generalized feedback • Extensive explanations
Reinforce and apply	8. Assess performance 9. Enhance retention and transfer	Quick check for understanding and connection to on-the-job application	• Clear success criteria • Direct job application • Next steps	• Comprehensive assessment • Theoretical connections • Future possibilities

unnecessary elaboration. By organizing your microlearning around these four components, you ensure that nothing essential is missing while preventing unnecessary expansion.

Content Selection Technique

With your instructional structure determined, you'll need practical tools to help you make objective decisions about what specific content to include or exclude. The challenge many learning designers and SMEs face is determining what's absolutely essential versus what's merely interesting or nice to know. Two content selection tools, which I call "Keep or Delete" and "The Five Whys," provide systematic approaches to content curation that minimize subjectivity and align decisions with learning outcomes. The third approach, the Inverted Pyramid, is a centuries-old writing style that prioritizes the most important information first. When applied consistently, each approach helps you achieve concision by systematically identifying what's essential versus what's extraneous.

Keep or Delete

Keep or delete is the fastest approach. For each piece of content, ask:

- Does it directly support the stated learning objective?
- Is this information directly essential for achieving the intended outcome of this microlearning solution?
- Would removing it significantly reduce understanding of the core concept?

These questions help you make quick decisions. If you answer no to any of them, delete the content. To determine what is essential for knowledge-based learning, focus on foundational concepts; for skills-based learning, focus on practice requirements; and for performance-based learning, focus on task completion necessities.

The Five Whys

If you are still hung up on a piece of content and aren't sure whether to keep it or cut it, try asking "Why?" five times:

1. Why is this information included?
2. Why is that reason important?
3. Why does that matter to the participant?
4. Why would omitting this information risk failure in achieving the learning outcome?
5. Why is this the best way to present it?

The Inverted Pyramid

The Inverted Pyramid serves two distinct but complementary purposes in microlearning design. It can be used as a strategic filter for content selection and as a structural method for writing content clearly.

As a decision framework, the Inverted Pyramid helps you determine the appropriate level of detail within a microlearning campaign (Figure 12-1). This application guides high-level decisions about content inclusion, helping you make strategic choices about depth and detail.

Figure 12-1. Inverted Pyramid

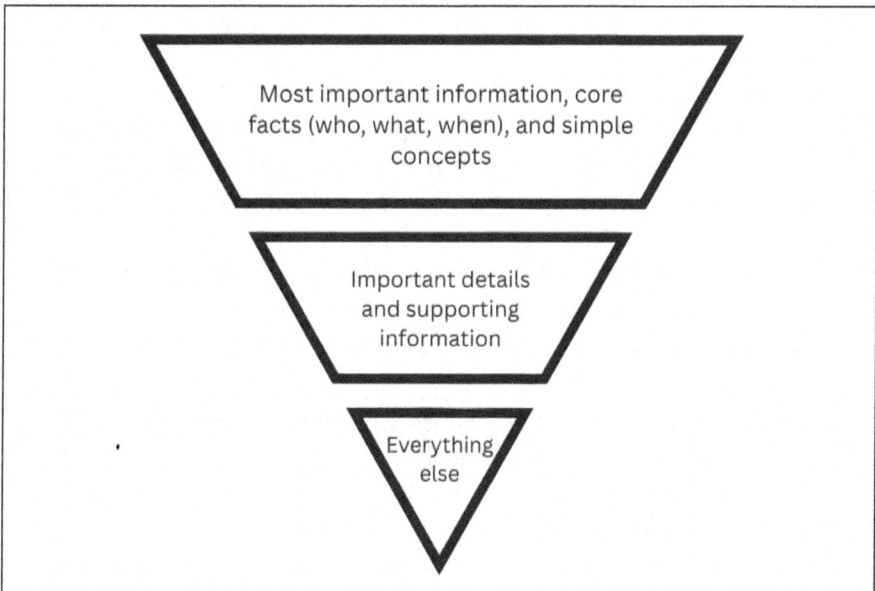

Most important information, core facts (who, what, when), and simple concepts

Important details and supporting information

Everything else

The Inverted Pyramid also serves as a tactical writing technique for structuring individual pieces of content. Use it to help organize individual text elements and ensure the most important content is encountered first, even if participants don't complete the entire experience. Follow these steps:

1. **Lead with essential information.** Place the most critical facts first.
2. **Follow with supporting details.** Add contextual information in descending order of importance.
3. **End with background information.** Place optional content at the end.

The Inverted Pyramid framework is particularly powerful when applied strategically across a microlearning campaign. It helps you make consistent decisions about depth across multiple products, ensuring each includes only what's necessary for its specific purpose.

🐝 Strategic Concision Using the Inverted Pyramid

Be Natural applied the Inverted Pyramid to create three distinct but connected microlearning products for its new organic moisturizer. Together, these products formed a strategic microlearning campaign with the ultimate outcome of building sales associates' confidence and competence.

Performance-Based Microlearning

The L&D team focused solely on top-level information (including product name, main ingredients, three main benefits, and suitable skin types) and omitted all supporting details and background information.

- **Format.** Display concise product information cards directly with products in stores.
- **Purpose.** Support both sales associates and customers at the point of decision.
- **Campaign role.** Provide performance support in the actual work environment at the moment of need.

Skills-Based Microlearning

The L&D team included top-level information plus important details about product application techniques and answers to common customer questions and omitted background about product development and detailed scientific information.

- **Format.** They created three brief scenario-based practice activities.
- **Purpose.** Develop consultation skills for matching products to customer needs.
- **Campaign role.** Build on essential information by developing specific skills needed for customer interactions.

Knowledge-Based Microlearning

The L&D team included all three levels, with core information first, followed by supporting details, and finally background on the research behind main ingredients.

While they included all three levels, each level still required concision—including only essential elements that directly support learning outcomes.

- **Format.** A series of four three-minute microlearning modules builds progressive understanding.
- **Purpose.** Build a foundation for understanding product line positioning and development.
- **Campaign role.** Provide deeper context and understanding for those who need it.

By applying the Inverted Pyramid across a campaign of microlearning products, BN successfully created a concise but comprehensive approach to product training. Each product was appropriately concise for its specific purpose while contributing to the larger goal of confident, effective sales interactions. This strategic approach demonstrates how concision frameworks can guide not just individual content decisions, but entire campaign architectures.

Content Element Techniques

Once you've made decisions about what to include, try these techniques to help you implement concision in different content elements.

Concision Techniques for Text

Organize text with a clear hierarchy to help readers find essential information:

- Use descriptive headings and subheadings.
- Start with essential information in each section.
- Structure information from most to least important.

This approach ensures that participants encounter essential information first, even if they don't complete the entire experience. It's particularly valuable for performance-based microlearning because time is limited. Figure 12-2 shows an example.

Figure 12-2. Before and After Concision

Before	After
"Safety is paramount in all manufacturing operations. Over the years, many standards have been developed to ensure worker protection. Among these standards, proper machine operation procedures are particularly important. When operating the packaging equipment, it's essential to follow proper startup procedures to prevent injuries."	"Always verify that the safety lock is engaged before loading the packaging equipment. This prevents the machine from activating during loading, which is the most common cause of hand injuries."

Concision Techniques for Visual Elements

Eliminate decorative elements that don't contribute to understanding:

- Remove background elements that don't add contextual value.
- Use simplified representations when detailed rendering isn't necessary.
- Apply visual hierarchy to emphasize the most important elements.

Figure 12-3 shows an example.

Figure 12-3. Before and After

Concision Techniques for Audio

Manage the amount of information in your audio:

- Aim for 125 to 150 words per minute for narration in English. (You will find information about speaking rates in other languages at tfcs.baruch.cuny.edu/speaking-rate.) When language-specific guidelines aren't available, start with a slightly slower pace than you'd use in English (roughly 110–130 words per minute) and adjust based on feedback from native speakers when possible.

- Use simple sentences with a clear subject-verb-object structure.
- Use strategic sound cues to replace verbal explanations.

The alert tone paired with a visual cue in the "after" example in Figure 12-4 addresses multiple learning needs while signaling importance without requiring a lengthy explanation.

Figure 12-4. Before and After

Before	After
"Now, we're going to take a look at how to properly lift heavy objects using the correct posture and approach to ensure that you don't injure your back or strain any muscles during the process. It's really important to follow these guidelines because back injuries are among the most common workplace injuries and can lead to significant time off work and potential long-term health complications."	"Let's examine proper lifting technique to prevent injuries." [*Alert tone sound effect + visual alert icon.*] "Follow these three steps to protect your back."

Application Across Microlearning Types

Now that we've established decision frameworks and content techniques, let's explore how these apply differently across knowledge-based, skills-based, and performance-based microlearning.

Knowledge-Based Microlearning

Knowledge-based microlearning focuses on helping participants acquire and retain information. Here, concision involves presenting only facts, concepts, and principles that directly support learning outcomes. The strategies in this section align with the Inverted Pyramid framework.

For knowledge-based microlearning, we focus primarily on the top layer of that pyramid—delivering essential who, what, and when information. Many knowledge products also benefit from selectively including simple concepts or principles, which correspond to the pyramid's middle (how) layer.

These additions support comprehension without overwhelming your target audience. The pyramid helps us decide how deep to go, while the following techniques, known as "progressive disclosure," will help us structure that depth so participants engage only with what they need, when they need it.

Knowledge-Based Concision Techniques

Effective knowledge-based microlearning requires layering information rather than overwhelming participants with comprehensive content all at once. Start with core concepts to ensure your target audience understands the essential elements without experiencing cognitive overload. Then, provide strategic options for deeper exploration; for example, "learn more" links and expandable sections can house supplementary details for those who need them. This progressive disclosure approach respects the diverse needs of your audience, allowing novice participants to focus on the fundamentals while giving experienced participants the option to access additional context that enhances their understanding.

Design Considerations for Knowledge-Based Concision

Effective knowledge-based concision requires strategic decisions about information hierarchy and cognitive support. Prioritize memorability by focusing on what participants absolutely need to recall and ensuring that each piece of information supports long-term retention goals. Group related information into chunks of three-to-five-items that align with working memory limitations and create meaningful cognitive units. Use memory supports by incorporating mnemonics, acronyms, and mental models that provide scaffolding for information retention without adding extraneous cognitive load. Remove nonessential background information by cutting historical context unless it's directly relevant to immediate learning objectives or participant performance needs.

Knowledge-based microlearning often fails when designers prioritize comprehensive coverage over focused learning. Interesting but nonessential facts will distract from core information and lead to competing cognitive demands that interfere with the retention of essential content. In addition, avoid providing too much theoretical background before practical information, which can overwhelm participants before they've grasped fundamental concepts. Maintain clear distinctions between "need to know" and "nice to know" content—this fundamental categorization drives every other concision decision in knowledge-based microlearning.

Skills-Based Microlearning

Skills-based microlearning focuses on helping participants perform specific procedures or techniques. Concision here means including only what's needed for effective practice while eliminating everything else.

Skills-Based Concision Techniques

Break complex skills into their essential components by identifying the critical decision points where participants typically struggle or make errors. Then, focus practice opportunities on these decision points, rather than requiring participants to practice the entire procedure from start to finish. Routine tasks that don't require significant decision making or cognitive effort can be eliminated because they become automatic with minimal repetition. This targeted approach creates more focused practice opportunities that concentrate learning effort exactly where participants need the most support, which improves skills acquisition efficiency while respecting time constraints.

Design Considerations for Skills-Based Concision

Skills-based microlearning succeeds when it concentrates cognitive effort on the most challenging aspects of skills development. Focus on decisions, not actions, by emphasizing points where judgment is required. Streamline demonstrations by showing only what's necessary for understanding the critical decision points and technique variations that your target audience typically struggles with. Create focused practice opportunities by isolating the most challenging aspects of specific skill components. Provide concise feedback by addressing only the most critical aspects of performance that directly influence skill acquisition and transfer to real-world application.

Skills-based concision fails when designers treat all skill components as equally important or challenging. Avoid including practice for skill components that are already mastered because this wastes valuable practice time that could be spent on genuinely difficult elements. If you overexplain simple procedures, you risk creating cognitive overload before participants tackle the content that actually requires mental effort. Be particularly careful about creating overly complex scenarios because authentic complexity can inadvertently shift the focus away from the specific skill components your target audience needs to develop.

Performance-Based Microlearning

Performance-based microlearning focuses on supporting immediate application in the workplace. Concision is paramount here because these products are typically accessed during work, when time and attention are limited.

Performance-Based Concision Techniques

Eliminate explanations of why and how whenever possible to create performance support that facilitates immediate action and focuses exclusively on what to do. Use imperative verb forms that directly guide action to reduce cognitive processing time and create clear, actionable direction. For example, "Select the customer account" is better than "You should select the customer account." Structure content in the precise sequence of required actions to mirror the actual workflow and minimize mental translation between the support tool and the task at hand. This streamlined approach creates microlearning products that integrate seamlessly into workflow and allow workers to access exactly what they need without disrupting their primary focus.

Design Considerations for Performance-Based Concision

Performance-based microlearning operates under entirely different constraints than knowledge- or skills-based approaches. The focus should be on immediate use. Eliminate all nonessential elements because workers using performance support are typically under time pressure and cognitively loaded with their primary task. Optimize for scanning by using bullet points, numbered steps, and a clear visual hierarchy that allows for rapid information retrieval. Design for context by considering when and where the microlearning products will be accessed, recognizing that performance support often occurs in less-than-ideal conditions with environmental distractions and competing priorities. Focus on triggers by helping participants recognize when to use the performance support, ensuring they can quickly identify the right tool for their specific situation without extensive decision making.

Performance-based concision fails when designers confuse performance support with training, leading to tools that hinder rather than help the workflow. Avoid including explanations and theory in performance support tools because they create unnecessary cognitive demands when workers need immediate, actionable guidance. Resist creating overly comprehensive resources that are difficult to navigate, which defeats the purpose of supporting performance. Most critically, consider the physical and cognitive constraints of the work environment; performance support that works perfectly in a quiet office may be completely unusable on a factory floor or during a customer interaction.

🐝 Concision Across Microlearning Types

Be Natural's L&D team applied concision principles to address three distinct learning challenges, demonstrating how the approach varies by microlearning type.

Knowledge-Based Challenge

Because new sales associates were struggling to retain product information during customer interactions, they missed average sales threshold patterns. Thus they were typically taking four to six weeks longer than necessary.

The concise solution was to replace the 20-minute comprehensive training module with a progressive disclosure:

- **Core (3 minutes).** Essential details only—name, key benefits, target customer
- **Support (5 minutes).** Ingredients and benefits (optional)
- **Advanced (5 minutes).** Research and competitive positioning (optional)

As a result, associates began reaching minimum sales thresholds, demonstrating better retention of essential information when addressing more advanced customer inquiries.

Skills-Based Challenge

The manufacturing team needed to improve their machine operation procedures, but the traditional two-hour training program was time-consuming and ineffective.

A task analysis revealed three critical error-prone decision points. The concise solution the team created included:

- Three 5-minute modules, each targeting one decision point
- Practice scenarios for each point
- A simple decision-tree job aid
- Optional supervised practice focusing on decision application

As a result, the team reduced floor training time while improving safety compliance by focusing exclusively on error-prone procedures.

Performance-Based Challenge

New hires in various work environments struggled to remember multiple systems and procedures, taking several weeks longer to reach independent or self-directed fluency in their role.

The concise solution was to replace comprehensive onboarding binder with targeted performance support using tablets at workstations or assistive overlays in software:

- Digital quick-reference cards organized by task (not system)
- 60-second how-to videos linked via QR codes at workstations
- AI chatbot providing step-by-step guidance for common processes

Each tool focused exclusively on guiding action with no background information unless absolutely necessary for task completion.

As a result, time to productivity decreased from four weeks to 2.5 weeks because the team provided exactly the right information at the moment of need.

> **Key Pattern**
> Effective concision requires understanding what the target audience actually needs for success, and then eliminating everything else—regardless of how interesting or traditionally important that content might seem.

Maintaining Balance

As you apply these concision techniques across different microlearning types, remember that the goal is balance—not brevity for brevity's sake. Every microlearning product exists to achieve specific outcomes, and effective concision means including what is necessary for those outcomes while eliminating everything else.

In knowledge-based microlearning, this means focusing on what participants truly need to know and remember. In skills-based microlearning, it means creating targeted practice on critical decision points. And in performance-based microlearning, it means providing exactly what's needed to complete a task successfully—no more, no less.

By applying these decision frameworks and techniques appropriately across different microlearning types, you can create experiences that respect participants' cognitive capacity while maximizing effectiveness. The result is microlearning that achieves its outcomes more efficiently, whether those outcomes involve knowing, performing, or applying something in the workplace.

Common Challenges and How to Overcome Them

Implementing concision consistently can be challenging. Here are some common barriers you might encounter and practical strategies to overcome them.

Stakeholder Resistance

Stakeholders often push back against concision, fearing that important information might be omitted. Comments like, "They need to know this background information" or "We've always included this context" are common resistance points.

To address stakeholder resistance, use data-driven approaches to build consensus:

- Conduct small pilot projects comparing concise and comprehensive versions, measuring retention and application.
- Share before-and-after examples with concrete metrics. (For example, "This approach improved knowledge retention by 35 percent.").
- Use the Five Whys technique in stakeholder meetings to challenge assumptions about what's truly necessary.

Finding the Balance Between Brevity and Depth

Creating truly concise microlearning is often like walking a tightrope. Lean too far toward brevity, and you risk creating superficial experiences that lack necessary context; include too much depth, and you lose the benefits of concision.

To find a balance, use a tiered content approach:

- Identify true must-know content through performance observations and data analysis.
- Create core microlearning products focused exclusively on essential content.
- Develop optional layers for those who need or want more depth.
- Use clear signposting to help participants navigate between layers.

If your budget doesn't allow for fully developed tiered content, create simple "Learn More" resources using existing documentation. Even basic PDF reference guides can provide depth while keeping your microlearning focused.

Editing Paralysis

Many learning designers find themselves stuck in endless editing cycles, struggling to determine what to cut and what to keep.

To avoid that cycle, create structured editing processes with clear stopping points:

- Begin with specific word or time limits for each component. (For example, "This introduction cannot exceed 30 seconds.")
- Use peer review with specific concision criteria.
- Implement the "rule of halves" for initial drafts (challenge yourself to cut content in half).

- Set firm deadlines for final edits to prevent diminishing returns.

If professional editing resources aren't available, use free readability tools and word count features to maintain objective standards for concision. Even simple tools can help maintain discipline in the editing process.

SME Management

Subject matter experts often provide excessive detail and resist efforts to streamline content, viewing simplification as "dumbing down" their expertise.

For best results, transform SMEs into partners in the concision process:

- Involve them in audience analysis to build understanding of participant constraints.
- Have them observe users struggling with complex content.
- Focus conversations on performance outcomes rather than content inputs.
- Celebrate their expertise by highlighting the most meaningful elements.

🐝 Overcoming the Challenges of Concision

Be Natural's L&D team faced stakeholder and SME pushback on their use of concision during the creation of some of their first microlearning products, but they found pragmatic ways to overcome both.

When discussing content for BN's sales onboarding microlearning campaign, the marketing director insisted that detailed brand history be included in every knowledge-based microlearning initiative focused on BN products. In response, the L&D team conducted a simple experiment with two groups of new hires: Group 1 received the concise microlearning products, while group 2 was given comprehensive versions that included historical information. After a week, the team tested both groups on their ability to answer customer questions. Group 1, which had used the concise microlearning products, outperformed on the main selling points; both groups performed equally poorly on historical information. The data convinced stakeholders that their request was hindering, not helping, sales effectiveness.

BN's manufacturing safety team struggled with concision when working with its engineering SMEs, who insisted on detailed explanations of the mechanical principles behind each performance-based microlearning product focused on safety procedures. The L&D team invited these SMEs to observe new operators using their documentation during supervised practice. Seeing operators overwhelmed by technical details but succeeding with streamlined guidelines shifted the SMEs' perspective. Together, they created a tiered approach: concise, action-oriented instructions for daily use, with optional technical resources for deeper understanding.

Chapter Summary

Designing with concision means making thoughtful decisions about what to include and exclude in your microlearning, ensuring every element serves a clear purpose in achieving learning outcomes. This principle is about respecting participants' cognitive capacity and focusing on what truly matters. Takeaways from this chapter include:

- **Concision requires decision frameworks.** Tools such as the Streamlined Events Framework and content selection techniques help you make objective decisions about what to include based on your microlearning goals.
- **Different microlearning types require different approaches to concision.** Knowledge-based microlearning benefits from progressive disclosure, skills-based microlearning from focused decision points, and performance-based microlearning from action-oriented structures.
- **Content elements can be optimized across text, visuals, and audio.** Techniques such as clear structure for text, visual simplification, and strategic use of audio cues all contribute to more concise, effective microlearning.
- **Managing stakeholders and SMEs is crucial for successful implementation.** Resistance to concision is natural, but data-driven approaches and collaborative techniques can help build consensus around more focused approaches.

- **The goal is balance, not brevity.** Effective concision means including what's necessary for desired outcomes while minimizing or removing everything else, creating experiences that respect both learning needs and real-world constraints.

By applying the principle of concision appropriately across your microlearning ecosystem, you can create experiences that achieve their outcomes more efficiently.

Looking Ahead

The next chapter explores Principle 5, Make Media Meaningful, which builds on concision by helping you select and design media elements that enhance rather than distract from learning. While concision focuses on what content to include, meaningful media addresses how to present that content most effectively, ensuring that every visual, audio, or interactive element serves a clear purpose in achieving your microlearning outcomes.

VISR Project Check-In

Given the frameworks and techniques for designing with concision, it is time for you to consider how this principle applies to your specific microlearning initiative. As you work through your selected microlearning solution from the part 2 opening activity, use this VISR reflection framework to evaluate how intentional content decisions can strengthen your project's effectiveness. Take a few minutes to reflect on each element:

Validate

- How does this principle challenge your assumptions about what content is truly necessary for your microlearning product?
- Are there elements you've included based on tradition or preference rather than learning necessity?
- What content are you including that participants could actually do without?

Innovate

- What would your microlearning products look like if you had to reduce content by 30 percent while maintaining effectiveness?
- How might structured approaches to concision help you create a more powerful microlearning products?
- Could techniques such as progressive disclosure or the Streamlined Events Framework transform your current approach?

Spark

- What new ideas does this principle generate for how you write across your microlearning campaign?
- Are there opportunities to create tiered content structures that balance concision with depth?

Refine

- How will you know if your concision efforts have maintained learning effectiveness while reducing cognitive load?
- Identify one specific area of your current microlearning products that could benefit from greater concision.
- What specific technique from this chapter could you apply to refine this element?

Consider reviewing your current microlearning content with the "Keep or Delete" technique, challenging each element to justify its inclusion based on its direct contribution to learning outcomes.

CHAPTER 13

Principle 5: Make Media Meaningful

> By the end of this chapter, you should be able to answer these questions:
> - How do media choices enhance or hinder learning outcomes in microlearning?
> - What criteria should guide your selection of media for different microlearning purposes?
> - How can you balance media richness with cognitive load considerations?
> - What practical approaches can help you document and justify your media decisions?
> - How does meaningful media support different types of microlearning solutions?

If you watch any competitive cooking show, you know that the judges usually evaluate contestants' dishes based on three criteria: how well the dish represents the assigned challenge, how good it tastes in terms of flavor and texture, and how visually appealing the presentation is. The most successful chefs understand that visual presentation isn't just a decorative afterthought; it's an integral part of the dining experience that enhances flavor perception and enjoyment. However, even the most beautifully plated dish will fail if it prioritizes appearance over taste or doesn't fulfill the challenge's requirements.

Similarly, in microlearning design, media choices shouldn't be made simply for visual appeal or because technology makes them possible. Media elements—whether they're images, audio, video, or interactive components—must serve a clear purpose in supporting learning outcomes. Organizations often fall into the trap of wanting microlearning to be more visual because it is "so short," which winds up overwhelming participants with unnecessary animations, complex graphics, or distracting videos that actually interfere with learning.

Making media meaningful means intentionally selecting and designing media elements that support learning objectives, respect cognitive limitations, and enhance engagement without causing distraction. We must choose the right media format for the right purpose at the right time, ensuring that every element contributes directly to understanding, retention, or application.

This fifth principle builds on the foundation established in previous chapters. Our understanding of tool capacity (Principle 1) helps us determine what media options are technically feasible. Appropriate context (Principle 2) guides us in selecting media that fits participants' environments and situations. Global equity (Principle 3) ensures our media choices are accessible and inclusive for diverse audiences. And balancing concision (Principle 4) reminds us that even media elements must be streamlined and purposeful.

In this chapter, we'll explore how to select, create, and implement meaningful media in your microlearning solutions. We'll examine how cognitive processing affects media perception, consider practical tools for making media decisions, and demonstrate how different types of microlearning—knowledge-based, skills-based, and performance-based—benefit from different media approaches. Through examples from Be Natural, you'll learn to create microlearning in which every media element serves a clear purpose and supports your learning outcomes.

Understanding the Principle

In microlearning, media elements appear everywhere—visuals in product tutorials, audio narration in onboarding, or animated scenarios in leadership programs. But just because a microlearning product can include media elements doesn't mean it should. Every media choice you make either enhances understanding or adds unnecessary complexity.

When used meaningfully, media functions like seasoning in a perfectly executed dish. It elevates the learning experience without overwhelming the main ingredients. Too much media, or the wrong kind, can overpower your message, confuse your participants, and increase cognitive load.

Before we explore how to make media meaningful, let's clarify terminology that often gets conflated:

- **Media** refers to any format used to present content—text, images, audio, video, animations, or interactive elements. Even plain text is a form of media.
- **Multimedia** refers to the intentional combination of multiple media formats in one experience, such as a narrated animation or an interactive scenario with layered visual and audio elements.

You can use media without creating multimedia. A simple, well-chosen image alongside text can be more effective than an elaborate multimedia presentation with animations, narration, and interactive elements. The key question isn't "Should I use multimedia?" but rather "What type of media best supports the outcome, for this audience, in this context?"

The Science of Learning and Media

Two foundational theories guide effective media choices in microlearning: cognitive load theory (CLT) and the cognitive theory of multimedia learning (CTML).

Cognitive Load Theory and Media

As we have discussed, CLT focuses on how our working memory manages information during learning. When media is thoughtfully selected and designed, it can help manage cognitive load in several ways:

- **Reducing intrinsic load** by making complex concepts more accessible through visualization
- **Minimizing extraneous load** by eliminating unnecessary decorative elements
- **Supporting germane load** by directing attention to essential relationships and concepts

Poorly chosen media does the opposite: It increases extraneous load, distracts from essential content, and makes learning more difficult.

The Cognitive Theory of Multimedia Learning

Developed by Richard E. Mayer, CTML provides a scientific foundation for understanding how people learn from words and graphics (Mayer and Moreno 2005). According to Mayer's research, three ideas have remained constant throughout the theory's development:

- **Dual channels.** Humans have separate information-processing channels for verbal and visual information. This means that we process narrations and text differently from how we process animations, videos, and other visuals.
- **Limited capacity.** Processing capacity in each channel is severely limited. We can handle only a few pieces of information at once in our working memory.
- **Active processing.** Meaningful learning requires cognitive engagement. Participants must select relevant material to process in working memory, mentally organize it into coherent verbal and visual structures, and integrate these with one another and with relevant knowledge from long-term memory.

These three ideas reveal why microlearning can be so effective: It respects cognitive limitations by design. While traditional long-form training often requires participants to sift through extensive content to identify what's important, microlearning does much of this sifting work by:

- Preselecting what's essential (what participants must focus on)
- Preorganizing information into logical, easy-to-process structures (how things fit together)
- Creating clear pathways for integration (how this connects to what participants already know)

This deliberate reduction doesn't cut corners, it channels cognitive resources toward what truly matters for performance. These cognitive processes translate into three practical design principles that are particularly relevant for microlearning:

- **The modality principle** suggests that participants learn better from graphics and narration than from graphics and on-screen text. This distributes processing across both channels rather than overloading the visual channel.
- **The redundancy principle** cautions against presenting identical content in multiple formats simultaneously. Reading the same text that's being narrated forces participants to process the same information twice, creating unnecessary cognitive load. In a sales-training video, for instance, having a narrator read verbatim what's written on-screen creates redundancy. Either simplify on-screen text to key points or rely primarily on narration.
- **The coherence principle** advises eliminating extraneous material that doesn't directly support learning outcomes. Background music, decorative animations, and interesting but irrelevant content all increase cognitive load without enhancing learning. For example, a manufacturing safety microlearning product about proper lifting technique doesn't need background music or animated characters—these elements increase cognitive load without contributing to the learning outcome.

Cognitive Theory of Multimedia: A Theory That Keeps Us Honest

Richard E. Mayer's cognitive theory of multimedia learning isn't just about academic e-learning. The theory helps us make smarter media choices in any learning experience. It reminds us that our target audience only has so much mental bandwidth, and our job is to help them use it wisely. From choosing a still image over an animation to stripping down a cluttered infographic, CTML gives us permission to do less—on purpose (Mayer and Moreno 2005).

Table 13-1 provides a comparison of how CLT and CTML apply to the function of learning.

Table 13-1. How CLT and CTML Are Similar But Focus on Different Aspects of Learning

Aspect	CTML	CLT
Purpose	Guides effective multimedia design to minimize extraneous processing and maximize meaningful learning	Manages mental effort (cognitive load) during learning to avoid overloading working memory
Core focus	How people learn from words and pictures (multimedia)	How information is processed within the brain's limited capacity
Key application	Selecting and arranging media formats	Breaking content into manageable parts
Memory systems	Dual channels (visual and auditory)	Working memory and long-term memory interaction

Understanding these theories helps us make better decisions about when to use media, what types to select, and how to implement them effectively.

How the Principles Connect

Media choices don't exist in isolation. The principle of making media meaningful builds directly on the principles we've explored so far.

- **Principle 1: Know Your Tools' Capacity.** Understanding your tools' capabilities helps you determine what media formats are technically feasible. Some platforms may limit file sizes or formats, while others offer robust multimedia support. Knowing these constraints ensures that you will select media that can function properly across your delivery environments.
- **Principle 2: Craft an Appropriate Context.** Media choices must fit participants' physical, mental, and technological contexts. A noisy factory floor demands different media than a quiet office; a stressed participant needs different media than a relaxed one. Understanding your personas and their environments helps you select media that works in their real-world conditions.
- **Principle 3: Ensure Global Equity.** Making media meaningful requires you to consider diverse needs to ensure accessibility and inclusion for all participants. This might mean providing alternative formats (such as transcripts for audio or descriptions for visuals), diversifying

representation in imagery, or designing for varying levels of technological access.

- **Principle 4: Design With Concision.** Media should enhance concision, not detract from it. Well-chosen visuals can often explain concepts more efficiently than text alone, while poorly chosen media adds complexity without adding value. Every media element should serve your learning outcomes while respecting participants' cognitive capacity.

These connections demonstrate that media becomes meaningful when it works in harmony with your tools, your participants, and your message. For example, high-definition video might seem like an engaging choice, but it fails the meaningful test if participants primarily access microlearning on low-bandwidth mobile devices (Principle 1) or in noisy environments where audio is difficult to hear (Principle 2).

By integrating these principles, you can create microlearning experiences in which every media element serves a clear purpose, works within your technical constraints, supports your participants' contexts, and remains accessible to everyone.

What Makes Media Meaningful?

We can now establish clear criteria for meaningful media in microlearning. Understanding what makes media truly meaningful requires examining both its positive contributions and any potential problems.

Media is meaningful when it makes content easier to understand, apply, or remember while serving a specific learning purpose rather than just an aesthetic one. Effective media choices respect participants' cognitive capacity and context, creating appropriate engagement without distraction. Perhaps most important, meaningful media supports accessibility and inclusion, ensuring that learning experiences work for everyone.

Conversely, media becomes problematic when it's added primarily for visual appeal or to break up text without serving the learning objectives. Problems also arise when media duplicates content unnecessarily across channels, overwhelming participants with excessive detail or sensory input.

Additional issues occur when media assumes technological capabilities beyond what's available or creates barriers to accessibility.

The best way to know if media is meaningful isn't based on how impressive it looks or sounds, but on how effectively it supports learning outcomes while respecting participants' cognitive limitations and contextual realities.

A Decision Framework for Media Selection

Before we explore specific applications across microlearning types, let's examine a practical decision-making tool (Figure 13-1) that can guide your media choices regardless of content or context.

Figure 13-1. The Media Decision Tree

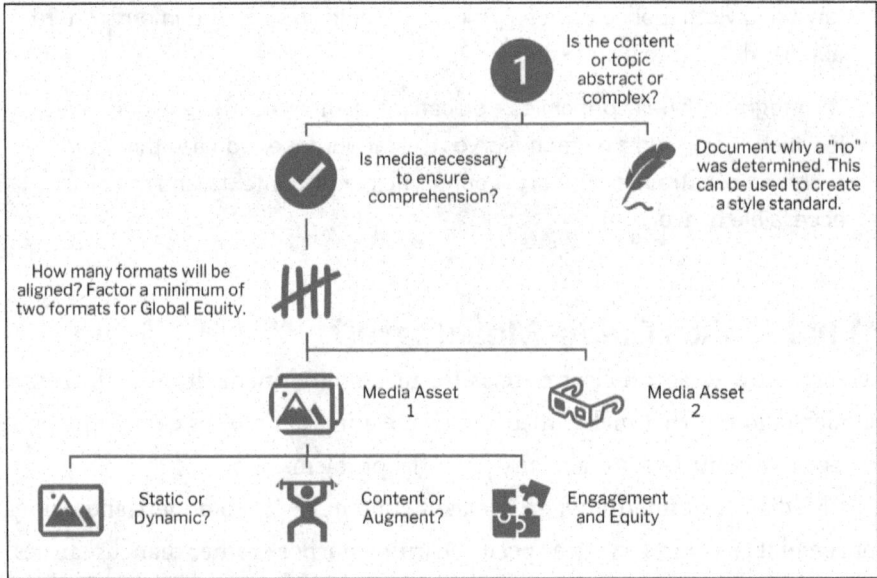

The media decision tree provides a systematic approach to determining what types of media are appropriate for your microlearning content. It can help you make objective decisions based on content characteristics rather than personal preferences or assumptions.

The decision process begins by evaluating whether your content is abstract, complex, or both:

- **Abstract content** involves concepts that can't be directly observed (such as leadership principles, company values, and strategic thinking).

- **Complex content** contains multiple interconnected parts or requires several steps to understand (such as detailed processes or multifaceted skills).

The decision tree then guides you through several questions:

- How many media formats would best serve your participants?
- Is static or dynamic media appropriate?
- Should the media serve as primary content or augmentation?
- How can you ensure engagement and global equity?

Document Your Media Decisions

After using the media decision tree, document your decisions using a few key questions. You can use these prompts informally to think through your choices, or you can formalize your responses by creating a simple tool to record, justify, and revisit those decisions. You can do this in a spreadsheet, a design document, or team review notes. The goal is to create a visible trail. This approach helps maintain alignment across your products and provides a rationale for stakeholders or collaborators (as well as style standards).

When assessing your content, consider whether it's abstract, complex, both, or neither, along with what specific aspects make it that way. You'll also want to evaluate how much prior knowledge your participants have, because this will influence your media strategy decisions.

Your media strategy should address which media formats you've chosen to use and why. Then, for each individual media element, determine the format (video, audio, image, or text), whether it's static or dynamic, and whether it serves as primary content or augmentation. Critical questions include what specific purpose each element serves and what equity considerations apply.

During integration planning, consider how the media elements will work together, as well as any technical constraints you need to address and how you'll measure their effectiveness. This approach is more valuable than just looking at a single microlearning product because it reflects the reality that complex skills like leadership typically require multiple complementary approaches. Microlearning campaign-level analysis also demonstrates how different media choices work together throughout the learning journey while showing how meaningful media extends beyond individual products to create a cohesive experience. Additionally, it reinforces the campaign-based approach to microlearning that we explored in earlier chapters.

🐝 Media Evolution: From Complex to Purposeful

Be Natural's L&D team learned that effective media decisions require matching media characteristics to learning purposes. This became clear as they worked across different types of microlearning challenges—from product knowledge to safety procedures to campus navigation.

Knowledge-Based Challenge: Product Understanding

BN's sales team struggled to understand the complex ingredient profiles of their natural products, so the L&D team used thoughtfully designed media to create a knowledge-based microlearning campaign. This interactive visualization used a layered approach to show each product's ingredient profile. The primary view highlighted essential active ingredients using simple visual representations. If participants tapped an ingredient, a secondary layer would appear with more detailed information about sourcing and benefits. It included audio pronunciation guides for complex ingredient names and used consistent visual language across all products (for example, color-coding for ingredient categories and simple icons for benefits). This approach respected cognitive load limitations while using visuals to make abstract chemical concepts concrete. Results showed that the sales representatives who used this microlearning program could recall key product benefits more accurately than those using traditional text-based product sheets.

Skills-Based Challenge: Safety Procedures

BN's manufacturing team needed to improve safety procedures for operating new packaging equipment. The L&D team created a skills-based microlearning campaign featuring a series of brief (30–60 second) video demonstrations of specific, high-risk machine operations procedures. Each video used a consistent three-part structure: overview of the procedure, demonstration of correct technique, and highlighted safety checks. Rather than creating a single lengthy video, the team broke the content into discrete skill components that employees could practice individually. Critical decision points (or moments requiring judgement) were emphasized with on-screen highlights and slow-motion sequences. The videos deliberately omitted background music and unnecessary visual elements to keep the focus on procedural details. Each skill component included a brief practice opportunity in which participants could identify correct and incorrect procedures from sample images. This resulted in a reduced number of safety incidents related to the equipment upon implementation.

Performance-Based Challenge: Campus Navigation

New BN employees avoided cross-functional collaboration, staying within their own departmental areas despite organizational expectations to work across teams. The honeycomb-shaped campus made it unclear where different departments were located and what support they could provide. This isolation created multiple performance problems: new hires felt disconnected from the broader organization, projects were delayed when critical expertise wasn't consulted, teams duplicated efforts by not leveraging existing solutions from other areas, and problem-solving suffered from lack of diverse perspectives.

The L&D team created a performance-based microlearning solution using targeted media to support the behavior of seeking appropriate cross-functional partners. The team developed an interactive way-finding system with QR codes placed at key decision points throughout the campus. When scanned, these codes displayed simple, context-specific visual directions using a consistent color system aligned with departmental wings. Each direction identified which teams occupied that area and specifically what they could help with (such as "marketing and creative services can help you with brand approvals, campaign collaboration, and content review.") Rather than showing distances, the visuals provided estimated walking times and recognizable landmarks from the participant's current position. The L&D team deliberately avoided complex 3D maps and elaborate animations in favor of simple directional arrows superimposed on actual photos of the environment, with department capabilities overlaid. This approach connected physical location to functional capability, making cross-functional collaboration immediately actionable.

Once the program went live, new hires reported feeling more integrated into the organization, and teams began consulting cross-functional partners earlier in projects. In addition, late arrivals at meetings started to decrease, and new hires reported less stress in onboarding surveys.

By tackling these three challenges, BN's team learned that systematic media decisions, guided by content characteristics and learning purposes, consistently outperformed intuitive or aesthetically driven choices.

Application by Microlearning Type

The specific application of meaningful media differs across knowledge-based, skills-based, and performance-based microlearning. Let's now explore how to tailor your media approach to each microlearning type, examining the unique considerations and techniques that will help you create truly meaningful media experiences.

Knowledge-Based Microlearning

Knowledge-based microlearning focuses on helping participants understand and remember information. Here, the media's primary role is to make abstract concepts concrete and to enhance retention through multiple processing channels. Specific techniques for knowledge-based media include:

- **Visual explainers.** Abstract concepts become more accessible when visualized. Use simplified illustrations, infographics, and diagrams to represent relationships and structures that are difficult to describe in words alone.
- **Progressive disclosure.** Layer information visually; starting with core concepts, allow participants to explore deeper details as needed. This approach supports schema development by allowing learners to build foundational mental models before adding complexity, which respects cognitive limitations while accommodating different knowledge needs.
- **Meaningful animations.** Use animation sparingly to demonstrate processes or changes over time, but keep animations simple and focused on the essential information rather than decorative elements.
- **Guided attention.** Use visual cues such as arrows, highlighting, or callouts to direct attention to key information, reducing extraneous cognitive load from visual searching.

Common pitfalls in knowledge-based media are shown in Table 13-2.

Table 13-2. Knowledge-Based Media Pitfalls

Common Pitfall	Adjustment Strategy
Animation that distracts rather than instructs	Animation works best when used sparingly to demonstrate processes or changes over time. This keeps the focus on the essential information rather than decorative movement.
Visual overload from multiple elements or decorative features	Media that directly supports understanding tends to be more effective than comprehensive visual libraries. Consistent visual language helps build mental models across related concepts.
Visuals that don't accurately represent the concept	Aligning visual elements with the concepts being taught strengthens comprehension. Meaningful interactivity encourages exploration rather than passive viewing.
Visualizations too complex or too simplistic for the audience	Matching the media complexity to the audience's knowledge level improves engagement. Multiple representation options accommodate diverse learning preferences and cognitive styles.

Skills-Based Microlearning

Skills-based microlearning focuses on helping participants develop or improve specific procedures or techniques. Here, media's primary role is to model desired behaviors, guide practice, and provide performance feedback. Techniques for skills-based media include:

- **Demonstration videos.** Show both expert and common novice performance to highlight critical differences. Focus camera angles on the most important elements of the skill.
- **Interactive sequences.** Break complex skills into step-by-step interactive elements that allow participants to practice decision points (when judgment is needed) rather than passively observe.
- **Comparative visuals.** Use side-by-side comparisons of correct and incorrect techniques to highlight important differences.
- **Audio coaching.** Provide narration that emphasizes what to look or listen for during skill execution, particularly for skills with subtle distinctions.

Common pitfalls in skills-based media are shown in Table 13-3.

Table 13-3. Skills-Based Media Pitfalls

Common Pitfall	Adjustment Strategy
Demonstrations showing procedures from varying angles or with different techniques	Using consistent perspectives to show procedural steps reduces cognitive load. Maintaining the same camera angles and approaches throughout helps learners focus on the skill rather than reorienting to the scene.
Emphasis only on perfect execution without showing errors	Demonstrations that include both expert and common novice performances help learners identify critical differences. Examples of typical mistakes and corrections support realistic learning.
Highly polished production that obscures critical details	Clarity often matters more than polish. Production choices that enhance rather than obscure the specific skills being demonstrated serve learners better.
Missing steps that experts perform automatically	Including all essential steps, even those that seem obvious to experienced performers, supports novice learning. Signaling highlights important elements while adequate processing time between steps aids comprehension.

Performance-Based Microlearning

Performance-based microlearning focuses on supporting immediate application in the workplace. Here, media's primary role is to provide guidance, contextual cues, and decision support when it matters most. Techniques for performance-based media include:

- **Quick-reference visuals.** Create stripped-down visuals that communicate essential information at a glance for in-the-moment support.
- **Contextual media triggers.** Use QR codes, near field communication (NFC) tags, or location-based notifications to deliver relevant media at the point of need.
- **Decision-support graphics.** Develop simple flowcharts or decision trees that guide real-time choices in complex situations.
- **Micro-demonstrations.** Create ultra-brief (five-to-15 seconds) visual demonstrations of specific actions that can be accessed exactly when needed (think animated gifs).

Common pitfalls in performance-based media are shown in Table 13-4.

Table 13-4. Performance-Based Media Pitfalls

Common Pitfall	Adjustment Strategy
Information not immediately relevant to the current task	Performance support is more effective when stripped down to the essential information needed for immediate action. Designing for scanning rather than reading supports time-sensitive situations.
Requirements for ideal viewing conditions or specific devices	Designing for actual work conditions—including bright sunlight, noisy areas, or workers wearing gloves—increases usability. Ensuring media works on available devices in real environments improves accessibility.
Solutions that work in controlled conditions but fail in the actual workplace	Accounting for environmental constraints and variables in the actual performance environment strengthens reliability. Testing solutions in realistic workplace conditions can reveal potential issues.
Dependence on perfect connectivity or advanced technical capabilities	Performance support that works with intermittent or no connectivity better serves real-world needs. Solutions that function within the available technical infrastructure will have better adoption rates.

Using Media in Microlearning

Table 13-5 summarizes how common media types support microlearning.

Table 13-5. Matching Media to Microlearning Types

Microlearning Type	Primary Purpose	Common Media Approaches	Be Natural Example
Knowledge-based	Build understanding or recall	Infographics, layered visuals, progressive disclosure, and audio glossaries	Ingredient visualization (sales)
Skills-based	Practice procedures or fluency	Step-by-step videos, slowed replays, comparisons, and short scenarios	Safety demo series (manufacturing)
Performance-based	Guide real-time task execution or decision making	Quick-reference visuals, QR-triggered media, and micro-demos	Wayfinding support system (onboarding)

Table 13-6 shows how media types align with each type of microlearning. Use this media selection matrix to help you document and justify your media choices in a systematic way—ensuring that each element serves both purpose and participants.

Table 13-6. Media Selection Matrix

Media Type	Knowledge-Based	Skills-Based	Performance-Based
Static images	Best for concept visualization and relationships	Useful for procedural steps and comparisons	Ideal for quick-reference guides and decision support
Video	Effective for complex processes and systems	Essential for modeling behaviors and techniques	Most useful as micro-demonstrations of specific actions
Audio	Helpful for verbal concepts and pronunciation	Valuable for coaching through practice	Useful for brief reminders and alerts
Interactive media	Beneficial for concept exploration	Critical for skills practice and feedback	Valuable for contextual decision support

The most effective microlearning often combines these approaches strategically, using each type of media for what it does best while maintaining overall cognitive efficiency.

Common Challenges and How to Overcome Them

Implementing meaningful media in microlearning isn't always straightforward. Let's examine a few common challenges and practical solutions.

Stakeholder Expectations vs. Cognitive Science

Stakeholders often request flashy, elaborate media because it looks impressive even when simpler media would be more effective. They may equate production value with learning value.

Here's what you can do: Educate with evidence by sharing before-and-after examples demonstrating how simplified media improved learning outcomes. Create quick prototype comparisons to show the cognitive load difference and use the media decision tree to provide objective justification for media choices.

Most important, focus your conversations on performance outcomes rather than aesthetic preferences.

Technical Constraints

Limited bandwidth, outdated devices, or restricted technology environments can limit media options, particularly for field or frontline employees or those in manufacturing settings.

Here's what you can do: Design for the lowest common denominator with progressive enhancement by creating core content that works across all technical environments. Develop media in multiple formats and resolutions while using adaptive delivery that detects device capabilities. Prioritize lightweight formats, such as graphics, over video when bandwidth is limited.

If you have limited resources, try this work-around: Create a single high-quality source file, and then generate multiple versions optimized for different environments. Free tools like Handbrake (for video compression) and GIMP (for image optimization) can help teams with limited budgets create multiple versions efficiently.

Global Equity in Media Selection

Creating media that is effective across diverse audiences with different languages, cultural backgrounds, and accessibility needs.

Here's what you can do: Design for inclusivity from the start—minimizing text embedded in images, for example, will facilitate translation. Use culturally neutral visual metaphors and examples and test media with representatives from diverse audience segments. Ensure that your color choices work for those with reduced visual capabilities and include transcripts for audio content and descriptions for any visual elements to assist with language and auditory needs.

Balancing Production Quality and Development Speed

High-quality media often requires significant production time and resources, creating tension between quality and the need for rapid microlearning development.

Here's what you can do: Develop a tiered production approach by creating reusable templates and media frameworks that maintain consistency. Establish a media component library for common elements and focus production resources on the highest priority elements. Use simple media for the initial launch, and make plans to enhance the content based on feedback.

If budget constraints limit professional media production, consider using smartphone cameras with simple stabilization for demonstrations, creating infographics in PowerPoint or Google Slides instead of with specialized tools, recording audio in quiet rooms with simple microphones rather than professional studios, and focusing on content quality over production polish.

🐝 Iterative Media Improvement: Quality Inspection

To solve persistent quality issues in its manufacturing process, Be Natural created a microlearning campaign about quality inspection. It initially developed text-based procedures with static images, but supervisors reported that quality issues were still occurring. The L&D team hypothesized that this was because static images couldn't effectively show the subtle differences between acceptable and unacceptable products.

The Redesign Process
The team redesigned the approach using comparative photography showing examples across the quality spectrum—from clearly unacceptable to borderline to excellent quality. Each image was annotated with specific features to observe. The team also added brief videos showing the process from the inspector's perspective, highlighting where to look and what to feel for.

Measuring the Impact
The L&D team tracked quality rejection rates before and after implementation and conducted a follow-up study in which inspectors used the original versus redesigned media approaches. The redesigned approach (with its purposeful media choices) reduced quality rejections and improved inspector confidence significantly.

The lesson was that the specific characteristics of the task (subtle visual and tactile discrimination) required media addressing those challenges, rather than generic process documentation.

Chapter Summary

Just as a skilled chef knows that visual presentation enhances the dining experience without overshadowing flavor, effective microlearning designers make purposeful media choices that enhance learning without creating cognitive overload. Throughout this chapter, we've explored how to make media meaningful in microlearning experiences. Takeaways from this chapter include:

- **Media should support outcomes, not just look appealing.** Every image, audio element, video, or interaction should serve a clear purpose in achieving your learning objectives. Decorative elements that don't contribute to understanding create unnecessary cognitive load.

- **Different microlearning types benefit from different media approaches.** Knowledge-based microlearning benefits from progressive disclosure and visual organization, skills-based microlearning requires demonstrations and guided practice opportunities, and performance-based microlearning needs quick-reference visuals and context-sensitive support.

- **CTML provides practical guidelines.** Following principles such as modality (combining visual and verbal channels), redundancy (avoiding unnecessary duplication), and coherence (eliminating extraneous content) helps ensure that media enhances rather than hinders learning.

- **Media decisions should be documented and justified.** Using tools like the media decision tree and media selection matrix helps teams make consistent, purposeful choices that align with learning objectives and respect participants' cognitive capacity.

- **Media must be accessible and equitable.** Providing multiple formats and considering diverse needs ensures that your microlearning reaches everyone uniformly, regardless of abilities, preferences, or learning environment.

By applying these principles, you'll create microlearning experiences in which media functions like the perfect seasoning in a well-prepared dish—enhancing understanding, engagement, and retention without overwhelming your participants.

Looking Ahead

Now that we've explored how media can enhance—or hinder—microlearning outcomes, the next chapter will shift from design decisions to action. Principle 6 focuses on creating microlearning experiences that elicit meaningful engagement and learner behaviors in real-world environments.

VISR Project Check-In

Whether you're deep into a project or still exploring your media options, this check-in will help you ensure that every media element earns its place on the plate. Take a moment to revisit your selected project from the part 2 opening activity and consider how the principle of meaningful media applies.

Validate

- How do the media elements in your current microlearning products serve your learning objectives?
- Have you been making media choices systematically or intuitively?
- What criteria have guided your media decisions so far, and how do they align with your content characteristics?

Innovate

- Could you redistribute content across channels to better manage cognitive load?
- Are there opportunities to replace text-heavy explanations with simple visualizations, or complex animations with static images plus narration?

Spark

- How might you layer media elements to address both abstract and complex aspects of your content?
- Might different products in your campaign benefit from different media approaches?
- Could you enhance performance support with just-in-time audio or visual guides?

Refine

- What specific media elements in your current design could be simplified or adjusted based on this principle?
- Which media choice would have the greatest impact on learning outcomes if refined?
- How can you balance ideal media decisions with your practical constraints (such as your budget, timeline, or technical capabilities)?

As you apply these considerations to your project, remember that making media meaningful isn't about using more media or creating flashier experiences; it's about making purposeful choices that enhance learning without creating distractions.

CHAPTER 14
Principle 6: Elicit Action

By the end of this chapter, you should be able to answer these questions:
- Why is eliciting action a culmination of the previous design principles?
- How can you layer actions effectively to achieve strategic microlearning outcomes?
- What role do confidence and competence play in encouraging meaningful action?
- How do desirable difficulties enhance learning while maintaining appropriate challenge levels?
- How should eliciting action differ between knowledge-based and performance-based microlearning solutions?

As I introduce the sixth principle, I'm reminded of preparing a mushroom tortellini soup as a way of showing some gratitude to a friend. Given her food sensitivities and vegan diet, I started with an unassuming pot of water and carefully built a rich, full-bodied vegetable broth, layering flavors intentionally. First, I bloomed dried herbs in the pot; then, I added in fresh herbs from my garden, a hint of lemon, a touch of olive oil infused with mushrooms, and sage. The process couldn't be rushed; each ingredient needed time to release its essence and harmonize with the others before the next addition.

This slow-simmering process mirrors how we elicit action in micro-learning. We typically begin by establishing foundational understanding, and then gradually add opportunities for participants to engage, practice, and apply what they're learning. Just as every ingredient in my broth serves a specific purpose, every action we design must serve the ultimate goal: real-world application. When organizations skip this principle, they often create well designed microlearning that participants passively consume but never apply, resulting in knowledge that quickly evaporates without changing behavior or performance.

Eliciting action means designing opportunities for participants to engage actively with microlearning content through reflection, practice, decision making, and application. It transforms passive content consumption into dynamic learning experiences that build capability and confidence through deliberate practice and meaningful feedback.

For example, when I was completing a survey for a cultural awareness training course I had recently taken, one of the questions asked if I was applying the "new knowledge." The answer was no. I remembered the information well enough to pass the test, but not well enough to apply it. The scenarios had been cartoon-based and didn't reflect real workplace challenges that I would face.

Looking back, I believe that had there been skills-based microlearning opportunities, such as a guided worksheet for structured practice during the onboarding period, key concepts would have been reinforced. I would have been able to assess how those concepts played out in my work. I could have determined if a technique from the course would be helpful for me. And, I would have been able to seek clarity from the organization's resource center on cultural sensitivity.

Furthermore, had there been an activity in which I sat down with my lead to understand specific aspects of my work that cultural sensitivity would intersect with, I would have begun to refine my skills. For true performance-based support, the organization could have provided a quick-reference digital tool that I could access in the moment when encountering a potential cultural sensitivity situation in my actual workflow.

Action isn't the result of a single element—it's the outcome of multiple design principles working together. The principle of eliciting action brings together everything we've explored so far. Our understanding of tool capacity (Principle 1) helps us select appropriate interaction methods. Appropriate context (Principle 2) ensures that actions reflect real-world conditions. Global equity (Principle 3) guides us in designing accessible and inclusive actions.

Designing with concision (Principle 4) helps us focus on essential practice opportunities. And meaningful media (Principle 5) supports action through appropriate visual and interactive elements. In other words, microlearning is more likely to succeed when the purpose is clear through strategic alignment, challenges feel appropriate, support balances guidance with independence, and the format fits the environment. My recent experience highlighted the value and importance of these principles for our microlearning product development efforts.

In this chapter, we will explore practical approaches to eliciting different types of actions, from simple interactions to complex practical applications. This chapter will examine how cognitive load considerations shape your action design, demonstrate the power of engagement techniques, and provide frameworks for developing action-oriented microlearning that builds both confidence and competence. Through examples from Be Natural, you'll learn to create microlearning experiences that don't just inform, but transform. As you read, reflect on how your own designs encourage—or miss—opportunities for action, and where scaffolding, confidence, and context might play a greater role. If you want to be super actionable try the VISR Check-In activity at the end of this chapter, then come back through!

Understanding the Principle

Eliciting action in microlearning means designing opportunities for participants to actively engage—rather than passively consuming content. It's the difference between serving up information and creating experiences that prompt meaningful involvement, whether that's through reflection, practice, decision making, or application. Effective microlearning doesn't just deliver content; it guides participants through a sequence of engagement. When we elicit action, we shift learning from something that happens to participants to something they do.

Principle 6 addresses a fundamental truth: Knowing isn't the same as doing. Most of us have experienced the gap between understanding a concept and applying it. Microlearning that fails to bridge that gap—no matter how well designed or bite-sized—ultimately falls short of driving meaningful performance.

Eliciting action can involve one or more kinds of engagement, depending on the type of microlearning. For example, performance-based microlearning might support only real-world application, while knowledge- or skills-based designs allow for scaffolding across multiple steps. These engagement types work together to create a progression from initial involvement to authentic workplace application.

Initial engagement gets participants involved from the start. This might be as simple as asking them to reflect on their current practice or as complex as presenting a realistic challenge that hooks their interest. These first actions activate prior knowledge and readiness. Structured practice builds on this foundation to provide opportunities—such as decision-based scenarios, guided walk-throughs, or skills drills—to apply knowledge and improve skills in a safe environment. The key is that participants are doing, not just processing. This practice environment then bridges to real-world applications that connect learning directly to performance. These actions reinforce what's been learned and build confidence through authentic use in the workplace.

At this point, you might assume that theory steps aside and practice takes over—but theory is exactly what helps us understand why actions succeed or fail.

The Agency Framework

In chapter 8, we explored how CLT and Gagné's outcome categories help us understand what kinds of content and learning outcomes we're targeting. Principle 6 builds on those foundations by turning our attention to the conditions that support action.

I like to use what I call the "agency framework" to address these conditions. Based on practical experience, research, and reflection across multiple settings, this approach is informed by the competence motivation theory (Elliot et al. 2017). The agency framework identifies three interdependent factors that influence whether a participant will take meaningful action:

- **Motivation.** The participant's willingness to act
- **Confidence.** The participant's belief in their ability to succeed
- **Competence.** The participant's actual capability to perform the task

This framework is a lens we can use in designing microlearning. It helps us ask questions, such as "Is the employee unmotivated, uncertain, or unprepared?" and "How can our designs address that?

Motivation: Willingness to Act

Motivation is the spark that drives engagement. Without it, even the most well-crafted microlearning will fall flat. Motivation can be intrinsic (driven by curiosity, personal growth, or pride in one's role) or extrinsic (driven by deadlines, rewards, recognition, or social pressure). In microlearning, motivation is shaped by three key factors that work together to create compelling engagement:

- The perceived relevance of the action to the participant's role or goals
- The challenge level that feels just right—not too easy, not overwhelming—which maintains interest without creating frustration
- The immediacy of payoff, even if small (such as a quick win that improves workflow), which provides the reinforcement that sustains motivation over time

Make the value of taking action is visible. If participants understand how the action will help them solve a problem or succeed at work, they're more likely to engage.

Confidence: Belief in Ability to Succeed

Confidence is what moves a participant from "I get it" to "I can do this." Participants who lack confidence may understand the concept but hesitate to take action, especially in uncertain or high-stakes environments. Confidence in microlearning is reinforced by a systematic approach that builds belief through experience. This begins with progressive challenges, also known as "desirable difficulties," which start with success and build. These challenges work in conjunction with feedback that affirms what's working and clarifies next steps while confirming what's expected throughout the process.

Build confidence by offering structured early wins. Avoid jumping straight into full application—scaffold the experience to help participants build their belief in their ability.

Competence: Capability Gained Through Practice

Competence is the ability to perform a task or behavior successfully. It doesn't come from exposure—it comes from practice. In microlearning, this means deliberately designing actions that require doing, not just thinking or reading. Competence develops through a deliberate progression that mirrors real-world performance demands. This relies on varied practice with feedback and reflection, ensuring alignment with context, so that what's practiced is what's performed. The process is completed through *support fading*, which means starting with guidance, and then removing it as the individual grows.

Don't mistake completion for competence. Include actions that require performance—whether it's a quick checklist, a short decision scenario, or a practice prompt—and tie them back to real tasks.

These three components reinforce one another. Motivation fuels engagement. Confidence keeps momentum going. Competence solidifies learning through doing. When microlearning design fails to elicit action, it is often because of a breakdown in one of these areas. By systematically evaluating which component needs strengthening—willingness, belief, or capability—you can target your design efforts where they'll have the greatest influence on participant action.

Connecting Actions to Outcomes

While eliciting action supports learning, it must also support something larger: the organization's goals. When microlearning actions are disconnected from strategic intent, even the most engaging product can feel like irrelevant noise.

In chapter 2, we introduced the MLR Framework as a tool to assess your organization's readiness for microlearning and to shape your approach based on six consideration points:

- **Outcomes** (What do you need to achieve?)
- **Purpose** (Why are you using microlearning?)
- **Evaluation** (How will you know it's working?)
- **Implementation** (How will it be delivered and supported?)
- **Spaced learning** (How will it be reinforced?)
- **Potential** (What long-term value are you building?)

Now, the framework can help us connect the actions we design to the performance we expect. It ensures that we're not just eliciting activity; we're eliciting the right kind of action, at the right time, for the right reason.

Actions, Readiness, and Microlearning Types

When your organization is just beginning its microlearning journey, your capacity to elicit action may be limited. That's not a failure; instead, it's an opportunity to align your ambitions with what your infrastructure can realistically support. The MLR Framework helps make those trade-offs visible. For example:

- **If readiness supports knowledge-based microlearning,** actions might include simple recall, reflection, or comparison tasks that reinforce important ideas.
- **If readiness supports skills-based microlearning,** you can design structured practice with feedback loops, guided decision making, or skill component exercises.
- **If readiness supports performance-based microlearning,** actions should be tightly aligned to the moment of need—checklists, cues, reference tools, or performance aids that directly support the task.

Designing actions with this strategic alignment in mind keeps your microlearning from being a string of disconnected moments. It becomes a targeted, performance-aligned experience with measurable value.

When designing for action, always ask three critical questions to ensure strategic alignment:

- What is this action ultimately supporting?
- Is it aligned with an outcome someone is accountable for?
- Will this help the organization perform better—not just help the employee learn better?

The Spectrum of Action Types

Eliciting action doesn't mean every interaction must be difficult or demanding. Different types of action serve different purposes in microlearning design, and understanding this spectrum helps you choose the right approach for your specific context and goals.

Action types exist on a continuum from simple engagement to complex challenge:

- **Simple interaction.** At the foundational level, even basic actions—like clicking to reveal, selecting a response, or acknowledging understanding—represent meaningful engagement compared with passive consumption. These actions create moments of agency and attention that, while not cognitively demanding, establish active participation patterns.

- **Reflection and pensiveness.** Prompting your target audience to think deeply about content, connections, or implications creates cognitive engagement without necessarily requiring difficulty. Questions like "How does this connect to your experience?" or "What would you do in this situation?" invite contemplation and meaning-making. These reflective actions build understanding and personal relevance.

- **Practice without penalty.** Exploratory practice in safe environments—such as sandbox scenarios, "try it and see" interactions, and low-stakes experimentation—builds confidence through success rather than challenge. This approach allows participants to develop familiarity and comfort before facing more demanding applications. Practice without penalty is particularly valuable when building initial confidence or introducing entirely new concepts.

- **Challenging practice (desirable difficulties).** When the goal is building knowledge retention or developing skills that transfer to many contexts, productive challenge becomes essential. This is where desirable difficulties (or carefully designed challenges that require effort but produce stronger long-term results) become foundational to your design. For campaigns focused on building capability over time, these challenging practice opportunities move from optional to essential.

- **High-stakes practice.** Some performance contexts require practice that mirrors real-world pressure and consequences. Simulations where errors have costs, scenarios with time pressure, or situations where "you only get one chance" prepare participants for authentic workplace demands. This action type is appropriate when real performance includes significant stakes.

- **Social and collaborative action.** Learning through interaction with others—including peer teaching, collaborative problem solving, group decision making, and structured peer feedback—creates action through social engagement. These approaches leverage collective knowledge and build skills in working with others while creating accountability through social dynamics.

- **Metacognitive action.** Prompting individuals to reflect on their own learning process (such as "What strategy did I use?" "How did I approach this?" "When would I apply this again?") creates action at the strategic level. These metacognitive prompts build participant autonomy and support transfer by making thinking processes explicit.

When to Use Which Action Types

The type of action you design should align with three key factors. Tables 14-1 through 14-3 provide guidance for selecting appropriate action types based on your specific context.

Table 14-1. Action Types by Microlearning Type and Purpose

Microlearning Type and Purpose	Appropriate Action Types
One-off interactions or simple awareness-building	Simple interaction, reflection
Campaign-based knowledge building	Reflection plus challenging practice (desirable difficulties)
Campaign-based skill development	Practice without penalty through to challenging practice (desirable difficulties)
Performance support	Simple interaction, high-stakes practice (if a learning component exists)

Table 14-2. Action Types by Learner Development Stage

Learner Development Stage	Appropriate Action Types
Building initial confidence	Simple interaction, practice without penalty
Building capability	Challenging practice (desirable difficulties), social action
Approaching mastery	High-stakes practice, metacognitive action

Table 14-3. Action Types by Organizational Constraints

Organizational Context	Appropriate Action Types
Limited technology	Social action, reflection
Time-constrained environment	Simple interaction, performance support
Robust infrastructure	Full spectrum of action types available

Key Insight for Campaign Design

When you're creating microlearning campaigns (sequences of products designed to build knowledge or develop skills over time) challenging practice through desirable difficulties becomes the foundation of your design approach, not just one option among many. Campaigns aimed at lasting capability building require the productive struggle that desirable difficulties provide.

In contrast, for single-interaction microlearning products, simpler action types often suffice. A one-time awareness piece might need only reflection. A quick performance support tool might require only simple interaction. But when your goal is building and retaining capability over weeks or months, desirable difficulties shift from optional technique to an essential design foundation.

Desirable Difficulties: The Foundation of Campaign Design

When designing microlearning campaigns—sequences of products aimed at building knowledge or developing skills over time; desirable difficulties become the primary lens through which you design action. While simpler action types (such as reflection prompts, basic interactions, and exploratory practice) serve valuable purposes in specific contexts, campaigns that truly build lasting capability require the productive challenge that desirable difficulties provide.

However, not all difficulty leads to learning, and not all learning sticks because it was easy. Some of the most effective learning conditions are those that feel slow, provoke determination, or even cause frustration in the moment, but produce stronger results over time. These are what researchers refer to as "desirable difficulties" (Sachdeva 2024).

Desirable difficulties are carefully designed learning conditions that temporarily challenge participants in ways that support long-term retention, flexible application, and transfer of knowledge or skill. This doesn't mean you should make learning hard for its own sake; however, it's important to create productive struggle when the individual is ready for it. That distinction matters.

What makes a difficulty desirable? A challenge is "desirable" only if it meets certain criteria:

- The employee has the background knowledge or skill to respond.
- The challenge promotes encoding or retrieval, not confusion or failure.
- The outcome is long-term retention and flexible use, not just immediate performance.

When difficulties are introduced to learning experiences too early, without proper scaffolding or clarity, they stop being desirable. They become barriers. And when employees equate ease with learning, challenging tasks may feel like failure—even when they're doing the real work of learning. This means we need to apply this concept carefully, with attention to employee readiness, contextual support, and progressive design.

Employee Readiness

Not everyone engaging with a microlearning product starts from the same level of experience or familiarity. Desirable difficulties work only when the person has enough foundation to interact with the challenge productively. When difficulty is introduced too early—before key knowledge or awareness has been established—it can backfire, leading to confusion or withdrawal. Readiness must be assessed in relation to both the content and the context.

For example, asking a new customer service representative to choose between different de-escalation techniques won't be productive if they haven't yet learned to recognize the warning signs of an escalating situation. They need to first understand what escalation looks like before they can meaningfully practice choosing how to respond to it. Build the foundation, and then introduce the challenge.

Contextual Support

A well-designed challenge includes built-in support not just for content, but for pacing and relevance. The environment in which the microlearning is delivered affects whether difficulty becomes productive or punitive. Factors such as available time, device access, psychological safety, or clarity of expectations all shape whether a challenge helps or hinders. Contextual support means ensuring that participants have what they need to engage—without over-directing or removing all friction.

Support might include tips, a replay option, minimal but timely feedback, or environmental realism that doesn't overwhelm.

Progressive Design

Desirable difficulty shouldn't be delivered at full intensity from the start. Complexity and autonomy should increase over time as individuals demonstrate capacity and interest. Progressive design respects the pacing of real performance growth: Initial actions should focus on access and basic use; later actions can shift toward synthesis, transfer, or adaptation. If microlearning ramps up challenges in this way, it encourages confidence while still preparing participants for everyday performance.

For example, begin with a short action tied to known context; then, follow it with a new variable, a delayed retrieval cue, or a reflection prompt that reuses prior knowledge in a new frame.

Common Forms of Desirable Difficulties

Desirable difficulties are challenges intentionally introduced during learning content that make the initial performance harder but enhance long-term retention and transfer. While these difficulties may slow learners down initially, they strengthen learning by requiring deeper cognitive processing.

There are several instructional techniques that create desirable difficulties in microlearning design:

- **Retrieval practice.** Prompt recall rather than repeating information.
- **Distributed practice.** Spread learning sessions over time rather than massing them together.
- **Interleaving.** Mix different types of content or skills rather than blocking them.
- **Varying contexts.** Change practice conditions rather than keeping them constant.
- **Reduced feedback.** Delay or limit guidance rather than providing immediate correction.

As discussed in chapter 5, distributed practice and interleaving are also forms of spaced learning—the key distinction is that spaced learning focuses on "when and how often," while desirable difficulties focus on "how hard" the cognitive challenge should be. Table 14-4 shows how to apply these techniques across the three types of microlearning.

These conditions often slow immediate performance while improving long-term mastery. In microlearning, that trade-off must be carefully considered, especially when actions are short, time-sensitive, or deployed in high-pressure environments.

Now that we know something about desirable difficulties, let's make sure we know what they are not:

- **They are not inherently difficult tasks.** A challenge is beneficial only if the individual has enough foundational knowledge to engage productively.
- **They are not punitive.** The goal is never to trick or frustrate the participant; it's to create a mental stretch that strengthens retention.

Spacing and interleaving are delivery strategies that *can* create desirable difficulties when they require effortful retrieval, but not all spaced learning creates cognitive challenge.

Table 14-4. Desirable Difficulties and Microlearning Examples

Technique	How It Creates Desirable Difficulty	Microlearning Example
Retrieval practice	Requires effortful recall from memory rather than passive review, strengthening retrieval pathways through active cognitive work	After introducing three conflict resolution strategies, participants explain in their own words when each approach works best, without referring back to the content
Delayed practice	Introduces forgetting intervals that force effortful retrieval rather than easy recognition, requiring reconstruction of knowledge	Participants practice a customer service protocol on day 1, then return on day 4 to demonstrate the same protocol without review, which requires them to retrieve steps from memory
Mixed practice (interleaving)	Requires active discrimination between similar concepts by switching contexts, preventing automatic responses and forcing thoughtful selection	A branching scenario alternates between product feature questions and customer objection handling, requiring participants to identify which skill applies to each situation
Varied context	Forces transfer and adaptation by changing conditions, requiring flexible application rather than rote repetition	Participants apply the same safety checklist across three different work environments (e.g., warehouse, office, and outdoor site), adjusting their approach to each context
Reduced feedback	Increases cognitive demand by requiring self-monitoring and error detection rather than relying on immediate external correction	During repeated practice of a quality inspection procedure, guidance decreases with each iteration, requiring participants to self-check and catch their own errors

Why Desirable Difficulties Matter in Designing to Elicit Action

When we design microlearning actions that are too easy, many participants demonstrate immediate performance but don't retain or apply the skill later. This creates a false sense of success. In contrast, well-scaffolded challenges (such as a delayed self-check, a tricky decision point, or a task in a slightly unfamiliar context) require more effort but deepen learning.

As microlearning designers, our job is to balance efficiency with effectiveness. This requires a deliberate approach that doesn't shy away from effort but instead designs it intentionally. At the same time, we must avoid overloading the individual by scaffolding content appropriately. Most important, we should resist defaulting to comfort by aiming instead for productive growth.

Before finalizing an action, ask yourself three key questions that reveal whether you've created an appropriate challenge:

- Does this require the individual to retrieve, adapt, or apply knowledge?
- Is the challenge appropriate for the individual's current knowledge or skill level?
- Will this action seem hard now but help later?

If you answer yes to one or more of these questions, you may have introduced a desirable difficulty. If not, you may need to either simplify the task or add support before raising the challenge.

Application by Microlearning Type

Eliciting action isn't a one-size-fits-all design task. As we saw in the action spectrum, different action types serve different purposes. The type of microlearning product shapes how and when action is prompted. A knowledge-based module may call for quick reflection or recall, a skills-based experience might ask for guided decision making, and a performance-based tool needs to support the task directly, in real time.

In this section, we'll explore how action is designed differently across product types, using examples that demonstrate the progression from knowledge-based to performance-based microlearning.

Knowledge-Based Microlearning

As we've discussed, knowledge-based microlearning focuses on helping participants understand and remember information. While it's tempting to stop at content presentation, effective knowledge-based microlearning should elicit actions that strengthen retention and build connections to application.

Techniques to Elicit Action

Retrieval practice activities transform passive learning into active engagement by requiring participants to recall information from memory rather than simply reviewing it. These techniques leverage the *testing effect*, which occurs when the act of retrieval itself strengthens memory. Effective retrieval practices in microlearning include a range of approaches that progressively challenge recall abilities.

These begin with quick-recall challenges that ask participants to produce essential information without prompts and extend to "teach back" prompts that ask participants to explain concepts in their own words, through either recording or writing. Additional techniques include fill-in-the-blank activities that test recall of essential terminology or steps and spaced retrieval notifications that prompt participants to remember previously learned content at strategic intervals.

Building on retrieval practice, meaningful connection activities help build bridges between new information and existing knowledge, which in turn creates stronger mental models (also known as schema creation). These techniques support deeper processing by encouraging participants to engage in four key types of cognitive work:

- Reflecting on how new concepts relate to familiar ones through guided comparison prompts
- Identifying personal examples of abstract concepts to create emotional and contextual hooks
- Connecting theoretical knowledge to workplace scenarios through simple case applications
- Considering the implications or extensions of important principles through "What if?" questions

The progression continues with concept application activities, which provide structured opportunities to use new knowledge in simplified contexts before full practical application. These activities help participants test their understanding while building confidence through different approaches:

- **Simple scenario responses** that require applying specific facts or concepts
- **Sorting exercises** that require categorizing information according to principles
- **Pattern recognition activities** to identify concepts in realistic examples
- **Decision-making scenarios** with limited variables to focus on knowledge application

Design Considerations

When designing actions for knowledge-based microlearning, consider how to support motivation, build confidence, and develop flexible competence through a systematic approach that addresses each component strategically.

Begin by supporting motivation through clear connections between knowledge and application. Participants need to understand why information matters before they will engage meaningfully with it. Show workplace relevance early and often—where possible, provide options for participants to choose how to explore and demonstrate knowledge. This foundation enables you to progressively build confidence by starting with simple recall before moving to application. Structure activities so initial successes build confidence for more challenging actions later. Immediate feedback that confirms correct understanding helps participants feel secure in their knowledge foundation.

Finally, develop flexible competence by varying the contexts in which knowledge is applied. Show concepts in multiple scenarios to prevent overly narrow understanding. Because teaching reinforces comprehension, build in opportunities for participants to explain concepts to others (even hypothetically).

Common Pitfalls

Avoid common mistakes when designing knowledge-based microlearning actions. Three key pitfalls threaten the effectiveness of knowledge-based microlearning, each undermining action in different ways:

- **Mistaking content consumption for meaningful action is the most common pitfall.** Simply clicking through slides or watching videos is passive consumption, not action that builds capability. Always include activities that require participants to process and generate responses.
- **Neglecting real-world application results in inert knowledge that participants can recall but not use.** Even knowledge-based microlearning should include prompts about how information applies to real situations.
- **Focusing exclusively on memorization undermines long-term retention and transfer.** While some information must be

memorized, knowledge is more valuable if participants understand the principles and relationships that they can apply flexibly.

Skills-Based Microlearning

Skills-based microlearning focuses on helping participants develop and refine specific capabilities through targeted practice. Unlike knowledge-based approaches, skills development requires actually doing something: participants must perform actions that build procedural fluency and decision-making abilities.

Techniques to Elicit Action

Guided practice provides structured opportunities to perform skills with appropriate support that gradually diminishes. These techniques help participants build confidence through scaffolded experiences that systematically build capability. This approach includes step-by-step walk-throughs in which participants follow a process with guidance and demonstrations paired with immediate practice opportunities. The progression continues as competence grows and support systems are gradually removed. Additional practice on difficult skill components further supports competence before integration.

Building on guided practice, decision scenarios present situations that require participants to apply skills in context. These techniques strengthen decision making and adaptability through varied challenge types. These challenges include branching scenarios in which choices lead to different outcomes and "What would you do?" situations with multiple valid approaches. Problem-solving challenges based on realistic workplace situations and comparative exercises evaluating different approaches to similar situations can also add additional variety to your microlearning product.

Feedback loops complete the cycle by providing information about performance quality to guide participant improvement and help refine their skills. These mechanisms include immediate feedback highlighting specific elements of performance and model comparisons showing expert versus novice approaches. The process also incorporates guided self-assessment using structured criteria and peer feedback through simple, focused review frameworks.

Design Considerations

When designing actions for skills-based microlearning, consider how to build motivation, help participants progress toward confidence, and develop adaptable competence through a comprehensive design approach.

Build motivation by connecting skills development directly to performance outcomes. Show the gap between current and desired performance to create purposeful engagement. When possible, let participants choose which aspects of a skill to focus on first, which gives them a sense of ownership of the learning process. This foundation enables you to create safe practice environments before high-stakes application. Remember, early failures in public can dramatically diminish confidence, so practice opportunities should initially be private. Design early experiences for success while gradually introducing more challenging conditions.

Finally, develop adaptable competence by varying practice conditions. Many skills practiced in only one context fail to transfer to new situations. Include varied scenarios, conditions, and applications to build flexible capability rather than rigid procedure-following skills.

Common Pitfalls

Avoid a few of the most frequent mistakes that L&D pros make when designing skills-based microlearning actions. Here are the three most critical errors that can undermine skills-based microlearning effectiveness:

- **Providing insufficient practice opportunities.** Skills require repetition to develop, yet many microlearning solutions provide minimal practice. Offering multiple brief practice opportunities distributed over time is more effective than creating a single, longer session.
- **Creating unrealistic practice scenarios undermines transfer to real performance.** Practice that doesn't reflect actual workplace conditions often fails to improve on-the-job performance. Incorporate authentic constraints, pressures, and variables that exist in the real environment. (Don't forget to use the personas we discussed in chapter 10.)

- **Failing to isolate difficult skill components for focused practice can slow development.** Many complete skills have specific elements that cause the most errors or hesitation. Identify these components and create targeted micropractice opportunities before integrating the full skill.

Performance-Based Microlearning

Performance-based microlearning focuses on supporting immediate application in the workplace. Unlike knowledge or skills development, which happen outside workflow, performance support is accessed during the actual task or decision moment, so it requires different design approaches for action.

Performance-based microlearning supports real-time application while building capability over time. This distinguishes it from pure performance support tools like job aids or checklists, which assist with tasks but don't create learning opportunities. Effective performance-based microlearning gradually reduces support as individuals internalize procedures, whereas job aids remain constant resources for complex or infrequent tasks.

Techniques to Elicit Action

These techniques focus on performance-based microlearning that develops independence through progressive challenge, not permanent support tools.

- **Progressive guidance systems.** Progressive guidance provides support that decreases as capability develops, creating learning through increasing independence. Initial interactions offer detailed step-by-step instructions with rationale for each decision. As individuals demonstrate competence, guidance reduces to key decision points and critical safety checks. Eventually, support fades to minimal verification prompts, with detailed guidance available only when requested. This progression transforms external support into internalized capability, rather than creating permanent dependence on job aids.
- **Contextual practice prompts.** Contextual prompts create deliberate practice opportunities during actual work, building skill

through repeated application with varying challenge.

These prompts present realistic scenarios at natural work pauses, requiring individuals to demonstrate procedures or explain decisions before proceeding. Early prompts provide immediate feedback and correction; later prompts delay feedback to encourage self-monitoring. Scenarios progress from standard situations to edge cases, building flexible expertise rather than rote responses.

- **Adaptive performance triggers.** Adaptive triggers prompt action based on a demonstrated need rather than fixed schedules, creating desirable difficulty through varied context. The system identifies patterns in performance data and provides targeted prompts when specific situations arise. For experienced workers, triggers appear only for high-risk or infrequent procedures. For developing workers, triggers provide more frequent practice opportunities that gradually space out as competence improves. This adaptation ensures the cognitive challenge remains appropriate to the capability level.

- **Collaborative verification protocols.** Peer-based verification distributes learning while building collective competence through structured interaction. Partners verify critical procedures using protocols that require explanation rather than simple confirmation— forcing articulation of reasoning strengthens understanding. These protocols begin with detailed checklists that both partners complete, progress to spot-checking specific high-risk elements, and eventually become brief confirmations between trusted colleagues. The structure creates accountability while developing expertise through repeated explanation and observation.

Design Considerations

When designing actions for performance-based microlearning, consider how to ensure immediate value, balance guidance and workflow, and account for the physical and technological environment through careful design decisions.

Begin by ensuring immediate value by focusing on the most critical needs in the moment. Performance support must deliver clear benefits that outweigh the cost of pausing to use it. Design for the context and urgency of the work situation, not ideal conditions. Simultaneously, balance guidance and workflow by minimizing disruption to the primary task. Support should integrate seamlessly into work rather than feeling like an interruption. The best performance support feels like part of the task itself rather than an addition to it.

Finally, account for the physical and technical environment where performance happens by designing for actual conditions, whether that's a noisy factory floor, a customer-facing retail environment, or a field location with limited connectivity. Support that works perfectly in ideal conditions may fail completely under practical constraints.

Common Pitfalls

Avoid some of the most frequent mistakes that learning designers make when designing performance-based microlearning actions. These three missteps can render performance support ineffective:

- **Creating performance support that interrupts rather than enhances workflow.** This mistake can dramatically reduce usage because participants will skip the support if it takes too long to access or feels too separate from the task. Design products that accelerate work rather than delaying it.
- **Providing too much information at the moment of performance.** This can overwhelm participants, especially if they're already under pressure. Focus only on what's needed for the immediate task, saving deeper explanations for knowledge building outside the workflow.
- **Making access too complicated during time-sensitive tasks.** If support requires multiple steps to access or complicated navigation, participants will abandon the product and it won't be used when most needed. Ensure that support is immediately accessible with minimal effort, especially in high-pressure situations.

🐝 Designing Actions Across Learning Types

Be Natural's approach to action design demonstrates how desirable difficulties create meaningful engagement across knowledge-based and performance-based microlearning.

Knowledge-Based Microlearning: Product Understanding with Retrieval Practice

BN's retail and sales team members needed to learn complex ingredient profiles for natural beauty products. Rather than providing reference guides employees could consult whenever needed, the L&D team designed micro-learning to incorporate retrieval practice as a desirable difficulty.

New employees explored the product information for five minutes, then (without access to the original content) they recorded a 30-second expla-nation of why a customer might choose that product. This forced effortful retrieval rather than passive review. Three days later, employees received a two-minute challenge asking them to recall the same product's key ben-efits and recommend it for a specific customer scenario, again without reviewing the material first. The delay created partial forgetting, requiring cognitive effort to reconstruct the information.

Results showed that employees using this retrieval-based approach re-tained product knowledge significantly better than those using traditional reference materials, and they also demonstrated greater confidence during actual customer interactions.

Performance-Based Microlearning: Safety Procedures With Reduced Feedback

BN's manufacturing team needed to internalize critical safety procedures for new packaging equipment. The L&D team created a performance-based approach incorporating reduced feedback as a desirable difficulty.

During the first week, operators practiced safety procedures with imme-diate step-by-step guidance displayed on tablets at their workstations. In week 2, guidance appeared only at critical decision points and operators had to recall the intermediate steps independently. By week 3, the system provided only a starting prompt and final verification checklist, requiring operators to execute the entire procedure from memory and self-monitor for errors.

This progressive withdrawal of support created increasing cognitive demand, forcing operators to develop independence and error detection skills rather than relying on external guidance. Safety incident rates for the new equipment decreased compared with traditional training approaches.

Common Challenges and How to Overcome Them

Even with the best intentions, implementing action-oriented microlearning presents challenges. Let's examine common obstacles and practical approaches to address them. Because you may also be dealing with an overarching challenge of resource constraints—whether related to the L&D department or the authoring or delivery platforms—I also offer some work-arounds for each challenge.

Stakeholder Resistance to Action-Based Learning

Many stakeholders misunderstand microlearning, believing that simply delivering small, "one and done" pieces of content is sufficient for learning transfer. This misconception leads them to question investments in action-oriented designs because they assume brief exposure to information should be enough for participants to apply it on the job.

Here's what you can do: Use data and demonstration to build buy-in while connecting to strategic outcomes identified in your MLR Framework. Try these approaches:

- Present research showing the performance gap between passive content consumption and active learning.
- Create small pilot implementations that measure both completion and application.
- Develop before-and-after comparisons showing how action-oriented approaches improve performance metrics that stakeholders already value.
- Frame conversations around business outcomes rather than learning activities.

If your resources are tight, try this work-around: Start small by creating peer-supported action pathways. When participants support one another through structured, low-tech activities, you build a microculture of growth without overloading L&D teams or requiring new systems. This approach can include several practical options:

- Action cards or conversation starters that fit into a stand-up meeting and reflection guides that teams can use during weekly huddles
- Brief practice prompts embedded into shift hand-offs or Slack threads
- Lightweight tools to distribute responsibility, support spaced learning, and normalize ongoing action as part of everyday routines

Lack of Support for Sustained Action Progression

Many organizations struggle to implement microlearning that truly elicits action because stakeholders often default to self-contained, one-time learning experiences that fit neatly within existing systems, especially LMSs. While these systems are effective for delivering content and tracking completion, they rarely support the kind of progressive, multitouchpoint actions that build real competence.

This tendency often reflects an organizational culture that values "checked boxes" over behavioral change and quick fixes over sustained development. As a result, even well-intentioned microlearning efforts can stall when they lack the scaffolding needed to support ongoing action and reflection.

Here's what you can do: To move past this limitation, it's essential to address both culture and capacity using the MLR Framework as a foundation. Try these approaches:

- Identify cultural champions who already value continuous growth and applied learning—bonus if they're outside the L&D function.
- Link progressive action to existing organizational values such as excellence, safety, innovation, or customer care.
- Showcase small wins. Create quick case studies or feedback loops that demonstrate the impact of sustained action over time.
- Design within reach. Instead of introducing brand-new systems, look for existing team meetings, feedback cycles, or manager check-ins that can support action progression.

If your resources are tight, try this work-around: Design peer-supported action progression where participants guide one another through structured activities. This builds a microculture of sustained development within teams while distributing the facilitation burden. Create simple tools such as action cards, reflection guides, or practice prompts that can be used in pairs or small groups during scheduled meetings or breaks.

These suggestions acknowledge that organizational culture plays a significant role in how actions are supported and valued, which may be an even more fundamental challenge than capacity limitations in many organizations.

Difficulty Orchestrating Progressive Actions Across Campaigns

Organizations can struggle to maintain coherence among multiple microlearning products, particularly when they form part of an extended campaign. This difficulty stems from several factors: the misconception that microlearning should be one-and-done, self-contained experiences; limited understanding of spaced learning principles (as outlined in the MLR Framework); and insufficient mapping and planning processes to coordinate actions across products. (See appendix A for help thinking through that.) Without deliberate orchestration, actions become isolated events rather than progressive steps that build capability over time.

Here's what you can do: Create a comprehensive action-mapping strategy that draws on spaced learning principles from the MLR Framework. Try these approaches:

- Develop documents that map how actions connect and build across multiple microlearning products. Sometimes, all you need is a simple table.
- Ensure that each action builds progressively on previous ones, enhancing motivation, confidence, and competence as introduced earlier in this chapter.
- Create clear connections between microlearning actions and on-the-job application opportunities where relevant.
- Review your complete sequence of planned actions across all products to identify missing elements or unnecessary repetition.

If your resources are tight, try this work-around: Start by identifying just three to five specific microlearning activities that directly support the primary learning outcomes of your campaign. For example, if your campaign focuses on customer service skills, you might prioritize activities for active listening, managing difficult conversations, and finding solutions. Create a flowchart showing how these few activities build up one another. Focus your limited resources on designing these activities effectively rather than creating numerous disconnected experiences.

🐝 Overcoming Technology Constraints in Leadership Training at BN

Be Natural's leadership development program focused on essential leadership skills, with giving effective feedback as a critical component. The original program included interactive videos, a simple diagram showing the key steps of giving effective feedback, and audio examples to help leaders practice and improve their feedback skills. This approach worked well for office-based leaders, but extending the training to manufacturing team leaders created challenges.

Manufacturing supervisors faced several practical constraints in implementing this program, including:

- Limited computer access during shifts (only two tablets were available for use on the factory floor)
- Noisy environments that made audio difficult to hear
- Poor network connectivity on the factory floor
- Company policies restricting personal devices in certain areas

These constraints were discovered when working through the implementation dimension of the MLR Framework. Rather than creating a completely different training program, BN's L&D team developed a practical hybrid approach.

First, they identified which feedback skills would have the biggest impact on team performance. Then, they created two complementary learning opportunities:

- **Durable laminated cards with QR codes that supervisors could scan during breaks.** These codes displayed simple text-based scenarios and practice activities that worked even with poor connectivity.
- **Leadership huddles of structured 15-minute discussions during shift changes.** Supervisors practiced giving feedback to one another on real workplace situations using pocket reference cards.

This approach maintained the practice-focused nature of the original program while working within the manufacturing environment's limitations. Within three months, employee feedback scores from manufacturing teams improved and were more aligned with the results seen in teams outside of manufacturing using the full technology solution.

This example shows how understanding your available tools (Principle 1), your work environment (Principle 2), and the need for globally equitable solutions (Principle 3) helps you create effective learning opportunities despite constraints. By focusing on the most important skills and providing practical ways to practice them, BN achieved strong results while adapting to manufacturing's specific workplace realities.

Chapter Summary

Throughout this chapter, we've seen how intentionally designed actions build both confidence and competence. Using an agency framework—focusing on motivation, confidence, and competence—provides a blueprint for creating microlearning that inspires meaningful engagement.

Desirable difficulties, when thoughtfully incorporated, strengthen learning by creating productive challenges that enhance long-term retention and transfer. In addition, different microlearning types require distinct approaches to action: Knowledge-based solutions benefit from reflection and retrieval practice, skills-based solutions thrive on guided practice with feedback, and performance-based solutions need streamlined support at the moment of need.

By applying these principles within the constraints of your organizational environment and technological capabilities, you can design microlearning that doesn't just inform, but transforms knowledge into action and improves performance in ways that align with strategic business outcomes.

Looking Ahead

The next chapter explores Principle 7, Avoid Overuse, examining how to prevent excessive application of microlearning approaches and techniques. Now that we've designed experiences that elicit meaningful action, we'll explore how to maintain balance—ensuring that our microlearning strategy remains focused and effective rather than becoming diluted through overextension.

VISR Project Check-In

Take a moment to connect this principle to the microlearning project you selected for the part 2 opening activity. Use the VISR reflection framework to evaluate how the principle of eliciting action applies specifically to your project.

Validate

- What moments in your current microlearning solution require learners to actively do something versus simply receive information?
- Are participants actively engaging with the content in ways that build both confidence and competence?
- Does your design incorporate appropriate levels of challenge?

Innovate

- If you're designing a campaign to build knowledge or skills, where could desirable difficulties create productive challenge?
- Could you add retrieval practice, varied conditions, or meaningful challenges that enhance long-term retention and application?

Spark

- Where could you replace content consumption with actions that require learners to think, decide, practice, or apply?
- Could gamification elements, reflection prompts, or peer feedback mechanisms enhance engagement while building agency?

Refine

- How does your microlearning solution connect to application in a workplace context?
- What simple adjustments could help bridge the gap between what employees do in training and what they need to do on the job?
- What desirable difficulties could you introduce to strengthen motivation, confidence, or competence in your current microlearning design?

CHAPTER 15
Principle 7: Avoid Overuse

By the end of this chapter, you should be able to answer these questions:
- What are the characteristics of overuse, and how does it lead to desensitization in microlearning?
- How can you create meaningful variety in your microlearning designs without overwhelming participants?
- What strategies help you avoid "page-turner" experiences and generic template traps?
- How does overuse affect cognitive processing and engagement?
- What signs indicate you might be overusing specific microlearning principles?

As we conclude our discussion of the seven principles that will help you maximize the power of microlearning, I have one more cooking analogy to share that relates well to this final principle and the delicate balance required in cooking, as well as microlearning. Most of us wouldn't mash potatoes without salt, pepper, and butter—but too much of any ingredient can ruin the dish. Similarly, if we serve the same potato recipe repeatedly, our dinner guests might start seeking variety or simply stop coming to the table. By occasionally introducing thoughtful variations—perhaps some chives or rosemary, or a splash of chicken broth—we can keep the dish interesting while maintaining its essential character.

The same principle applies to microlearning. Organizations frequently discover that after successfully implementing their first microlearning initiatives, they begin applying the same formula to every learning need. L&D teams develop a successful template that soon becomes overused, leading to what participants describe as "yet another page-turner," just in shorter form. The familiarity breeds complacency, and participants slip into *cognitive autopilot*—clicking through without meaningful engagement. When formats become predictable, participants' brains no longer fully activate to process the content, reducing learning effectiveness despite well-crafted material.

Avoiding overuse means deliberately introducing meaningful variety into your microlearning strategies, thoughtfully varying formats, approaches, and interactions to prevent desensitization. Your goal isn't constant novelty, but strategic variation that maintains coherence across your learning ecosystem while keeping participants cognitively engaged. Avoiding overuse means moving beyond generic templates to create experiences that stimulate different aspects of learning, capture attention in fresh ways, and support knowledge transfer through diverse presentation methods.

You must learn to recognize when familiarity has crossed into predictability—when participants no longer fully engage because they've become desensitized to your approach. This desensitization isn't just a result of repetitive formats; it can occur with interaction patterns, visual styles, delivery schedules, or assessment methods that have become too predictable.

This seventh principle completes our design principles by ensuring your microlearning remains effective over time.

Rather than operating in isolation, avoiding overuse works with every principle we've explored: It pushes you to use the full range of your tools' capabilities instead of defaulting to familiar features, encourages you to use a variety of approaches to match changing contextual needs, recognizes that different audiences need different approaches, ensures concise presentation doesn't become formulaic, supports rotating media formats while maintaining purposefulness, and promotes varying engagement patterns rather than repeating identical interactions.

Without this principle, even the most carefully designed microlearning becomes predictable through repetitive implementation. When participants can anticipate exactly what comes next, they shift from deep processing to surface-level engagement—clicking through content without meaningful cognitive effort.

In this chapter, we'll explore how to recognize when you're slipping into overuse. We'll examine the cognitive science behind desensitization and practical frameworks for introducing strategic variety. Through examples from Be Natural and other organizations, you'll learn to create microlearning that remains fresh and effective by varying your approach while still honoring the principles we've explored throughout this book.

Understanding the Principle

Overuse in microlearning occurs when the same formats, patterns, interactions, or approaches are repeated so frequently that participants become desensitized to them. You don't need to abandon effective approaches; you can introduce strategic variety, however, to maintain engagement while preserving the benefits of familiarity.

Overuse manifests in several ways that can compound negative effects:

- **Template overuse** occurs when organizations use identical layouts, sequences, or structures across all microlearning products, creating a predictable visual and navigational experience that participants can complete without conscious attention.
- **Delivery method overuse** involves consistently delivering microlearning through the same platform or channel so participants approach each new learning opportunity with the same mental framework and expectations. This further desensitizes the individual from the start.
- **Interaction pattern overuse** develops when teams repeatedly use the same types of activities or assessments, leading participants to engage in familiar response patterns rather than fresh thinking.
- **Media overuse** happens when organizations rely on a single media type—such as always using video or always using text—preventing engagement of different cognitive processing channels and learning preferences.
- **Scheduling overuse** creates predictability through rigid, unchanging timelines that allow participants to mentally prepare for

learning time rather than encountering learning as an integrated part of their workflow.

The danger in each case isn't the consistency itself; in fact, consistency often benefits learning by reducing extraneous cognitive load. The danger lies in the cognitive disengagement that results when participants can predict every aspect of the experience. If participants can anticipate exactly what will happen next, their brains shift from active processing to autopilot, fundamentally undermining the learning process regardless of content quality.

The Science of Learning and Overuse

When we discussed CLT in chapter 8, we focused primarily on how working memory limitations affect individual learning experiences. But overuse introduces two additional cognitive challenges that operate differently.

Cognitive overload is immediate and task specific. It occurs when working memory capacity is exceeded during a single learning experience. Signs include confusion, frustration, and inability to process new information.

Cognitive fatigue, however, develops over time through repeated exposure to similar stimuli. Unlike overload, fatigue doesn't necessarily impair immediate understanding. Instead, it gradually reduces our depth of processing, motivation to engage, attention to detail, and ability to transfer learning to real-world situations (Behrens et al. 2023). Cognitive fatigue affects these processes in several ways:

- **Depth of processing.** When microlearning formats become too predictable, participants might skim through text or click "next" without truly processing information, like automatically clicking through a familiar quiz format without considering the questions carefully.
- **Motivation to engage.** A sales team initially excited about a new microlearning campaign, for instance, might gradually lose interest when every product follows exactly the same pattern. By the fifth microlearning product, the team is completing it merely to check a box rather than with genuine curiosity.
- **Attention to detail.** Manufacturing safety training that always uses the same scenario format, for example, might cause participants to

miss critical safety warnings because they've begun to skim familiar-looking content.

Research in cognitive psychology also shows that repeated exposure to similar stimuli leads to *habituation*—a decreased response to familiar patterns. When participants can predict exactly what will happen in a microlearning experience, their brains no longer fully activate to process the content. This isn't because they lack interest in the subject matter, but because predictability triggers automatic, rather than deliberate, processing. For example, onboarding training that becomes predictable might be completed successfully (participants pass all the quizzes), but when faced with real customer interactions, new employees struggle to apply what they've learned.

The paradox for microlearning designers is clear: The very templates and patterns that make our solutions efficient to produce and easy to navigate can ultimately reduce their effectiveness through desensitization.

Key Ways to Avoid Overuse

By understanding several key ways to avoid overuse, you can make more informed decisions about when, how, and for whom to introduce variations in your microlearning design.

Introduce Strategic Variety

Avoiding overuse requires introducing thoughtful variations that refresh engagement without creating confusion or unnecessary complexity. The ultimate goal is *cognitive refreshment*—reactivating attention and engagement by introducing variations that require active processing. This can be achieved in several ways:

- **Employ novel challenges.** Presenting unexpected problems or scenarios that require new thinking and prevent participants from relying on automatic responses
- **Change interaction patterns.** Varying how participants engage with content (from clicking to dragging, typing to speaking, or response-based to reflective) to maintain attention and prevent mechanical completion

- **Vary media formats.** Alternating between text, images, audio, video, and interactive elements to engage different processing channels and maintain interest
- **Adjust delivery contexts.** Changing when and where microlearning appears (in workflows, during scheduled times, or triggered by events) to prevent participants from tuning out familiar patterns
- **Alternative assessment approaches.** Switching between different ways of checking knowledge, skills, and performance (multiple choice, scenarios, peer discussion, and application tasks) to encourage deeper processing

By incorporating these refreshment techniques, you can create *productive unpredictability*—enough consistency for cognitive efficiency, but enough variation to prevent automatic processing. Plan this variation intentionally, considering which elements benefit from consistency (such as navigation patterns) and which need regular refreshment (such as scenarios or interaction types).

Balance Variety and Consistency

Finding the right balance between variety and consistency is perhaps the most challenging aspect of avoiding overuse. Too much consistency breeds familiarity and disengagement; too much variety creates confusion and cognitive overload.

Successful balance requires understanding which elements benefit from consistency versus those that need strategic variation. Navigation patterns, terminology, branding elements, and basic interaction models should remain consistent to reduce extraneous cognitive load, creating a reliable foundation that participants can navigate without conscious effort. Conversely, content presentation, scenario contexts, media formats, and assessment approaches benefit from thoughtful variation to maintain engagement, preventing the predictability that leads to automatic processing.

In addition, timing and frequency matter significantly in implementing variation. Consider introducing at least one significant variation every two to three products in a campaign, ensuring changes are noticeable enough to reactivate attention without creating confusion. For long-term initiatives, plan more substantial refreshes quarterly to prevent long-term fatigue while maintaining program coherence.

Coherence across variations serves as the unifying thread that prevents variety from becoming chaos. Use visual or thematic elements to maintain a sense of unity even as you vary other components. For example, Be Natural maintained consistent branding while varying interaction models across its onboarding campaign, demonstrating how strategic consistency enables effective variation.

🐝 Leadership Development Refresh: Implementing Strategic Variety

When Be Natural experienced rapid growth, the company created a leadership development program designed entirely using microlearning campaigns to accommodate busy schedules while building future leadership talent. Despite this thoughtful approach, the program began showing classic signs of overuse about eight months after implementation.

The L&D team noticed several concerning patterns:

- Declining session feedback as initial enthusiasm gave way to lukewarm responses
- Superficial engagement with participants completing products faster than expected
- Limited real-world application despite leaders being able to recite principles
- Diminishing discussion board participation
- Increasingly similar action plan submissions (suggesting templated responses rather than genuine thinking)

The issue wasn't the content itself but the delivery pattern. Every product followed the exact same format—introduction video, text-based screens, reflective activity, and multiple-choice check-in—creating a predictable rhythm that no longer actively engaged participants' cognitive processes.

Strategic Variety Implementation

Instead of completely redesigning the program, BN's L&D team implemented strategic variety while maintaining core leadership principles and learning objectives. They developed a multifaceted approach:

- **Delivery variations alternated between different approaches.** The team interspersed traditional e-learning modules with brief virtual peer discussions. They also transformed text-based products into interactive infographics and scenario-based decision points, podcast-style audio learning for commutes, and occasional five-minute video conferences at milestone points.
- **Contextual enhancements replaced generic scenarios with rotating business situations relevant to BN.** Real company challenges were anonymized and incorporated, participants contributed scenarios through a simple submission tool, and advanced participants received more nuanced scenarios with greater complexity.
- **Assessment diversity moved beyond standard multiple-choice.** The team alternated self-assessments with peer feedback activities, coaching, brief video response options, micro-application assignments, and leadership challenge simulations providing two-minute skill practice opportunities.
- **Responsive delivery made contextual adjustments.** The team achieved this by triggering some content through specific business events rather than calendar scheduling, providing supervisors with reinforcement guides, offering self-directed path choices, and ensuring mobile-first accessibility across contexts.
- **Delivery initiation balance strategically mixed push and pull approaches.** Some of the content was scheduled and delivered to leaders (weekly leadership insights pushed via email), while other resources could be accessed on-demand (conflict resolution guides available through searchable library). This balance prevented notification fatigue while ensuring critical developmental content reached everyone.

Outcomes and Lessons Learned

BN's strategic approach yielded meaningful improvements including more consistent leadership approaches across departments, fewer escalated team conflicts, and a strengthened leadership pipeline as employees voluntarily participated before formal promotion consideration. They described the refreshed program as more relevant to their daily work, with many read-ily applying concepts from the microlearning campaigns in novel situations.

The L&D team learned valuable lessons about balancing consistency (in program objectives, leadership principles, and quality standards) and variety (in the delivery methods, contexts, media formats, and assessment approaches). This allowed the team to introduce productive unpredictability without sacrificing the coherence of the learning experience.

Monitor Engagement Patterns

Effective avoidance of overuse requires actively monitoring engagement patterns, or how participants interact with your microlearning ecosystem over time. Unlike traditional training, which might focus only on completion and assessment scores, a strategic approach to avoiding overuse requires tracking multiple engagement indicators, including:

- **Completion rates over time.** Unlike traditional training completion rates that measure whether participants finish a single program, this metric tracks how completion rates change across similar products in a microlearning campaign to identify engagement fatigue patterns. Watch for declining completion rates across similar products or within a campaign. If your first product has a 95 percent completion rate but that drops to 60 percent by the fifth, it may indicate engagement fatigue rather than content difficulty.
- **Performance on similar assessments.** Compare performance across products using similar assessment approaches. Consistently high scores with decreasing time spent might indicate that participants are going through the motions rather than engaging deeply. This pattern often indicates insufficient cognitive challenge; participants may need assessments that better elicit action (Principle 6) through desirable difficulties, varied formats, or increased complexity.
- **Time spent with different product types.** Analyze whether participants spend appropriate time with each product type. Unusually quick completion of what should be comfortably challenging activities signals potential disengagement.

- **Participant feedback about engagement.** Directly ask about the learning experience through short pulse surveys. Questions like "Did this seem different from previous products in the campaign?" can reveal a perception of sameness.
- **Signs of autopilot learning versus engagement.** Look for patterns that suggest mindless clicking versus deliberate interaction. For example, consistent response times across varied complexity levels often indicate automatic processing and question if the complexity is really there.

Measure Learning, Not Just Engagement

Try to avoid the trap of mistaking activity for achievement. When assessing potential overuse, distinguish between surface-level engagement metrics and real learning outcomes. A participant might diligently complete every microlearning product in your campaign (high engagement metrics) while processing the content so superficially that little knowledge transfer occurs (poor learning outcomes).

For example, in a pharmaceutical sales training program, representatives might complete all brand-focused knowledge in the microlearning campaign with perfect scores yet struggle to explain important differences among medications when speaking with providers. This gap between completion and application often signals that cognitive fatigue has led to superficial processing.

This fatigue may stem from repetitive microlearning patterns or from the work environment itself (Principle 2). Remember, high mental load, stress, or demanding contexts can push learners toward autopilot completion rather than deep engagement.

Be Aware of Pattern Tolerance

Understanding your audience's characteristics is crucial for effective variation. Not all participants experience overuse fatigue at the same rate or in the same ways, so there are some things to keep in mind:

- **Prior knowledge plays a role in fatigue.** Experts (seasoned or senior employees) often detect patterns more quickly than novices (junior employees or new hires) and may become disengaged sooner with repetitive formats. For mixed-expertise audiences, consider optional complexity paths.

- **People adapt based on learning preferences.** While some participants value consistency and predictability, others seek novelty. If possible, offer some elements of choice in how content is experienced.
- **Some people need accommodation for cognitive differences.** Participants who process information holistically versus sequentially may respond differently to pattern variations. Ensure that your variation strategy accommodates different cognitive approaches.
- **Others need adjustments for job context.** In high-stress environments such as emergency medicine or air-traffic control, consistency in training format may actually be beneficial, allowing cognitive resources to focus entirely on content rather than navigating unfamiliar structures.

Application by Microlearning Type

In previous chapters, separate discussions of knowledge-based, skills-based, and performance-based microlearning served us well, but for a chapter on avoiding overuse, it presents an interesting opportunity.

Rather than falling into a predictable pattern—which would ironically demonstrate the very problem we're trying to avoid—I'm taking a different approach here. Just as you should occasionally refresh your microlearning formats to prevent habituation, I refreshed our chapter format to model the principle in action. The comprehensive BN case study demonstrates strategic variety applications for both knowledge-based and performance-based microlearning. Skills-based variety, while equally important, follows similar principles of varying practice scenarios, feedback mechanisms, and skill-building progression concepts thoroughly explored in previous chapters.

Chapter Summary

Avoiding overuse in microlearning is essential for maintaining engagement without sacrificing learning effectiveness. Throughout this chapter, we've explored how:

- Overuse leads to desensitization, causing participants to engage on autopilot rather than with meaningful cognitive processing. This happens when templates, formats, or delivery patterns become too predictable.
- Cognitive science indicates that overload and fatigue affect learning differently. Overload overwhelms participants in the moment, while fatigue erodes engagement over time through repetitive experiences.
- Different microlearning types require different approaches to variety. Knowledge-based solutions benefit from differing information representation and performance-based solutions from variations in at-the-moment-of-need support, while skills-based variety (although not detailed in this chapter) follows similar principles.
- Strategic variety isn't about constant novelty, but purposeful variation that maintains coherence while refreshing engagement. This means making intentional decisions about what to vary and when.
- Signs of potential overuse include declining completion rates, reduced assessment performance over time, and participant feedback indicating monotony or predictability.

The principle of avoiding overuse completes our design framework by ensuring that well-crafted microlearning experiences remain effective over time. By introducing variety while maintaining consistency in key areas, you can create microlearning that continually engages participants' cognitive processes rather than merely capturing their clicks.

Looking Ahead

As we conclude our exploration of microlearning design principles, we shift our focus from crafting effective individual experiences to implementing successful microlearning initiatives across your organization. In part 3, we will explore how pilot programs serve as both validation tools and learning opportunities—providing concrete data that informs both the MLR Framework and your design approach.

The principle of avoiding overuse becomes especially important as you scale because patterns that might be barely noticeable in a single product become amplified across an entire learning ecosystem. Whether you're validating existing approaches, testing variations of a principle such as avoiding overuse, or launching something entirely new, pilot programs establish crucial baseline data that connects back to every aspect we've covered. This data helps you assess organizational readiness (part 1) while refining your application of design principles (part 2), creating a continuous improvement cycle that strengthens your microlearning strategy over time.

VISR Project Check-In

Take a moment to connect this principle to the microlearning project you selected for the part 2 opening activity. Use the VISR reflection framework to evaluate how the principle of avoiding overuse applies specifically to your project.

Validate
- Does your approach rely too heavily on a single format or interaction pattern?
- If you're improving existing microlearning, what patterns might participants already be tired of?
- If you're converting traditional training, are you simply shortening without adding variety?
- For new initiatives, have you considered how to build sustainable variation from the start?

Innovate
- Based on your identified audience and constraints, how might you introduce meaningful variety?
- If you're working with limited tools (as noted in your constraints), what creative variations are still possible?
- How could you rotate among different approaches while working within your technical limitations?

Spark
- What new possibilities emerge when considering your desired outcome through the lens of variety?
- For knowledge-based solutions, could different representation formats enhance retention?
- For skills-based learning, might varied practice scenarios deepen mastery?
- For performance support, could contextual variations better aid real-world application?

Refine
- How might you incorporate strategic variety specifically for your target audience and their context?
- What specific element in your current plan could benefit from thoughtful variation to avoid future desensitization?

Remember that avoiding overuse isn't about constant novelty; it's about strategic variety that maintains engagement while respecting your participants' need for some consistency and familiarity.

PART 3

Launching Microlearning

Part 1 helped you assess your organizational readiness, and part 2 provided design principles tied to foundational theories of learning. Part 3 focuses on implementation: how to launch microlearning through pilot programs, measure their impact, and scale what works. I hope this final section will serve all readers, whether you have read the book sequentially or only part 1 or 2.

This final section provides practical guidance for moving from assessment and design to actual implementation. The approaches presented here are tested frameworks from my practice that you can adapt to your organizational context. While I can't account for every variable you might encounter, these tools and strategies will give you a solid foundation for launching microlearning initiatives that align with your current capabilities and build toward more ambitious goals.

Opening Activity: Preparing to Pilot

If you worked through the part 2 opening activity, you identified and refined a microlearning project through seven design principles using the VISR framework. Part 3 will help you pilot that project.

If you're starting here, you'll need to do some foundational work before you can continue:

- **You need a specific project to pilot.** The opening activity in part 2 will help you define your project type, target audience, desired outcomes, and constraints.
- **You need to understand your organizational readiness.** The part 1 opening activity provides this foundation by helping to clarify what microlearning means to your organization and what you hope it will address.
- **You need to understand the different microlearning types.** Chapter 1 establishes these definitions and explores microlearning as a concept, method, and product.

Once you have this foundation in place, chapter 16 will help you design effective pilots, understand different pilot types, track capacity, measure impact, and scale successful approaches. For a complete set of implementation tools, including the Microlearning Campaign Blueprint and Microlearning Product Design Guide, see Appendix A.

Microlearning Is a Journey, Not a Race

What I've learned about implementing microlearning effectively is that the most enduring initiatives start small, are adjusted through experimentation, and scale strategically based on results, creating a journey of continuous improvement. Pilot programs provide a low-risk way to test and validate your approach before committing significant resources, helping you understand not only whether your microlearning design works, but whether your organization can realistically support it.

Microlearning success grows through cycles of piloting, learning, and scaling over time. Chapter 16 will show you how to navigate this journey strategically, connecting back to your readiness assessment from part 1 and the design principles you explored in part 2.

CHAPTER 16
Pilots, Plans, and Impact

> By the end of this chapter, you should be able to answer these questions:
> - How do you connect implementation back to your assessment and design principles?
> - What implementation approaches best align with your organization's readiness level?
> - How can you use pilot programs to test and refine your microlearning approach?
> - What metrics should you use to measure the impact of your microlearning initiatives?
> - How do you move from successful pilot programs to comprehensive microlearning strategies?

Have you ever watched a chef develop a new recipe for their restaurant? They don't immediately add it to the menu and serve it to hundreds of customers. Instead, they create small test batches, gathering feedback from trusted staff, adjusting ingredients and techniques, and scaling up production only after they've refined the recipe to perfection. The chef understands that testing in a controlled environment allows for low-risk experimentation, iterative improvement, and confidence before full-scale implementation.

This same approach applies to microlearning implementation. Rather than immediately launching organization-wide initiatives, the most successful L&D teams typically start with focused pilot programs that allow for experimentation, learning, and refinement before scaling. When you create numerous small learning pieces without strategic alignment and then throw them at the wall like spaghetti to see what sticks, you're more likely to feel "burned" by microlearning when it doesn't work for your organization.

Pilot microlearning programs can provide a more intentional middle ground between theoretical design and full implementation. They give you valuable data while limiting risk and building organizational capability, which can turn random experimentation into evidence-based practice.

Throughout parts 1 and 2, we explored how to assess your organization's readiness for microlearning and how to apply sound design principles to actual microlearning campaigns and products. Now, in this final chapter, we'll bridge theory with practice by examining how pilot programs serve as both validation tools and learning opportunities—providing concrete data that will inform your MLR Framework assessment (chapters 2–7) and your design approach. We'll explore different types of pilot programs, how to measure their impact, and how to use what you learn to build comprehensive microlearning strategies. The pilot approaches and implementation strategies in this chapter represent tested frameworks from my own experience helping organizations launch microlearning. Every organization has unique variables I can't account for, so consider them as starting points you can adapt to your specific context, constraints, and goals.

I recommend pilot programs because they are not only a way to test content, design, and impact, but they also offer a chance to determine relatively quickly if your L&D team has the skills and bandwidth to scale microlearning initiatives. Running a pilot program can reveal where your team's current capacity might fall short and where capabilities are strong but underleveraged. It can also help you recognize the areas where your organization is less capable or less culturally open. Pilot programs also allow for iterative adjustments. If you haven't completed the part 3 opening activity, consider doing so first to clarify your implementation approach before diving into pilot strategies.

Whether you're conducting your first microlearning pilot program or refining your approach based on previous implementations, this chapter will help you connect the insights from your organizational assessment and design principles to practical implementation strategies that create measurable impact. Where you need deeper understanding of underlying principles—like learning science foundations or detailed assessment methodology—I'll point you to relevant chapters that provide that depth.

Let's take a look at Be Natural's complete implementation journey. This illustrates how the concepts around pilot programs, planning, and impact work together as an integrated approach.

🐝 Be Natural's Strategic Pilot Approach to Microlearning Implementation

When BN began its microlearning journey, the company faced multiple performance challenges across different departments. Rather than launching organization-wide initiatives, the organization's L&D team adopted a systematic pilot approach that demonstrated the strategic value of testing, measuring, and scaling microlearning implementations.

Phase 1. Converting Existing Content—The PPE Safety Pilot Program

BN's microlearning implementation began when the company faced declining personal protective equipment (PPE) compliance. The safety data told a compelling story: Minor incidents were increasing, especially in teams with newly promoted supervisors, while safety attitude surveys averaged only 2.4 out of 5. Teams with higher safety violations consistently missed their quarterly bonuses, which included safety metrics as a component. Rather than implementing formal remediation, the company chose to test a microlearning campaign that addressed issues identified in the data.

The pilot program converted specific sections of the comprehensive safety training course into five targeted products focusing on proper PPE standards, peer-to-peer safety conversations, safety's impact on teammates, bonus implications of violations, and efficiency benefits of proper PPE. This level-setting approach aimed to test whether microlearning could improve both safety metrics and sentiment scores before investing in converting additional training content.

The pilot program incorporated multiple approaches (including pensive, persuasive, performance, and practice) to address both compliance behaviors and enforcement challenges, while connecting safety directly to tangible outcomes such as quarterly bonuses. The campaign converted traditional safety content into practical microlearning activities that were delivered during daily safety huddles, with magnetic cutouts and visual prompts to reinforce learning in the work environment. This strategic approach worked because it provided measurable evidence of impact before committing to larger content conversion efforts.

Phase 2. Complementing Current Training—Sales Team Development

Building on the success of the safety pilot program, BN expanded its approach to sales team development. The L&D team created a microlearning campaign to extend the company's quarterly product knowledge workshops by implementing six weeks of spaced microlearning to reinforce key product features and provide scenario-based practice. This pilot program tested whether microlearning reinforcement improved knowledge retention and application without disrupting the existing training approach. The results demonstrated how microlearning could enhance rather than replace existing effective training programs by building organizational confidence in the approach while validating capabilities for more advanced implementations.

Phase 3. Developing New Initiatives—Customer Service Enhancement

As BN's capabilities grew, the company moved to address performance gaps that traditional training hadn't covered. For example, a microlearning campaign on empathetic communication was developed to address customer service issues identified in quarterly reviews. This pilot program tested whether microlearning could effectively address a specific performance gap without requiring a comprehensive training program. The results demonstrated the organization's growing sophistication in identifying opportunities for microlearning to fill gaps that formal training programs had missed.

Phase 4. Testing Technology and Delivery Approaches—Platform Evaluation

With proven content approaches established, BN turned to optimizing delivery mechanisms. When considering a new learning technology platform, the L&D team created identical microlearning content and then delivered it through three different mechanisms:

- The existing LMS
- A dedicated microlearning app
- Manager facilitated team discussions

This pilot program helped the company determine which delivery approach generated the most engagement and retention before investing in new technology. It demonstrates how successful content pilot programs can create a foundation for informed infrastructure decisions.

Phase 5. Supporting Self-Driven Development—Leadership Advancement

BN's most complex pilot program tested autonomous learning approaches. For the BN leadership development program, the L&D team tested a library of on-demand microlearning products that managers could access as needed versus a structured sequence delivered on a predetermined schedule. This pilot program helped BN understand the balance between structure and autonomy that would best serve its leadership development goals.

Strategic Impact and Scaling Insights

This unified approach shows how strategic piloting creates a pathway from initial testing to comprehensive microlearning strategies, with each phase informing and strengthening the organization's overall microlearning capability:

- Validate different implementation approaches from content conversion to new initiative development.
- Build organizational capabilities systematically so each phase builds on previous successes.
- Test technology and delivery methods based on proven content strategies.
- Measure meaningful impact beyond completion rates to performance outcomes and business results.
- Create evidence for scaling decisions through systematic capability building across multiple contexts.

Designing Effective Pilot Programs

It's simple to say, "Go run a pilot!" but it's much more difficult to cope with the dozens of details that need attention as you begin the process. In the Be Natural examples, you can see a lot of variety as well as consistency in approaches. I've identified seven guidelines that consistently separate successful pilot programs from those that struggle to provide useful insights.

1. Set Clear Objectives

What do you want to learn from the pilot program? Do you want to know if retained knowledge translates into better performance more rapidly or at all? Are you testing to see if your target audience performs better if they have self-directed options?

Effective pilot programs focus on answering specific questions rather than broadly testing microlearning. Clear objectives might include:

- Determine whether spaced microlearning improves knowledge retention compared with traditional training.
- Evaluate whether performance-support microlearning reduces error rates in specific procedures while on the job.
- Assess whether participants engage more with push or pull delivery methods.
- Measure how different microlearning formats affect skills development in specific areas.

By defining clear objectives, you can create a focused framework for evaluation and ensure that your pilot program provides actionable insights (specific findings that directly inform your scaling decisions).

2. Select the Right Approach Based on Your Needs

Try to find the context that best aligns with your goals. For example, if you're focusing on skills acquisition, you may lean toward a pilot program to test microlearning that complements an established training program, curriculum, or workshop—or anything not clearly established in an LMS. You may need to test delivery technology as part of your microlearning pilot if that could be a potential solution to skills acquirement.

The approach you select should align with your objectives and your organization's readiness level as assessed through the MLR Framework. Organizations I've worked with that have lower readiness typically start by converting existing content, while those with higher readiness might experiment with new initiatives or self-driven approaches.

3. Use Multiple Metrics

In any pilot program, you'll want to move beyond completion rates as your go-to metrics. Ensure that your pilot has several pathways for gathering data that connect learning experiences to actual performance outcomes. This means considering not just engagement data, but also how participants apply what they've learned and the resulting business impact.

Using multiple metrics creates a more complete picture of your microlearning initiative's effectiveness and helps you articulate value to stakeholders beyond simple completion statistics. We'll explore specific measurement approaches in greater detail in the next section on measuring the impact of pilot programs. (These measurement approaches build on the evaluation methodology introduced in chapter 4.)

4. Establish an Iterative Improvement Process

Many opportunities to run pilot programs are constrained by entities or individuals outside your L&D business unit, but whenever possible, repetition is valuable because no one pilot program will tell you everything you want to know about developing a new microlearning initiative. Results from one pilot can refine your initiative, and you can then test again with some adjustments before scaling the solution.

The pilot programs I've seen succeed include planned review points and mechanisms for incorporating feedback. Consider including:

- Midpilot check-ins to identify and address immediate issues
- End-of-pilot evaluations to assess outcomes against objectives
- Postpilot debriefs with stakeholders to gather qualitative feedback
- Dedicated time to implement changes before scaling

This iterative approach embodies the philosophy of starting small, learning, improving, and then scaling that makes microlearning implementation most effective.

5. Target Specific Audiences

Narrow your audience! Dialing in on a population with specific needs as opposed to targeting a broad, sweeping audience will give you stronger insights into your future capacity and capabilities for a particular initiative.

Targeted pilot programs provide clearer data and more actionable insights. Consider selecting audiences that:

- Represent a clearly defined job role or function.
- Face specific performance challenges that microlearning might address.
- Share key characteristics with the broader population you'll eventually serve (so pilot insights transfer when you scale).
- Are accessible for feedback and assessment.

This focused approach allows you to understand how microlearning works in specific contexts before expanding to diverse audiences with varied needs.

6. Consider Your L&D Organizational Structure

The way your L&D function is set up will also affect the approach you choose. If your L&D team's work is decentralized, you'll want to collaborate with one another and with other units. Create teams that represent all L&D practitioners across the organization. Even if your pilot program serves only one L&D function and its stakeholders, you will glean valuable information to reflect on and take back to the group or team. Here are some things to consider:

- In centralized L&D functions, ensure that pilot program objectives align with your broader learning strategy.
- In decentralized functions, coordinate across teams to avoid duplication and leverage shared insights.
- Identify executive sponsors who can remove barriers and provide visibility.
- Create clear communication channels for sharing pilot program progress and results.

Remember: You never need to adhere to these suggestions as hard-and-fast rules. Just be sure to set clear goals, create shared governance, develop a measurable approach, and meet regularly as a team to communicate your progress and findings.

7. Create a Clear Road Map

Effective pilots benefit from clearly mapping how participants will progress from their current state to the desired outcome. Performance journeys provide this road map.

Performance journeys are the mapped pathways that outline how a persona moves from one level of competence to another. This could involve different stages of learning (from initial exposure to mastery) with microlearning solutions at each point. They help ensure that learning is not just a one-time event but a continual process of improvement, with specific microlearning products tailored to each stage of the journey. Concepts such as distributed practice and spaced repetition play important roles in designing these learning pathways. Effective performance journeys include:

- Clear competency milestones that participants should reach
- Microlearning products mapped to specific competency development needs
- Assessment points that measure progress toward performance goals
- Feedback mechanisms that guide continued development
- Recognition of achievement at milestones

When designing your pilot, create a miniature performance journey that illustrates how participants will progress from their current state to the desired performance outcome through microlearning initiatives.

Approaches to Pilot Programs

The three most common approaches to pilot programs are:

- Converting a pre-existing training course into a microlearning initiative
- Creating a microlearning initiative to complement a current training curriculum, program, or workshop

- Developing a brand-new microlearning initiative unrelated to current content or training programs, curriculum, or workshops

These three approaches represent the most common implementation scenarios I've encountered. Organizations typically start with what they have (converting content), extend what's working (complementing training), or address gaps that traditional training hasn't solved (developing new initiatives). Understanding which scenario fits your situation helps you design more strategic pilot programs. Let's examine each one in more detail, along with other specialized approaches.

Converting Existing Content

This approach focuses on transforming traditional training into microlearning formats. Think of it like breaking down a lengthy cookbook chapter into individual recipe cards—each one is focused, actionable, and easier to use when you need it. It's particularly useful for organizations with established training programs that suffer from low completion rates or poor retention. This approach works best when your MLR Framework assessment shows strong delivery capabilities but gaps in design experience in the implementation dimension (see chapter 6 for more information).

Try to do a few key things when converting existing content:
- Identify which parts of the content can be broken into smaller chunks.
- Focus on key concepts or skills that need frequent reinforcement.
- Maintain essential learning objectives while eliminating "nice to know" content.

For guidance on chunking and creating focus, review chapter 12 for practical techniques. If you need to know more about the "why" behind the importance of chunking content and stripping away nonessentials, chapter 8 provides information about science of learning, specifically cognitive load.

Complementing Current Training

This approach uses microlearning to enhance or extend existing training programs rather than replacing them. It's like adding a flavorful sauce or seasoning to an already good dish—you're not changing the main course; you're just making it more memorable (or adding variety!). It's ideal for organizations that already have effective formal training but want to increase retention or application. This approach works across knowledge reinforcement, skills practice, performance support, and behavior change initiatives.

Do a few things before complementing your current training with microlearning:

- Map out how microlearning fits into larger programs or workshops.
- Design it to incorporate desirable difficulties, like spaced retrieval or varied practice contexts, that deepen learning rather than duplicating what was already covered.
- Coordinate timing between formal training and microlearning sequencing, whether that's placing microlearning as a precursor, alongside, or as a post-training reinforcement.

Developing New Microlearning Initiatives

This approach creates entirely new microlearning solutions for needs that haven't been addressed through formal training. It's appropriate when identifying performance opportunities that traditional training hasn't addressed effectively.

Do a few things before developing brand-new microlearning initiatives:

- Identify the performance gap or opportunities.
- Align microlearning directly with job-specific competencies or performance objectives.
- Determine if the need varies across different audience groups.

More Advanced Approaches

The following approaches require more organizational maturity and are typically pursued after establishing foundational capabilities.

Testing Technology and Delivery

One specialized approach to developing a pilot program focuses on evaluating different technologies or delivery mechanisms for microlearning. It's valuable when considering new platforms. I typically recommend this approach when organizations are experiencing technology limitations that constrain their microlearning effectiveness, or when they're considering significant platform investments that need validation.

Make sure to do a few things before testing technology and delivery approaches in a pilot program:

- Test delivery platforms (such as mobile, desktop, and tablet applications).
- Evaluate how different technologies support spaced learning (distributed practice) techniques.
- Compare engagement and effectiveness across delivery methods.
- Test accessibility and inclusivity features (including screen reader compatibility, captions, multilingual support, and navigation options).

Supporting Self-Driven Development

This less common approach tests microlearning strategies that give participants more control over their learning experiences. Supporting self-driven development is useful for organizations exploring more autonomous, pull-based learning cultures in which employees seek out and engage, versus traditional training in which the organization pushes learning content out to employees.

Try a few things before supporting self-driven development:

- Determine how much control participants should have or what you want to explore with respect to self-directed engagement.
- Test different ways of pushing versus allowing pull strategies.
- Assess whether participants engage because they find value in the learning content or because they feel required to complete it.

After selecting your pilot type, it helps to consider the resources and capabilities necessary for execution.

Tracking Capacity During Your Pilot Program

Beyond testing your microlearning products, pilot programs provide valuable information about your team's ability to develop and sustain microlearning initiatives. Rather than trying to track everything at once, start by organizing capacity indicators into manageable categories.

Consider beginning with just one or two indicators per category if comprehensive tracking seems overwhelming. The goal is to gather practical insights that inform scaling decisions, not to create burdensome measurement processes. I recommend using three buckets that represent the indicators noted previously:

- **Development capacity focuses on tracking how efficiently your team creates content.** This includes monitoring your development timeline compared to estimates, which reveals whether your planning assumptions are realistic and helps you build more accurate project schedules. Additionally, identifying content creation bottlenecks and accelerators shows you where workflows slow down or speed up unexpectedly, providing insights for process optimization.

- **Organizational support needs involve monitoring cross-functional requirements that affect your pilot program's success.** This means assessing the level of support required from other departments, which helps you understand dependencies and resource needs for future scaling. Furthermore, tracking the time and effort spent on stakeholder alignment reveals how much coordination is actually needed—often one of the most underestimated aspects of microlearning implementation.

- **Participant enablement focuses on assessing what participants need to succeed with your microlearning approach.** This includes evaluating technical guidance and facilitation requirements, which directly affects your staffing and support planning for scaled implementations. Additionally, monitoring engagement support, especially for pull-based approaches in which participants must actively seek out learning, helps you understand the level of ongoing support needed to maintain participation.

This information helps you plan resource needs for scaling microlearning initiatives. For example, if your pilot reveals that stakeholder alignment consumes your project time, you'll know that you need to allocate more resources to this area when scaling. Or you and your team may need to work on refining the overall approach to aligning stakeholders.

Track your progress, starting with the initial conception of the pilot program and continue through post-pilot evaluations. Use a review or debrief after the pilot to gauge your team's capacity and capability, assessing workload distribution, bottlenecks, and team efficiency. This informal but practical approach helps you plan realistic resource needs for scaling microlearning initiatives.

As discussed in chapter 7, capability frameworks provide structured measurement, but capacity is best assessed through real-world application like pilots.

Measuring the Impact of Pilots

Measuring the impact of your microlearning pilot programs goes beyond tracking completion rates. Meaningful assessment connects learning experiences to performance outcomes and provides actionable data for refinement.

Qualitative and Quantitative Assessment Methods

Comprehensive impact measurement combines quantitative metrics with qualitative insights. Quantitative methods provide data that demonstrates measurable impact and can be tracked over time. These approaches include:

- Assessment scores and knowledge checks that show learning retention and comprehension
- Performance data from business systems that reveal actual workplace application and results
- Engagement analytics from learning platforms that indicate participation patterns and completion rates
- Time-to-competence measurements that track how quickly participants achieve proficiency levels

Qualitative methods, on the other hand, offer deeper insights into the participant experience and contextual factors that influence success. These approaches include:

- Open-ended participant feedback surveys and interviews that capture personal experiences and perceived value
- Written manager observations and feedback that provide supervisory perspectives on behavior change and application
- Focus groups with participants and stakeholders that reveal collective insights and shared challenges
- User experience testing sessions that identify usability issues and design improvements

This mixed-method approach provides both the *what* (quantitative data showing impact) and the *why* (qualitative insights explaining factors influencing success or challenges). The following sections provide specific examples of the quantitative and qualitative metrics you can apply in your pilots.

Meaningful Metrics That Go Beyond Completion Rates

While completion rates offer baseline engagement data, they tell you little about actual learning or performance impact. Consider the more meaningful metrics outlined in Table 16-1.

Table 16-1. Microlearning Metrics

	Metric	Measurement Methods
Knowledge-based microlearning	Knowledge retention over time	Surveys, follow-up interviews, and spaced knowledge checks
	Ability to apply concepts in scenarios or simulations	Observation checklists, manager assessments, and performance rubrics
	Confidence ratings on important knowledge areas	Self-assessments, peer evaluations, and supervisor ratings
Skills-based microlearning	Quality of skill demonstration in practice scenarios	Rubric scoring, peer evaluations, and expert assessments
	Time to competence compared with traditional approaches	Milestone tracking, supervisor sign-offs, and performance timelines
	Error reduction during skill application	Error logs, quality checks, and incident reports
	Skill change against baselines and benchmarks	Pre- and post-assessments, industry standards, and internal competency frameworks
Performance-based microlearning	Direct performance indicators in target workflows	Productivity metrics, output quality measures, process completion rates, and xAPI tracking
	Frequency of reference to performance support tools	Usage analytics, access logs, and user engagement data
	Problem resolution time or quality	Helpdesk tickets, customer satisfaction scores, and resolution tracking

Microlearning and Performance Data

The most valuable microlearning assessment connects learning experiences directly to workplace performance. Consider these approaches:

- **Baseline performance data.** Gather performance metrics before implementing microlearning to establish a comparison point, or use microlearning to create the performance baseline.
- **Control groups.** When possible, compare performance between groups that received microlearning and those that didn't.
- **Performance observation.** Use structured observation to assess behavior change after microlearning implementation. Ensure key indicators are clearly defined using neutral, unbiased language.
- **Workflow integration.** If microlearning is embedded in workflows, track usage patterns and corresponding performance outcomes.
- **Manager assessments.** Gather structured feedback from managers about observed performance changes.

From Your Pilot Program to a Comprehensive Strategy

Successful pilot programs provide the foundation for broader microlearning strategies. The transition from focused experimentation to comprehensive implementation requires thoughtful planning and strategic expansion.

Using Data to Inform Scaling Decisions

The purposes of measurement include validation of approach, proof of concept, strategic decision making, and continuous improvement. These processes can be used to evaluate and refine your microlearning:

- **Regular data reviews.** Schedule check-ins to examine metrics and identify trends.
- **Root cause analysis.** If an area shows limited impact, investigate why.
- **Stakeholder input.** Share data with stakeholders to gather their perspectives on results.

- Documentation of insights: Capture what you're learning for future microlearning initiatives.
- Action planning: Develop specific refinements based on data insights.

Pilot programs are often the most valuable method for testing both the effectiveness of content and an L&D team's ability to deliver at scale. A comprehensive evaluation of pilot program results—spanning knowledge acquisition, skills acquisition, and performance improvement—will provide valuable insights into resource needs, capacity gaps, and the suitability of microlearning initiatives for broader implementation.

As you scale successful pilot programs, use the design principles from part 2 (chapters 8–15) to ensure your expanded microlearning products maintain the same learning effectiveness that made your pilot program successful. This transformation involves five interconnected areas: systematically scaling successful approaches, building reusable organizational assets, applying design principles at enterprise level, developing sustainable content strategies, and creating systems for content reuse and adaptation. Together, these elements transform isolated pilot successes into comprehensive organizational microlearning capabilities.

Scaling Successful Approaches

When your pilot program demonstrates positive impact, consider some of these approaches to scaling it:
- **Phased expansion.** Gradually introduce successful microlearning to additional audience segments rather than immediate organization-wide deployment.
- **Capability building.** Develop tools and templates based on successful pilot programs to enable broader implementation with efficiency and the same level of quality.
- **Train-the-trainer approaches.** Equip additional L&D team members or business partners to develop similar microlearning.
- **Technology investment.** With proof of concept established, invest in platforms that support broader implementation.
- **Process documentation.** Create standard operating procedures based on what worked in your pilot program.

I've learned from organizations that scale successfully that gradual, capability-building approaches outperform aggressive rollouts, which overwhelm teams and compromise quality.

Building on What Works

Rather than viewing each microlearning initiative as an isolated project, build a connected ecosystem through:

- **Template development.** Create standardized templates based on successful pilot formats.
- **Content libraries.** Develop reusable content modules or snippets. You may be familiar with the term *shareable content objects*, which can be incorporated across multiple microlearning experiences.
- **Design pattern documentation.** Capture effective design patterns that can be replicated in future initiatives.
- **Measurement frameworks.** Standardize how you measure impact across initiatives to enable comparison and improvement.
- **Stakeholder playbooks.** Document successful approaches to stakeholder engagement and management for use in project discussions.

This systematic approach transforms individual successes into organizational capabilities that support sustainable microlearning implementation.

Applying the Design Principles at Scale

As you move from pilot programs to a comprehensive strategy, the design principles from part 2 will become even more critical. As a refresher, those principles are:

- **Principle 1: Know Your Tools' Capacity.** Ensure your technology infrastructure can support broader implementation without compromising experience quality.
- **Principle 2: Craft Appropriate Context.** Maintain contextual relevance as you expand to diverse audience segments. Effective scaling benefits from assessing adaptation needs before more broadly distributing existing content.

- **Principle 3: Ensure Global Equity.** Address accessibility and inclusivity needs that may become more varied at scale while adapting methods to suit different audience contexts.
- **Principle 4: Design With Concision.** Resist the temptation to add content as initiatives expand in scope.
- **Principle 5: Make Media Meaningful.** Maintain media quality and purposefulness in larger initiatives.
- **Principle 6: Elicit Action.** Preserve active engagement elements that worked in your pilot program.
- **Principle 7: Avoid Overuse.** Introduce strategic variety to prevent desensitization as microlearning becomes a regular part of the organizational learning experience.

These principles provide a framework for maintaining quality as you scale from focused pilot programs to a comprehensive program.

Developing a Content Strategy for Sustainable Growth

Sustainable microlearning implementation requires a content strategy that balances creation efficiency with learning effectiveness. This strategy can include:

- **A modular content approach.** Design content in reusable modules that can be recombined for different purposes.
- **Maintenance planning.** Establish processes for reviewing and updating microlearning content to ensure continued relevance.
- **Governance structures.** Define roles and responsibilities for content creation, approval, and management.
- **A content prioritization framework.** Create criteria for determining which performance needs warrant microlearning development.
- **A resource allocation model.** Develop a system for allocating development resources based on potential business impact.

Reusing and Adapting Content Across Initiatives

Strategic content reuse can maximize your return on investment. Here are some things you can try:

- **Content mapping.** Catalog existing content by topic, learning objective, and format to identify reuse opportunities.
- **Contextual adaptation.** Develop processes for adapting core content to different contexts or audiences.
- **Content refreshment cycles.** Establish schedules for updating content to ensure continued relevance.
- **Cross-functional asset sharing.** Create mechanisms for sharing microlearning assets across departments or functions.
- **Continuous improvement process.** Implement systems for gathering feedback on content effectiveness to guide refinement.

The organizations I work with that struggle with content reuse typically try to force existing content into new contexts rather than thoughtfully adapting it. This shortcut usually backfires. However, I've also seen successful microlearning that transforms disconnected products into a strategic content ecosystem that efficiently addresses organizational performance needs.

Applying the MLR Framework in Implementation

Implementation doesn't signal the end of your microlearning journey; instead, it creates new insights that inform continued assessment and refinement. This brings us full circle: The MLR Framework from part 1 provides a structure for this ongoing improvement cycle.

Reassessing Readiness After Pilot Programs

Many pilot programs reveal readiness factors that weren't apparent upon the initial assessment, including:

- **Technical readiness insights.** Pilot programs test technological capabilities in real conditions, revealing strengths and limitations.
- **Audience readiness reality.** Participant engagement with pilots shows actual (versus assumed) readiness to use and adopt microlearning as a new approach.
- **Stakeholder readiness validation.** Leadership support of pilot programs indicates a true commitment to microlearning approaches.
- **L&D team capability evidence.** Development and implementation experience demonstrates your team's capacity for microlearning.

Use these insights to update your MLR Framework assessment, creating a more accurate picture of your organization's readiness for different types of microlearning.

Identifying Growth Opportunities

Implementation data also highlights specific areas for organizational capability development including:

- **Technical infrastructure needs.** Identify platform limitations or integration challenges revealed during implementation.
- **Skills development priorities.** Recognize L&D team skills gaps that affected pilot program's quality or efficiency.
- **Process improvement opportunities.** Note workflow bottlenecks that slowed development or implementation.
- **Measurement capability needs.** Identify limitations in your ability to assess microlearning impact.

Addressing these specific capability gaps creates a focused development plan that increases your organization's capacity for effective microlearning.

Using Pilot Program Data to Change Levels

Remember that the MLR Framework identifies three levels of microlearning implementation:

- **Knowledge-based microlearning,** focused on information retention and recall
- **Skills-based microlearning,** centered on practice and capability development
- **Performance-based microlearning,** integrated with workflows to support real-time execution

Successful pilot programs build capabilities that support your company's ability to move toward more and more challenging implementations.

Building Organizational Capabilities Through Implementation

Each implementation cycle also builds capabilities across five key dimensions of your organization:

- **Technical infrastructure,** which includes testing and refining delivery platforms and measurement systems
- **Content development expertise,** which builds skills in creating effective microlearning experiences
- **Integration mechanisms,** which help develop approaches for embedding learning in workflows
- **Evaluation sophistication,** which means advancing from basic metrics to performance impact measurement
- **Stakeholder engagement,** which involves building relationships and credibility through demonstrated success

Document your lessons learned and capability improvements over time to create a road map for continued organizational growth in microlearning effectiveness.

As you move forward with your implementation journey, you'll find practical tools in appendix A—the Microlearning Campaign Blueprint and Product Design Guide—that can help you plan your campaigns and design your products. These tools will also help you translate the pilot program approaches we've discussed into actionable plans. Whether you're starting by converting existing content, complementing current training, or developing entirely new solutions, these tools will help you create microlearning that aligns with both your organizational readiness and sound design principles.

Chapter Summary

Successful microlearning implementation requires a strategic approach that connects assessment insights and design principles to practical execution. Throughout this chapter, we've explored how:

- Pilot programs provide the ideal starting point for microlearning implementation, offering low-risk experimentation and valuable learning opportunities.
- Different approaches to pilot programs—from converting existing content to testing new initiatives—serve various implementation objectives and organizational contexts.

- Comprehensive measurement approaches that go beyond completion rates connect microlearning to performance outcomes and business impact.
- The transition from successful pilot programs to comprehensive strategy requires thoughtful planning, content reuse, and capability building.
- Implementation creates new insights that inform ongoing assessment and refinement through the MLR Framework.

Remember that microlearning implementation isn't an endpoint but the beginning of a continuous improvement cycle that will strengthen your approach over time. By starting with focused pilot programs, measuring meaningful impact, and scaling strategically based on results, you can create microlearning solutions that truly maximize value for both participants and the organization.

A Final Note

Maximizing the power of microlearning emerges not from any single product or campaign but from a systematic approach that connects learning to performance through experiences that respect how people naturally learn and develop. By applying the frameworks, principles, and tools from this book, you're well positioned to create microlearning that delivers meaningful impact in your unique organizational context.

APPENDIX A
Implementation Tools

Building on the pilot program approach described in chapter 16, the tools in this appendix—the Microlearning Campaign Blueprint and the Microlearning Product Design Guide—provide structured frameworks to help you move from concept to implementation. These practical resources connect strategic thinking to tactical execution, ensuring that your microlearning initiatives are both effective and sustainable. I've based these tools on what I've seen work across different organizational contexts. Treat them as templates to customize rather than rigid requirements—your organization's specific needs, constraints, and capabilities should guide how you adapt them.

The Tools—An Overview

The Microlearning Campaign Blueprint helps you design a coordinated series of microlearning experiences that achieve broader performance goals. I use the Microlearning Campaign Blueprint when working with organizations that are planning comprehensive microlearning initiatives or converting existing training programs. It ensures strategic alignment while providing practical guidance for development and implementation. This tool:

- Aligns campaign objectives with business outcomes
- Defines the purpose and potential use cases for your campaign
- Structures the implementation approach across multiple products
- Establishes consistent measurement frameworks
- Coordinates product sequencing and timing

The Microlearning Product Design Guide helps you create stand-alone microlearning products or individual components within a campaign that align with campaign objectives and design principles. This guide ensures learning effectiveness while supporting practical implementation. This tool:

- Defines the specific use case for each microlearning product
- Identifies the target audience and desired performance outcomes
- Structures content for optimal engagement
- Plans content access approaches that fit work contexts
- Guides development decisions that support learning objectives and the participants' contexts
- Establishes measurement approaches for each product

When to Use Each Tool

Your implementation approach determines which tool to start with:

- **For comprehensive initiatives addressing multiple learning needs,** begin with the Microlearning Campaign Blueprint to establish a strategic framework before developing individual products.
- **For focused solutions addressing specific performance gaps**, start with the Microlearning Product Design Guide to create a targeted product that addresses the immediate need.
- **For existing training conversion,** use the Microlearning Campaign Blueprint to structure the overall approach. Then use the Microlearning Product Design Guide for each module that's being converted.
- **For technology pilot programs,** use the Microlearning Product Design Guide to create test products that evaluate platform capabilities.

Most organizations I work with begin with individual products using the Microlearning Product Design Guide, and then expand to campaigns as they build experience and demonstrate success.

How These Tools Connect to the Broader MLR Framework

These implementation tools connect directly to the MLR Framework explored in part 1 and the design principles discussed in part 2. In addition, the

Microlearning Product Design Guide incorporates the seven design principles, ensuring that your microlearning experiences maintain quality and effectiveness.

Both tools also prompt consideration of your organization's readiness level, helping you design implementations that align with your current capabilities while building toward more advanced approaches. They also reflect the learning science concepts introduced in chapter 8. Finally, they both encourage structured approaches to measuring impact that connect learning experiences to performance outcomes.

By using these tools, you can create a direct line from strategic assessment through principled design to practical implementation—ensuring that your microlearning initiatives are both effective and sustainable.

The Microlearning Campaign Blueprint

This blueprint was first developed for *Microlearning: Short and Sweet* and has been revised over the years to help guide users. It highlights many of the key points I make in part 1 (in particular about readiness) and why I address the specific design principles in part 2. Let's look closer at each piece.

Campaign Title

A campaign title is the overarching focus that unifies all products in a campaign. It should clearly communicate the performance area being addressed.

Campaign Outcomes

Campaign outcomes are the specific, measurable results that signify success. Include both learning metrics and business impact measures when possible; for example, "reducing errors by 10 percent in Q2" or "increasing compliance by 30 percent over the next year." Include approaches to evaluating or collecting the data for those outcomes.

Purpose

What is the primary focus of your campaign?

- **Augment.** Accelerate knowledge, skills, or performance beyond the standard.
- **Remediate.** Address identified performance gaps or deficiencies.
- **Reinforce.** Sustain knowledge and skills from previous training.

- **Supplement.** Add to existing training programs or experiences.

Note: A campaign can serve multiple purposes simultaneously. For example, a sales training campaign might both remediate current performance gaps while also augmenting high performers' capabilities. Select all applicable purposes and complete implementation details for each.

Use Cases

What are the reasons for your campaign?
- **Pensive.** Develop critical thinking and problem-solving skills.
- **Persuasive.** Modify behaviors or influence attitudes.
- **Performance.** Support execution of specific work tasks.
- **Post instruction.** Follow a larger training event (such as a workshop).
- **Practice based.** Provide opportunities to work on skills.
- **Preparatory.** Serve as prework for an upcoming event or activity.

Note: Both campaigns and individual microlearning products can serve multiple use cases. For example, a single product might be both pensive (encouraging reflection) and persuasive (motivating behavior change). Select all applicable use cases that your campaign will address.

Spaced Learning

Spaced learning refers to the timeframe and rhythm for completing the campaign, specified for each purpose you selected. This encompasses:
- **Overall duration.** The total period over which the campaign will run (for example, four weeks or three months)
- **Distribution pattern.** How microlearning products are spaced over time (such as weekly, biweekly, or variable spacing)
- **Learning intervals.** The intentional spacing between related concepts to optimize retention
- **Repetition strategy.** How key concepts are revisited throughout the campaign with increasing intervals
- **Reinforcement timing.** Strategic points where previous knowledge is deliberately reinforced
- **Practice scheduling.** When skills application opportunities occur relative to initial learning

Note: Effective spaced learning often follows increasing intervals between exposures rather than fixed schedules. Consider how spacing can be designed to match the forgetting curve for your specific content and audience.

Implementation Details

Implementation details encompass the specific information about how participants will access and engage with the campaign, including:

- **Delivery approach.** How content will reach participants (push versus pull delivery)
- **Access points.** Where participants will find and engage with the content (an LMS, a mobile app, an email, or team meetings)
- **Change management.** Strategies for adoption and engagement
- **Technology platforms.** Specific tools or systems used for delivery
- **Integration points.** How the campaign connects with existing workflows or systems
- **Support mechanisms.** Resources to help participants engage
- **Tracking methods.** How participation and engagement will be monitored
- **Product planning.** Each individual microlearning product within the campaign should include:
  - » *Product title.* A clear name that communicates purpose and aligns with the overall campaign
  - » *Outcomes.* Specific results each product should achieve, directly connected to campaign goals. They can have individual outcomes or contribute to larger outcomes that build across the campaign.
  - » *Use cases.* Which use cases each product addresses (there can be multiple per product)
  - » *Sequencing.* Where this product fits in the overall learning journey

Note: After completing the blueprint, use the Microlearning Product Design Guide to develop detailed designs for each individual product.

Template: Microlearning Campaign Blueprint

Campaign Title *What is the general focus of all products?*		Campaign Outcomes *What measure or measures signify success?*	
Purpose *What focus will the campaign have to best serve the performance of the participant?* ☐ Augment ☐ Remediate ☐ Reinforce ☐ Supplement		**Use Cases** • *What is the primary reason for the campaign?* • *Are there secondary or tertiary uses?* ☐ Pensive ☐ Persuasive ☐ Performance ☐ Post-instruction ☐ Practice-based ☐ Preparatory	

Spaced Learning *How long does each pathway have to complete the campaign?*	**Implementation** • *What is the timeline for dropping the campaign? Will it be all at once or over time?* • *When will communications be dropped or provided to each pathway?*		
Augment			
Remediate			
Reinforce			
Supplement			

316 | Appendix A

Products What are the topics of the campaign?	Outcomes What is the outcome of the topic? (It should contribute to measuring the campaign goal.)
Product 1	
Product 2	
Product 3	
Product 4	
Product 5	
Product 6	
Product 7	

Microlearning Campaign Blueprint Example

Campaign Title	Bee Safe: What Helps or Harms Our Hive	Campaign Outcomes	BN goal: 0 safety infractions related to PPE during next quarter.
	To reduce safety infractions, while encouraging an attitude of valuing safety of self and others.		BN goal: Cumulative score for valuing safety and others on the attitude and dispositions survey averages a 3.75 out of 5 by end of next quarter.
			Possible measures:
			• Safety reports (which include daily, weekly, and monthly data)
			• Supervisor/Foreman personnel reports for PPE infractions (e.g., verbal, suspension, etc.)
			• Observation both by floor supervisor, but also team member to team member
			• Team assessment survey focused on safety policy, BN safety philosophy, and situational awareness

Purpose	☐ Augment ☐ Remediate ☒ Reinforce ☐ Supplement	Use Cases	☒ Pensive ☒ Persuasive
			☐ Performance ☐ Post-instruction
			☒ Practice-based ☐ Preparatory

Implementation	
Spaced Learning	
Augment	Not applicable
	It may be determined later that this may be used as part of training. For example, when a team gets a new employee, perhaps the campaign cycle runs again for the benefit of integrating the new team member or members.
Remediate	Not applicable
	This is a consideration for future use of the campaign, whether in part or in whole. Given the philosophy of "safety of self and others" by BN there is consideration for making the entire team go through the campaign if a member has an infraction.
Reinforce	4, 6, and 8 weeks
	The pilot provides an opportunity to see if duration and exposure to content yield different results. Based on plant shift the campaigns will be executed in 4-, 6-, and 8-week formats. The same amount of content and activities will be covered, just in shorter timeframes. 4-week and 6-week formats will have additional observation checkpoints.

Supplement	No applicable	Though the campaign is based off the current training materials it is not a variation of it, it reinforces key pieces, specifically on PPE and the BN Safety Philosophy.
Products		**Outcomes**
Product 1	Use and Wear – Focus on Variations to What is "Right" vs "Risk"	Floor workers will consider possible variations and circumstances against BN PPE policy. They will reflect, assess, and share on the "right" types of PPE and how to wear them. Additionally, they will address "risk" in the same manner, while also presenting how they would resolve "risk". [Pensive and Performance/Practice Call to Actions]
Product 2	Use and Wear – Focus on Speaking to Teammates and Supervisors	Supervisor and managers will explore different techniques for addressing "risk" situations in the moment and how to manage the situation. Team members and supervisors will respectively identify approaches that seemed to work for the team versus an individual team member to build confidence in communicating effectively to that coworker. [Pensive, Persuasive, and Performance/Practice Call to Actions]
Product 3	Self and Others – Focus on Self Creating Harm to Others	Individuals will be tasked with creating a list of ways that unsafe behavior can impact their team members. Supervisors will present the information in aggregate to the team and include any "risks" and causes that may have been overlooked. Team members will have the opportunity to reflect and share any insights. [Pensive, Persuasive, and Performance/Practice Call to Actions]
Product 4	Self and Others – Focus on Bonus	Supervisors, infographics, and digital slides and video will deliver information on how simple safety infractions have created loss not only for the company, but for the employees via bonuses. Data will be company and team specific. Team members will consider and discuss options for how to stabilize their team's bonus related to safety for the next quarter. [Pensive and Persuasive Call to Actions]
Product 5	Self and Others – Focus on Efficiency	Team members will pair off and develop a scenario that they find less than efficient due to improper use and/or wear of PPE to present to the entire team and supervisor. Supervisor and team determine if PPE is a factor of inefficiency and then how to correct it. [Pensive, Persuasive, and Performance/Practice Call to Actions]

Microlearning Product Design Guide

Use this tool as you create individual microlearning experiences that align with both campaign objectives and design principles. Let's take a look at each field in the Microlearning Product Design Guide.

Product Number

Use the product number field to give each product a sequential identifier that you can use to track each product within your campaign (for example, 1, 2, 3 or A, B, C).

Product Title

In the product title field, assign a clear, descriptive name that communicates the purpose and focus of the microlearning product. The title should be engaging and convey what participants will gain from the experience. (You can transfer your title from the Microlearning Campaign Blueprint.)

Use Case

The use case field holds the purpose, or the primary reason for creating this microlearning product. Select from these options:

- **Pensive.** Develop critical thinking and problem-solving skills.
- **Persuasive.** Modify behaviors or influences attitudes.
- **Performance.** Support execution of specific work tasks.
- **Post instruction.** Follow a larger training event (such as a workshop).
- **Practice-based.** Provide opportunities to develop skills through practice.
- **Preparatory.** Serve as prework for an upcoming event or activity.

Note: A single microlearning product can serve multiple use cases simultaneously. For example, a product might be both pensive (encouraging reflection) and persuasive (motivating behavior change). Select all applicable use cases that your product addresses.

Design Considerations and Product Details

The design considerations column captures the key factors that will shape your product development across four areas: who will use it (participants), what it covers (content), how participants will access it (content access, such as email, LMS, or mobile), and what format you'll develop (development, such as video, infographic, or interactive module). These considerations work together to ensure your microlearning product fits the audience's needs and your organization's capabilities.

Participants

In the participants field, identify the specific individuals or groups engaging with this microlearning product. This includes:

- Their current knowledge and skill levels related to the topic
- Relevant characteristics of their work context (See Principle 2: Context)
- Challenges they face that affect performance
- Motivation factors that will drive engagement

Note: Personas are a helpful tool for ensuring relevant participant characteristics are holistically represented.

Content

The content field is for the subject matter or the specific knowledge, skills, or performance-based topic that the product addresses. It should:

- Focus on only essential elements needed to achieve the desired performance.
- Eliminate "nice to know" information that doesn't directly support performance.
- Consider what can be effectively addressed in a microlearning format.
- Align with the selected use cases.

Content Access

The content access field shows the physical or digital locations where participants will access the microlearning content. This includes:

- Delivery platforms (such as an LMS, a mobile app, or an email)
- Physical contexts (such as at a workstation, in meeting rooms, or even on factory floors)

- Integration points with existing systems or workflows
- Considerations for access limitations or barriers

Content access also considers the timing for when participants will engage with the microlearning product. This includes:

- Relationship to when the knowledge or skill is needed (before, during, or after)
- Frequency considerations (one-time versus repeated engagement)
- Timing relative to other learning experiences (if part of a sequence)
- Contextual triggers that prompt engagement

Development

The modalities field shows the specific formats and engagement approaches used in the microlearning product. This includes:

- Visual elements (images, videos, animations, and infographics)
- Audio components (narration, sound effects, and music)
- Interactive features (activities, questions, and simulations)
- Text-based content (explanations, instructions, and prompts)
- Physical elements (printed materials, job aids, and hands-on tools)

Note: Consider which modalities best support the content and learning context while managing cognitive load appropriately.

Possible Measures

The possible measures field lists the specific metrics and approaches used to evaluate the effectiveness of the outcomes anticipated by the microlearning product. This includes:

- Direct feedback from participants (reactions and perceived value)
- Learning measures (knowledge checks and skills demonstrations)
- Application indicators (behavior change and task execution)
- Performance impact (business metrics and outcomes)
- Collection methods (surveys, observations, and system data)

In addition, this field should highlight the desired performance, which includes the specific, observable behaviors or outcomes that participants should demonstrate after engaging with the microlearning product. This should:

- Focus on what participants will do differently.

- Be specific and measurable when possible.
- Connect directly to on-the-job application.
- Align with broader campaign goals (if part of a campaign).

Note: Whenever possible, connect measurement approaches directly to the desired performance outcomes. There may be times a microlearning product is created for information only or self-testing to build individual confidence.

Template: Microlearning Product Design Guide

Product Number:		Product Title:	
Use Case	Design Considerations	Product Details	Possible Measures
	Participants		
	Content		
	Content access		
	Development		

Microlearning Product Design Guide Example

Product 1: PPE: Use and Wear			
Use Case	Design Considerations	Product Details	Possible Measures
Pensive and performance	Participants	All team members in a crew or shift	Supervisor will set up scenarios and place the magnetic PPE on the employees for the crew or shift.
	Content	Repurposed from the e-learning module: Bee Natural Safety Training	Supervisor will prompt: • Are they wearing the appropriate PPE for the situation? • If no, what should they be wearing and why? • If yes, how does the PPE assist in keeping them safe?
	Content access	During the daily safety huddle	Supervisor can also ask crew or shift members to set up scenarios to test their team members.
	Development	Magnetic cut outs to use on wall in meeting area for daily safety huddles (need graphic artist) Safety prompts and activities created by L&D team	

Design Principles Checklist

Use this checklist at two key points:

- After completing your product design template to ensure your plan incorporates the design principles
- After development to verify your finished product meets these standards (within reason of your organization's context and level of readiness)

This tool references the seven design principles detailed in part 2 (chapters 8–15). If you need deeper understanding of any principle, refer to the relevant chapter for comprehensive guidance.

Design Principles Checklist

Principle	Considerations	Addressed?
1. Know Your Tools' Capacity	• Does this design work within your technical constraints? • Have you leveraged the strengths of your available tools?	☐ Yes ☐ No ☐ Partially
2. Craft an Appropriate Context	• Does the design connect to the participants' real-world context? • Is it relevant to their actual work environment?	☐ Yes ☐ No ☐ Partially
3. Ensure Global Equity	• Is the design accessible to all intended participants? • Have you considered diverse needs and preferences?	☐ Yes ☐ No ☐ Partially
4. Design With Concision	• Have you focused on essential content? • Have you eliminated unnecessary information to balance cognitive load?	☐ Yes ☐ No ☐ Partially
5. Make Media Meaningful	• Do your media choices enhance learning? • Does each element serve a clear purpose? • Do the media elements interfere with cognitive load?	☐ Yes ☐ No ☐ Partially
6. Elicit Action	• Does the design prompt active engagement? • Are participants doing more than passively consuming (or is the intent to create passive microlearning)?	☐ Yes ☐ No ☐ Partially
7. Avoid Overuse	• Does this product vary from other recent microlearning? • Have you considered potential desensitization?	☐ Yes ☐ No ☐ Partially

APPENDIX C
Who to Follow

The field of microlearning is evolving rapidly, with new research, technologies, and implementation strategies emerging constantly. While recommended reading lists provide valuable foundational knowledge, they represent a snapshot in time, often pointing to works that, though excellent, may not reflect the latest thinking or practical applications.

Instead of simply suggesting books to add to your shelf, this appendix connects you with active practitioners and researchers who are shaping the field right now. These thought leaders are:

- Publishing current research and insights that build on foundational work
- Experimenting with emerging technologies like AI, xAPI, and adaptive learning
- Sharing real-world implementation experiences from diverse organizations
- Responding to contemporary challenges such as hybrid work, designing for neurodiversity, and changing expectations
- Building communities in which practitioners can learn from one another

The Value of Following Active Voices

Following these practitioners provides several advantages over static resources:

- **Real-time learning.** You'll discover new research, case studies, and best practices as they emerge, not months or years later when they appear in formal publications.
- **Practical application.** These experts regularly share implementation challenges, solutions, and lessons learned from actual microlearning and general training and performance-based initiatives across different industries and contexts.
- **Interactive learning.** Many of these thought leaders engage with their communities, answer questions, and provide feedback on ideas, creating opportunities for direct learning and networking.
- **Trend awareness.** You'll stay aware of emerging trends and technologies that could affect your microlearning strategy, from AI integration to novel ways to design inclusively.
- **Diverse perspectives.** This curated list represents voices from different geographic regions, industries, and specialties, ensuring you're exposed to varied approaches and contexts.

How to Use This Resource

These thought leaders are categorized by key themes in this book:

- **Learning science foundations.** Experts grounding microlearning among other approaches in cognitive science and evidence-based practice
- **Data and learning analytics.** Specialists in measuring and optimizing program and training effectiveness
- **Process infrastructure and workflow learning.** Practitioners focused on embedding learning in organizational systems
- **People infrastructure and organizational change.** Leaders in building organizational capabilities for learning success
- **Emerging trends.** Innovators exploring AI, new technologies, and future applications

- **Universal design and accessibility.** Advocates ensuring all learning experiences serve everyone equally

Consider following thought leaders across multiple categories to develop a well-rounded perspective. The combination of their ongoing insights with the foundational principles in this book will provide you with both theoretical grounding and practical, up-to-date guidance for your microlearning initiatives.

Remember: The goal isn't to follow everyone, but to identify the voices that resonate with your specific context, challenges, and learning goals. Start with a few from areas most relevant to your current needs (or curiosity!), then expand your network as your expertise and interests grow.

Learning Science Foundations

Lauren Waldman

Waldman is a learning scientist quadruple-certified in neuroscience who merges brain science with practical learning design. She's pioneering the translation of neuroscience research into actionable learning strategies and cognitive-friendly design approaches.

- **LinkedIn:** linkedin.com/in/lauren-waldman-4666bab
- **Publications:** *Joining Forces With the Brain* (2023)
- **Additional platforms:** Learning Pirate (learningpirate.com)

Clark Quinn

Quinn combines more than 40 years of learning technology experience with deep cognitive science expertise. His work on games, mobile learning, engagement, and learning experience design provides essential frameworks for effective learning implementation.

- **LinkedIn:** linkedin.com/in/clarkquinn
- **Publications:**
  - » *Make It Meaningful* (2022)
  - » *Learning Science for Instructional Designers* (2021)
  - » *Millennials, Goldfish & Other Training Misconceptions* (2018)
  - » *Revolutionize Learning & Development* (2014)

- **Additional platforms:**
  - » Quinnovation (quinnovation.com)
  - » Learning Development Accelerator (ldaccelerator.com)

Ruth Colvin Clark

Clark provides evidence-based approaches based on foundational research of Richard E. Mayer and John Sweller that directly inform effective elearning design principles. Her research on cognitive load theory and multimedia learning is foundational to creating effective elearning experiences.

- **LinkedIn:** linkedin.com/in/ruth-colvin-clark-1190714
- **Publications:**
  - » *Evidence-Based Training Methods*, 3rd edition (2019)
  - » *E-Learning and the Science of Instruction* (with Richard Mayer; 2023)
- **Additional platforms:** ruth@clarktraining.com

Patrick Chun

Chun co-founded a global soft skills measurement standard that uses microlearning methodologies to develop empathy, intercultural awareness, and professional etiquette. His work demonstrates practical, scalable microlearning implementation across diverse cultural contexts.

- **LinkedIn:** linkedin.com/in/patrickchun
- **Publications:**
  - » *World Civility Index and Inner Development Goals* (2025)
  - » UN Sustainable Development publications
- **Additional platforms:** IITTI World Civility Index

Nidhi Sachdeva

Sachdeva specializes in evidence-informed microlearning design using cognitive science principles. Her research bridges the gap between education and practical implementation, particularly in formal higher education contexts.

- **LinkedIn:** linkedin.com/in/nidhi-sachdeva-toronto
- **Publications:**
  - » "No Pain, No Gain" (*TD*, August 2024)
  - » "Let's Focus on 'Learning' in Microlearning" (*The Learning Scientists* blog)

- **Additional platforms:**
  - » Science of Learning newsletter (scienceoflearning.substack.com)
  - » "How Learning Happens" YouTube Playlist (bit.ly/48ZLfa1)

Emmanuel Burguete

Burguete contributes to learning science foundations and evidence-based instructional design practices that inform effective microlearning development. His most notable research on brick-based design aligns with the foundations and principles of microlearning design and led to the creation of the Eduscript Doctor pedagogical scenario kit. Within this framework, microlearning is conceived as an optimized pedagogical brick, the most granular form of a learning scenario.

- **LinkedIn:** linkedin.com/in/emmanuel-burguete
- **Publications:**
  - » "Integrating microlearning into MOOCs: Design and validation of a pedagogical scripting kit" (Doctoral thesis on microlearning)
  - » "Empirical validation of a brick-centric learning design methodology and its implementation through the Eduscript Doctor pedagogical scenario kit" (*Education and Information Technologies*, vol. 30, 2025)

Data and Learning Analytics

Megan Torrance

Torrance leads practical xAPI implementation in corporate environments and founded the xAPI Learning Cohort. Her expertise in learning data and analytics provides essential insights for measuring learning effectiveness and creating adaptive experiences.

- **LinkedIn:** linkedin.com/in/megantorrance
- **Publications:**
  - » *Data & Analytics for Instructional Designers* (2024)
  - » *Agile for Instructional Designers* (2019)
  - » "Making Sense of xAPI," *TD at Work* (2017)
- **Additional platforms:**
  - » TorranceLearning

> » xAPI Learning Cohort
> » *Tangents* Podcast

Colin Hahn

Hahn uses talent analytics to drive decisions by reducing uncertainty. He draws from continuous improvement and operations disciplines in support of organizational performance.

- **LinkedIn:** linkedin.com/in/colinjhahn
- **Publications:** "See Metrics in a Different Light" (*TD*, February 2025)
- **Additional platforms:** SEWI-ATD Performance Improvement SIG

Alaina Szlachta

Szlachta brings research-based approaches to data strategy and learning analytics implementation. She helps organizations collect and strategically leverage data to make decisions about learning effectiveness.

- **LinkedIn:** linkedin.com/in/drszlachta
- **Publications:**
  - » *Measurement and Evaluation on a Shoestring* (2024)
  - » "The Weekly Measure" (Substack)
- **Additional platforms:** dralainaszlachta.com

Talented Learning Research and Consulting

Talented Learning provides fiercely independent, research-based insights on learning technology strategy—from analytics and benchmarks to system selection and implementation—that help organizations maximize business impact.

- **LinkedIn:** linkedin.com/company/talented-learning
- **Publications:** Annual RightFit Solution Grid
- **Additional platforms:**
  - » TalentedLearning.com
  - » Annual Learning Systems Awards
  - » *The Talented Learning Show* (podcast)
  - » youtube.com/@TalentedLearning

Will Thalheimer

Thalheimer's research-focused approach helps L&D professionals make evidence-based decisions about learning effectiveness and measurement strategies, particularly around spaced learning and retention. He's also spent more than 20,000 hours reviewing scientific research on learning, memory, instruction, and performance; providing resources and insights through publications and presentations.

- **LinkedIn:** linkedin.com/in/will-thalheimer-6590a41
- **Publications:**
  - » *The New Learning-Transfer Evaluation Model* (2024)
  - » *Performance-Focused Learner Surveys* (2022)
  - » *Performance-Focused Smile Sheets* (2016)
- **Additional platforms:** Work-Learning Research (worklearning.com)

Process Infrastructure and Workflow Learning

Keith Keating

Keating bridges learning and business operations by building the infrastructure that embeds learning into the flow of work. Through his frameworks like the Value Creation Compass and the Trusted Learning Advisor model, he helps organizations integrate development into everyday processes — aligning skills, performance, and business outcomes. His work demonstrates how L&D can be systematized like any other core business function, ensuring learning is not a side project but part of the organizational workflow itself.

- **LinkedIn:** linkedin.com/in/dr-keith-keating-1976963a
- **Publications:**
  - » *Hidden Value: How to Reveal the Impact of Organizational Learning* (2025)
  - » *The Trusted Learning Advisor* (2023)
  - » *Exploring the Beliefs of Organizational Learning* (Doctoral Research, 2022)
- **Additional platforms:** keithkeating.com

Brandon Carson

Carson brings more than 25 years of Fortune 200 experience (including organizations like Delta, Walmart, Starbucks, and Home Depot) and focuses on digital transformation's impact on learning strategy. His work on edge technologies and learning implementation is highly practical.

- **LinkedIn:** linkedin.com/in/brandoncarson

- **Publications:**
  - » *L&D's Playbook for the Digital Age* (2023)
  - » *Learning in the Age of Immediacy* (2020)
- **Additional platforms:** L&D Cares (ldcares.org)

Heidi Kirby

Kirby focuses on process infrastructure and organizational systems that enable effective learning implementation and scaling across complex organizations.
- **LinkedIn:** linkedin.com/in/heidiekirby
- **Publications:** "Leadership Competencies for Instructional Designers: Identifying Critical Incidents Used to Lead Design Projects That Improve Performance" (Dissertation, 2022)
- **Additional platforms:** Get Useful Stuff (getusefulstuff.com)

Kimo Kippen

Kippen brings extensive C-level experience in learning strategy and organizational development, providing insights into process infrastructure needed for successful learning initiatives.
- **LinkedIn:** linkedin.com/in/kimoandtheworld
- **Publications:** "Empowering Teams to Innovate" (ATD Blog, April, 2023)
- **Additional platforms:**
  - » Aloha Learning Advisors (alohalearningadvisors.com)
  - » Shape the Future Consortium (stfconsortium.org)

Margaret Spence

Spence challenges organizations to ask: Who gets left behind? She leads at the intersection of human-centered leadership, AI governance, upskilling, and women's leadership development—ensuring an equitable future of work for all.
- **LinkedIn:** linkedin.com/in/margaretspence
- **Publications:** *Leadership Self-Transformation: 52 Career-Defining Questions Every High-Achieving Woman Must Answer* (2017)
- **Additional platforms:**
  - » *What's Your Possible?* podcast (whatsyourpossible.co)
  - » The Undisruptable Woman Substack (margaretspence.substack.com)
  - » Inclusion Learning Lab

People Infrastructure and Organizational Change

Guy W. Wallace
Wallace's Lean-ISD methodology provides systematic approaches to developing people infrastructure and organizational capabilities needed for effective learning implementation and performance improvement.
- **LinkedIn:** linkedin.com/in/guywwallace
- **Publications:**
  - » *The 5th Management Foci: The Managers Guide to Performance Based Alignments, Processes, Practices, Resources, and Avoiding Foo Foo* (2024)
  - » *Overview of the PACT Processes for Performance Based Instruction* (2024)
  - » *The L&D Pivot Point: Performance Improvement Consulting* (2023)
- **Additional platforms:**
  - » Professional L&D Archive (guywwallace.wordpress.com)
  - » EPPIC

Tracie Cantu
Cantu help teams scale their impact, align with the business, and drive results through smarter systems, not bigger teams.
- **LinkedIn:** linkedin.com/in/traciemcantu
- **Publications:** *Running L&D Like a Business* (2026)
- **Additional platforms:** Your CLO (yourclo.net)

Bob Mosher
Mosher champions the 5 Moments of Need framework, essential for understanding when and how microlearning can support performance in workflow contexts and just-in-time learning delivery.
- **LinkedIn:** linkedin.com/in/bob-mosher-53b5091
- **Publications:** *Innovative Performance Support* (with Conrad Gottfredson; 2010)
- **Additional platforms:**
  - » Apply Synergies (applysynergies.com)
  - » 5 Moments of Need (5momentsofneed.com)
  - » *Performance Matters* podcast (performancematters.podbean.com)

JD Dillon

JD is an expert in frontline enablement, helping deskless employees do their best work every shift by embedding support within the workflow. He combines real-world experience with tech know-how to share practical, proven ways to elevate performance and boost business results.

- **LinkedIn:** linkedin.com/in/jddillon
- **Publications:**
  - » *The Modern Learning Ecosystem* (2022)
  - » *The Frontline Enablement Playbook* (2026)
- **Additional platforms:** Learn Geek (learngeek.co)

Emerging Trends

Josh Cavalier

Cavalier is a leading expert in applying generative AI to L&D with more than 30 years of experience. His practical frameworks for AI integration in learning design and his AI Task Enablement Scale provide actionable guidance for leveraging AI in learning experiences.

- **LinkedIn:** linkedin.com/in/joshcavalier
- **Publications:** *Applying AI in Learning and Development: From Platforms to Performance* (2025)
- **Additional platforms:** Brainpower Weekly AI show (joshcavalier.com/brainpower)

Markus Bernhardt

Bernhardt advises senior leaders on how to move beyond AI adoption hype to deliver systemic, measurable value. His research and practical guides focus on governance, workforce transformation, and the operating models that turn AI into business impact.

- **LinkedIn:** linkedin.com/in/markus-bernhardt
- **Publications:**
  - » *The Endeavor Report 2.0: State of Applied Workforce Solutions* (2025)
  - » Your Applied Workforce Solution Playbook
- **Additional platforms:** Endeavor Intellegence (endeavorintel.com)

Karl Kapp

Kapp co-authored the definitive microlearning guide and continues research-ing gamification's role in "bite-sized" learning as well as focusing on innovative action-first learning concepts. His innovative work bridges learning science with practical implementation, making complex concepts accessible for practitioners.

- **LinkedIn:** linkedin.com/in/kkapp
- **Publications:**
  - » *Action-First Learning* (2025)
  - » *Microlearning: Short and Sweet* (with Robyn Defelice, 2022)
  - » *Play to Learn: Everything You Need to Know About Designing Effective Learning Games* (with Sharon Boller, 2017)
- **Additional platforms:**
  - » karlkapp.com
  - » "L&D Easter Eggs" LinkedIn newsletter (linkedin.com/newsletters/6599686641453977600)
  - » Karl's YouTube channel (youtube.com/ProfKapp01)

Michelle Lentz

Lentz combines more than 20 years of learning strategy experience with cut-ting-edge AI implementation. Her work as a learning and AI strategist for Innovate Elevate on AI integration in corporate learning provides practical guidance for organizations adopting AI-enhanced learning.

- **LinkedIn:** linkedin.com/in/michellelentz
- **Publications:** "Partner With AI for Instructional Design" *TD at Work* (February 2025)
- **Additional platforms:**
  - » Innovate + Elevate Strategies (innovate-elevate.ai)
  - » michelleslentz.com/published-writing

Debbie Richards

Richards focuses on emerging learning technologies including AR and VR and their integration with learning. She is an ATD facilitator specializing in

AI workshops. Her expertise helps organizations understand and implement cutting-edge technology trends in learning design.

- **LinkedIn:** linkedin.com/in/debbierichards
- **Publications:**
  - » "Seeing the Possibilities With Augmented Reality" *TD at Work* (January 2019)
  - » "Preparing Your Organization for New Technologies" *TD at Work* (September 2023)
- **Additional platform:** L&D Cares (ldcares.org)

Universal Design and Accessibility

Gwen Navarrete Klapperich

Navarrete Klapperich specializes in universal design principles and accessibility implementation, ensuring learning experiences are inclusive and usable by individuals with diverse abilities and needs. She also provides training in disability etiquette and learning.

- **LinkedIn:** linkedin.com/in/gwennavarreteklapperich
- **Publication:** "Enhance Accessibility in Virtual Training Environments" *TD at Work* (December 2024)
- **Additional platform:** Accessibility and Universal Design for Learning Resources (kitaconsult.com/accessibility-and-udl)

Sarah Mercier

Mercier focuses on inclusive design practices and accessibility standards that ensure learning is designed for everyone, regardless of ability or technological access. Her work also bridges data and analytics with process and workflow learning, making inclusion not just a design principle but a measurable, operational reality.

- **LinkedIn:** linkedin.com/in/sarahcmercier
- **Publication:** *Design for All Learners: Create Accessible and Inclusive Learning Experiences* (2025)
- **Additional platform:** Build Capable (buildcapable.com)

Megan Kohler

Kohler specializes in designing inclusive learning approaches with an emphasis on personal belonging. Providing research-based, practical guidance for creating learning that serves diverse populations effectively.

- **LinkedIn:** linkedin.com/in/mkohler26
- **Publications:**
  - » *The Multi-Disciplinary Instructional Designer Integrating Specialized Skills into Design Toolkits* (with Chris Gamrat, 2023)
  - » Various publications (scholar.google.com/citations?user= Wx7gvdwAAAAJ&hl)
- **Additional platforms:** Megan Kohler Consulting (megankohler.org)

Nicole L'Etoile

L'Etoile brings certified expertise in accessibility (CPACC) and inclusive design, helping organizations implement learning that meets accessibility standards and serves anyone with disabilities.

- **LinkedIn:** linkedin.com/in/nicoleletoile
- **Additional platforms:**
  - » Design With Accessibility in Mind blog (letoile-education.com/blog)
  - » L'Etoile Education (letoile-education.com)

Connie Malamed

Malamed blends visual design and learning science to guide the creation of effective learning. Though not explicitly focused on universal design and accessibility, her work and research will help maximize your design efforts. She helps professionals elevate their visibility for career advancement and promotes practices to make learning accessible.

- **LinkedIn:** linkedin.com/in/conniemalamed
- **Publications:**
  - » *Visual Language for Designers* (2011)
  - » *Visual Design Solutions* (2015)
- **Additional platforms:** The eLearning Coach blog and podcast (theelearningcoach.com)

Diane Elkins

Elkins specializes in accessibility implementation and inclusive design practices, helping organizations create earning experiences that are truly universal and accessible to all.

- **LinkedIn:** linkedin.com/in/dpelkins
- **Publications:** E-Learning Uncovered series (2009–present)
- **Additional platforms:** Artisan Learning (artisanlearning.com)

Amy Vaughan

Vaughan's work centers on neurodiversity and universal learning design, informed by both professional practice and lived experience as a neurodivergent parent. She supports organizations in creating learning experiences that benefit individuals today while strengthening future leadership capacity.

- **LinkedIn:** linkedin.com/in/amykatevaughan
- **Publications:** "Mind the Neurodivergent Mind" (*TD*, November 2024)
- **Additional platforms:** shillidayvaughan.com

References

APMG International. n.d. "Change Management Professional Development." International Institute for Learning. iil.com/change-management -professional-development.

Aunger, R., S. White, K. Greenland, and V. Curtis. 2017. *Behavior Centered Design: A Practitioner's Manual,* version 1. London School of Hygiene and Tropical Medicine.

Bano, Y., and V. Shanmugam. 2020. "Review on Strategies for Bridging the Employability Skill Gap in Higher Education." *International Journal of Recent Technology and Engineering,* 7.

Behrens, M., M. Guba, H. Chaabene, O. Prieske, A. Zenon, K.-C. Broscheid, L. Schega, F. Husmann, and M. Weippert. 2023. "Fatigue and Human Performance: An Updated Framework." *Sports Medicine* 53:7–31.

Bjork, R.A., and E.L. Bjork. 2020. "Desirable Difficulties in Theory and Practice." *Journal of Applied Research in Memory and Cognition* 9(4): 475–479.

Bozarth, J. 2024. "Microlearning 2024: Current State and Future Implications." The Learning Guild, April 15. learningguild.com/research/microlearning -2024-current-state-and-future-implications.

Burguete, E., B. Coulibaly, and V. Komis. 2025. "Empirical Validation of a Brick-Centric Learning Design Methodology and Its Implementation Through the Eduscript Doctor Pedagogical Scenario Kit." *Education and Information Technologies* 30:5009–5057.

Butt, N., and N.F. Warraich. 2022. "Multitasking Behavior in the Workplace: A Systematic Review." *Journal of Social Research Development* 3(2): 229–247.

Carson, B. 2021. *L&D's Playbook for the Digital Age.* ATD Press.

Day, M. 2024. "Build a High-Value Credentialing Program." *TD at Work.* ATD Press.

Dillon, J.D. 2022. *The Modern Learning Ecosystem: A New L&D Mindset for the Ever-Changing Workplace.* ATD Press.

Dirksen, J. 2015. *Design for How People Learn,* 2nd ed. New Riders.

Elliot, A.J., C.S. Dweck, and D.S. Yeager, eds. 2017. *Handbook of Competence and Motivation: Theory and Application,* 2nd ed. The Guilford Press.

Franksiska, R., and A. Yuniawan. 2023. "Employee Multitasking at Work: A Systematic Literature Review." *Journal of Psychological and Educational Research* 31(1): 125–146.

Hockman, A. 2023. "Improve Training with Active Engagement." *TD at Work.* ATD Press.

Kornmeier, J., Z. Sosic-Vasic, and E. Joos. 2022. "Spacing Learning Units Affects Both Learning and Forgetting." *Trends in Neuroscience and Education* 26:100173. doi.org/10.1016/j.tine.2022.100173.

Lake, K., and S. Bhaduri. 2024. *L&D Trends 2024: The Future of Workforce Learning and Effective Measurement.* Brandon Hall Group.

LinkedIn. 2024. "2024 Workplace Learning Report." LinkedIn Learning. learning.linkedin.com/content/dam/me/business/en-us/amp/learning-solutions/images/wlr-2024/LinkedIn-Workplace-Learning-Report-2024.pdf.

Lowenthal, S. 2025. "3 Best Practices of Bridging the Learning and Doing Gap." eLearning Industry, April 28. elearningindustry.com/bridging-the-learning-and-doing-gap-3-best-practices.

Maydeu-Olivares, A., and T. D'Zurilla. 1997. "The Factor Structure of the Problem Solving Inventory." *European Journal of Psychological Assessment* 13:206–215.

Mayer, R.E. 2024. "The Past, Present, and Future of the Cognitive Theory of Multimedia Learning." *Educational Psychology Review* 36:8.

Mayer, R., and R. Moreno. 2005. A Cognitive Theory of Multimedia Learning: Implications for Design Principles. researchgate.net/publication

/248528255_A_Cognitive_Theory_of_Multimedia_Learning_Implications
_for_Design_Principles.

Mercier, S. ed. 2025. *Design for All Learners*. ATD Press.

Mincemoyer, C., N. Verdiglione, and B.H. Levi. 2020. "Cognitive Mapping for iLookOut for Child Abuse: An Online Training Program for Early Childhood Professionals." *Online Journal of Distance Education and eLearning* 8(2): 80–89.

Neovation Corporation. 2020. "OttoLearn Implementation Guide." OttoLearn Client Success Team. ottolearn.com/microlearning-resources /ottolearn-implementation-guide-download.

Osterman, P. 2022. "How American Adults Obtain Work Skills: Results of a New National Survey." *ILR Review* 75(3): 578–607.

Perkins, R.A. 2003. "The Role of Context in Instructional Design: A Case Study Examining the Re-Purposed Master's Degree Courses for Use in Malawi." Doctoral dissertation. Virginia Polytechnic Institute and State University, Blacksburg, Virginia.

Po"ttker, H. 2003. "News and Its Communicative Quality: The Inverted Pyramid—When and Why Did It Appear?" *Journalism Studies* 4(4): 501–11.

Richardson, M.X., O. Aytar, K. Hess-Wiktor, and S. Wamala-Andersson. 2023. "Digital Microlearning for Training and Competency Development of Older Adult Care Personnel: Mixed Methods Intervention Study to Assess Needs, Effectiveness, and Areas of Application." *JMIR Medical Education* 9:e45177.

Sachdeva, N. 2024. "No Pain, No Gain: Incorporating Desirable Difficulties Into Training Leads to Long-Term Retention and Lasting Learning." *TD*, August. td.org/content/td-magazine/no-pain-no-gain.

Sachdeva, N. 2025. "Microlearning as a Vehicle for Rosenshine's Principles of Instruction: Bridging Cognitive Science and Instructional Practice." *Opus et Educatio* 12(3). journals.bme.hu/oee/libraryFiles/ downloadPublic/135.

Sankaranarayanan, R., J. Leung, V. Abramenka-Lachheb, G. Seo, and A. Lachheb. 2023. "Microlearning in Diverse Contexts: A Bibliometric Analysis." *TechTrends*, 67:260–276. doi.org/10.1007/s11528-022-00794-x.

Soderstrom, N.C., and R.A. Bjork. 2015. "Learning Versus Performance: An Integrative Review." *Perspectives on Psychological Science* 10(2): 176–199. doi.org/10.1177/1745691615569000.

Tessmer, M., and R.C. Richey. 1997. "The Role of Context in Learning and Instructional Design." *Educational Technology Research and Development* 45(2): 85–115.

Thalheimer, W. 2006. "Spacing Learning Events Over Time: What the Research Says." Work-Learning Research. docslib.org/doc/1186527 /spacing-learning-events-over-time-what-the-research-says.

Tipton, S. 2024. "Improve Retention with Drip-Feed Learning." *TD at Work*. ATD Press.

Torgerson, C., and S. Iannone. 2019. *Designing Microlearning*. ATD Press.

Torgerson, C., and S. Iannone. 2020. "Making Bite-Sized Work: 5 Tips for Creating Effective Microlearning." Bull City Learning and Bull City Blue, February 20.

van Merriënboer, J.J.G., and J. Sweller. 2005. "Cognitive Load Theory and Complex Learning: Recent Developments and Future Directions." *Educational Psychology Review* 17(2): 147–177. doi.org/10.1007/s10648 -005-3951-0

Waxman, J.B., and S.J. Goldie. 2023. "Cognitive Theory of Multimedia Learning: Applying Cognitive Load Theory to the Design of Educational Multimedia." *Perspectives from the CHDS Media Hub*. Center for Health Decision Science, Harvard T.H. Chan School of Public Health.

Wentworth, D. 2021. "Aligning the L&D Strategy With Business Goals." Brandon Hall Group, November 1. brandonhall.com/aligning-the-ld -strategy-with-business-goals.

Index

Page numbers followed by *f* and *t* refer to figures and tables, respectively.

LinkedIn, 38
LMS. *See* learning management systems (LMS)
location-based notifications, 141, 230

M

maintenance capacity, 102
maintenance planning, 305
manager infrastructure, 73–74
manager support, 73–74, 100
manual spacing, 77–78
manufacturing safety, 58, 116, 214, 221, 272
Mayer, Richard E., 220–221
measurement frameworks, 304
measurement overreach, 46
media. *See also* multimedia
    challenges in, 232–234
    definition of, 219
    iterative, 234
    for knowledge-based microlearning, 228–229
    and load theory cognitive, media meaningful, 223–224
    in microlearning, 231–232
    overuse of, 271
    for performance-based microlearning, 230–231
    principles of, 218–219
    and science of learning, 219–223
    for selection framework, 224–228
    for skills-based microlearning, 229–230
    tree of decision, 224*t*
media decision tree, 224, 224*f*, 225, 232, 235
media selection matrix, 232*t*
memorization, 21, 120, 139, 255–256
mental states, 153, 163, 166–167, 174. *See also* emotional states
metacognitive action, 247
micro-demonstrations, 230
microlearning
    as concept, 10–11
    and global equity, 179–180
    knowledge-based (*See* knowledge-based microlearning)
    and LAER (listen acknowledge explore, respond), 21
    media in, 231–232
    as method, 11–13

    performance-based (*See* performance-based microlearning)
    as product, 13–14
    rules for, 9
    skills-based (*See* skills-based microlearning)
    types of, 17–18, 43–44
microlearning campaigns, 14–15
    completion rates in, 277
    customer challenge simulators in, 116
    design of, 248–249
    Inverted Pyramid in, 201–202
    media in, 225
    overuse in, 109
Microlearning Readiness (MLR) framework, 25–36
    application levels of, 29–30
    as baseline, 31
    and change management, 32–33
    components of, 19–21
    dimensions of, 28–29, 28*f*
    L&D function level of, 30
    level of organizational function, 30
    outcomes, purpose, and potential in, 38–42
    pilot initiative level of, 29–30
misaligned expectations, 46
mobile accessibility, 141–142
modality principle of multimedia, 221
modular content approach, 305
motivation. *See also* competence; confidence
    in agency framework, 242
    analysis of, 166
    of audiences, 154
    competence theory of, 242–243
    definition of, 243
    designing for, 255, 257
    and engagement, 155, 184, 244, 272
    in learning science, 108
    mapping strategies for, 264
motor accessibility, 176
motor skills, 123–124, 131, 161, 181–182, 196
multimedia, 219, 219–220, 221–222. *See also* media

N

near field communication (NFC) tags, 230
neurodiversity, 176, 178, 181–183

notification systems, 71
  for action, 254
  email, 13
  location-based, 230
  manual, 70
  platform-based, 71
  push, 12
  for scheduling, 71–72, 77
novel challenges, 273

O

objection handling, 21
objectives and key results (OKRs), 40
organizational evaluation culture, 56–58, 74,
  76, 152–153, 155–156, 166, 263–264
organizational readiness, 2, 22, 30, 34, 108,
  166, 284, 308
overuse, 269–282
  and completion rates, 280
  and consistency, 274–275
  of delivery methods, 271
  and engagement patterns, 277–278
  of media, 271
  in microlearning campaigns, 109
  and pattern tolerance, 278–279
  of scheduling, 272–273
  and science of learning, 272–273
  in spaced learning, 128
  and strategic variety, 273–277
  of templates, 271

P

participant understanding, 74
pattern recognition, 254
pattern tolerance, 278–279
peer-learning networks, 146
pensiveness, 246, 289
people infrastructure, 56–57, 59, 71–74, 76,
  79, 103
performance analytics, 54
performance-based microlearning
  in action-based learning, 258–260
  context in, 162
  in Gagné's Conditions of Learning,
    124–125, 161
  implementation of, 90
  in people infrastructure, 56–57
  in pilot initiatives, 307
  readiness for, 43
  spacing in, 75

  targets of, 124, 126
  tools for, 139
  uses of, 18, 34, 140–142, 203, 213
performance data
  and adaptive triggers, 259
  for algorithm-controlled spacing, 76
  baseline, 302
  for implementation, 88, 90
  for outcomes, 40
  as quantitative assessment method, 300
  scaling of, 100
  for technology tracking, 69, 70
performance improvement, 1, 11, 17, 45, 68,
  114, 303
persona development frameworks, 165,
  167–169
phased expansion, 303
physical accessibility, 154, 157
physical environments, 153–154, 157, 159,
  161, 166–167
pilot programs, 287–309
  for assessment methods, 300–301
  for audience targeting, 294
  capacity tracking during, 298–300
  content for, 305–306
  and current training, 296–297
  data for, 302–303, 307
  existing content for, 296
  growth of, 305, 307
  implementation cycles of, 307–308
  improvement process for, 293–294
  metrics for, 293, 301, 301t
  needs-based, 292–293
  objectives for, 292
  readiness assessment for, 306–307
  road maps for, 295
  scaling of, 303–305
  for self-driven development, 298
  structure of organizational, 294–295
PowerPoint, 234
practice without penalty, 182, 246
process documentation, 234, 303
process infrastructure, 55–56, 62–63, 70–73,
  76, 78–79, 103
processing capacity, 126, 220
productive unpredictability, 274, 277
progressive design, 250
progressive disclosure, 138, 206, 209, 228
progressive guidance systems, 258
progressive implementation, 186, 187

About the Author

Robyn A. Defelice, PhD, is a learning strategist, author, and speaker who empowers L&D teams to navigate complex challenges through collaboration and practical solutions. With more than 25 years of experience spanning manufacturing to healthcare, government agencies to financial services, higher education to pharmaceuticals, and startups to Fortune 500 companies, she applies evidence-based and systems-driven approaches to help organizations demonstrate real business value through learning.

Robyn is the co-author of *Microlearning: Short and Sweet* (ATD Press, 2019) with Karl M. Kapp, and a contributing author to *The Multi-Disciplinary Instructional Designer* (Routledge, 2022). She has also been researching how long it takes to develop training for more than a decade and consulting L&D leaders on operational maturity.

When she's not consulting or speaking at conferences, Robyn experiments in the kitchen, building on the foundational lessons her mother taught her years ago. She appreciates how often she can relate what she's doing in the kitchen to her work—especially to the subject of microlearning—in an effort to make it more palatable!

About ATD

atd The Association for Talent Development (ATD) is the world's largest association dedicated to those who develop talent in organizations. Serving a global community of members, customers, and international business partners in more than 100 countries, ATD champions the importance of learning and training by setting standards for the talent development profession.

Our customers and members work in public and private organizations in every industry sector. Since ATD was founded in 1943, the talent development field has expanded significantly to meet the needs of global businesses and emerging industries. Through the Talent Development Capability Model, education courses, certifications and credentials, memberships, industry-leading events, research, and publications, we help talent development professionals build their personal, professional, and organizational capabilities to meet new business demands with maximum impact and effectiveness.

One of the cornerstones of ATD's intellectual foundation, ATD Press offers insightful and practical information on talent development, training, and professional growth. ATD Press publications are written by industry thought leaders and offer anyone who works with adult learners the best practices, academic theory, and guidance necessary to move the profession forward.

We invite you to join our community. Learn more at **td.org**.